AN APPROACH TO
DESCARTES' 'MEDITATIONS'

AN APPROACH TO DESCARTES' 'MEDITATIONS'

by

FREDERICK BROADIE

UNIVERSITY OF LONDON
THE ATHLONE PRESS
1970

Published by
THE ATHLONE PRESS
UNIVERSITY OF LONDON
at 2 Gower Street London WC1
Distributed by Tiptree Book Services Ltd
Tiptree, Essex

Australia and New Zealand
Melbourne University Press

U.S.A.
Oxford University Press Inc
New York

485 11111 X

Printed in Great Britain by
Alden & Mowbray Ltd
at the Alden Press, Oxford

I DEDICATE THIS BOOK
TO MY MOTHER, IN MEMORY

'For I know that my redeemer liveth'

For from the sole fact that God created me it is most probable that in some way he has placed his image and similitude upon me, and that I perceive this similitude (in which the idea of God is contained) by means of the same faculty by which I perceive myself—that is to say, when I reflect on myself I not only know that I am something imperfect, incomplete and dependent on another, which incessantly aspires after something which is better and greater than myself, but I also know that He on whom I depend possesses in Himself all the great things towards which I aspire and the ideas of which I find within myself, and that not indefinitely or potentially alone, but really, actually and infinitely; and that thus He is God.

Descartes: *Meditation III*

PREFACE

THE EDITORS of a recent compilation of pieces on (or about) Descartes[1] began their introduction as follows: 'Descartes' *Meditations* probably rivals Plato's *Republic* as the work most frequently read or recommended as an introduction to philosophy. Its qualifications for this purpose are obvious: it is important, relatively short, well written, and seems—in the beginning at least —readily understandable. One of the most influential works in the history of Western thought, the *Meditations* has often been considered the keynote of modern philosophy.' I believe, however, that it is only too often on the level where it is readily understandable that it is influential, and especially in our own day. The trouble is that since the work is short and well written one has finished it before one has properly begun to grasp the vast issues with which Descartes engages. And they can never be simple to understand, as he himself tells us: 'And, truth to say, there are not so many in the world who are fitted for metaphysical speculations as there are for those of Geometry.' This great creative worker in both fields was in a position to know. He writes, in his Preface to the Reader, 'On the contrary, I should never advise anyone to read it excepting those who desire to meditate seriously with me, and who can detach their minds from affairs of sense, and deliver themselves entirely from every sort of prejudice. I know too well that such men exist in a very small number. But for those who, without caring to comprehend the order and connections of my reasonings, form their criticisms on detached portions arbitrarily selected, as is the custom with many, these, I say, will not obtain much profit from reading this 'Treatise.' I have taken him at his word, and accordingly the present work is not so much a text book, or a commentary, as an attempt to reconstruct his 'Treatise' afresh. Therefore, it is not a series of reflections, but

[1] Sesonske and Fleming, eds., *Meta-Meditations: Studies in Descartes* (Belmont, California, 1965).

vii

a sustained attempt to discover what is central in the *Meditations*, and to treat the work as Descartes urged us to. What I have done has, I believe, helped me; and taken slowly, and above all in conjunction with the *Meditations* itself, may also help others to those bursts of vision in which one knows for oneself, and on one's own authority, *why* someone is great.

Clearly then, in the nature of the task, Descartes will have to be quoted more often than one might like. But the quotations have been carefully chosen to illustrate their own meaning most effectively just where they appear, and it will be a waste of time reading this book if they are skipped. The whole point is to try to open up just how much is contained in Descartes' own writing.

For helping me to prepare this final draft, as well as for compiling the index, certain acknowledgements are due. Without the sustained, gallant, and imaginative help of Delia Harverson, Sarah Waterlow, and Alexander Broadie, not only would this book have been long delayed, but it would have been open to more criticisms than it now is. I thank them and shall remain grateful.

Thanks are also due to Mr A. G. Dewey of the Athlone Press for his suggestions, always tactfully given, and for his encouragement.

Finally to Alexander Altmann, wherever you are, thank you. He will understand.

4 February 1969   F.B.
Department of Philosophy
Edinburgh University

CONTENTS

NOTE

Quotations from Descartes are taken generally from *The Philosophical Works of Descartes*, translated by Elizabeth S. Haldane and G. R. T. Ross, 2 vols. (Cambridge, 1911), and are reproduced by permission of the Cambridge University Press. References to the *Meditations*, which appears in volume one of Haldane and Ross, and to the *Objections and Replies*, which occupies the whole of volume two, are by volume and page number only; references to other works included in volume one name the work in question.

Haldane and Ross employ square brackets to distinguish readings based upon contemporary French translations of works originally published by Descartes in Latin. Insertions for which the present writer is responsible are shown within angle brackets ⟨ ⟩.

CHAPTER ONE

THE SUB-TITLE of Descartes' First Meditation is worth more than a passing glance. It reads: 'Of things which may be brought within the sphere of the doubtful.' And what Descartes could not begin by guaranteeing was that everything bearing the claim to be knowledge would not end by being cast into that sphere. For the point of his enterprise was to see how far he could go in doing just that. There are types of religious faith which are said to be consistent with doubt; but no claim to knowledge would, I think, be allowed that held itself to be consistent with doubt. In other words one cannot know something and doubt it at the same time: and if at any time one knows then one cannot doubt; and if at any time one doubts then one cannot know. Perhaps no other thinker in the history of philosophical enterprise was as remorseless as Descartes in tracing out both the implications and the presuppositions of this conceptual contrast. This, at any rate, is what the First Meditation is about.

But as well as the foregoing logical considerations underlying Descartes' concern with the relation of knowledge to doubt, there is also an important psychological consideration. For it may be that in our unreflective state we are, from practical considerations, prone to take as true what may not be. For instance there appear to be good practical reasons for believing that there exists a world external to and independent of ourselves—we do manage, largely, to stay alive. But does this prove that there is in fact a world answering to this description? Or that what we learn about *via* the senses is more real than what we learn about by taking thought? For the unreflective the answer is plainly yes to both these questions. But since it is also a fact that we all start by being unreflective, and pick up the habits of the unreflective as we learn to live at all, without the psychological power to distance ourselves from these habits we might indeed learn to repeat what a reflective person may say, but not, so to say, to live reflectively. And for

Descartes, the method of doubt has for one of its aims the creation of just such a distance. In other words by getting into the habit of doubting, we give thought a chance to operate. Thus reflection becomes possible, and the question of what is real and what is not, or the question of whether something is more real than something else, is more likely to be decided by the mind than by the senses. And for Descartes, as we shall see, without this not only is the road to knowledge closed to us, but so also is the road to an understanding both of ourselves and of God.

Even the great Hobbes seems not to have realised the significance of what Descartes understood himself to be doing, and replying to his surprisingly feeble objections Descartes writes:

The reasons for doubt here admitted as true by this Philosopher were propounded by me only as possessing verisimilitude, and my reason for employing them was not that I might retail them as new, but partly that I might prepare my readers' minds for the study of intellectual matters and for distinguishing them from matters corporeal, a purpose for which such arguments seem wholly necessary. (ii, 60)

But still more pointed is his reply to the writers of The Second Set of Objections, who, it seemed to him, might have been suggesting that he hadn't much to show for his first two Meditations obviously worthy of publication:

Nothing conduces more to the obtaining of a secure knowledge of reality than a previous accustoming of ourselves to entertain doubts especially about corporeal things; and although I had long ago seen several books written by the Academics and Sceptics about this subject and felt some disgust in serving up again this stale dish, I could not for the above reasons refuse to allot to this subject one whole Meditation. I should be pleased also if my readers would expend not merely the little time which is required for reading it, in thinking over the matter of which the Meditation treats, but would give months, or at least weeks, to this, before going on further; for in this way the rest of the work will yield them a much richer harvest. (ii, 31)

From the start it is evident that what Descartes has in mind is an enquiry. Accordingly, he doesn't begin by ruling out the possibility of knowledge. On the contrary he shows himself immensely sensitive to the distinction between true and false belief. What he wants to be able to show beyond all further doubt

2

is that truth is possible, not that it isn't. But if it is then it must be recognisably so, for otherwise he cannot know whether he knows, or whether he doesn't. How, then, assuming something somewhere is true, can one know it to be so? The answer he will move towards is this:—only if, in a sense we shall later examine, doubt is actually not possible. But, of course, unless you try to doubt you cannot know whether it is or not.

In the first place Descartes offers as his reason for doubting the (presumable) truth that he has believed to be true what later turned out not to be. Error, therefore, is possible. This he takes himself to know to be true. However, as we shall see, his method doesn't depend upon his knowing even this for certain. He begins with the empirical fact that certainly some of his beliefs about the world have been false; and why, indeed, may not all his beliefs, past and present still be just that? But even if all his beliefs are not in fact false, and even if only one is, he is just as badly placed. For the very first step of his enquiry might be a false one.

It is now some years since I detected how many were the false beliefs that I had from my earliest youth admitted as true, and how doubtful was everything I had since constructed on this basis; and from that time I was convinced that I must once for all seriously undertake to rid myself of all the opinions which I had formerly accepted, and commence to build anew from the foundation, if I wanted to establish any firm and permanent structure in the sciences. (i, 144)

The goal, thus, is a permanent and comprehensive system of knowledge; but the immediate task is to establish whether knowledge is possible at all. Nevertheless, we shall find that for Descartes it is a necessary condition for something's being properly regarded as knowledge that it should be capable of being part of such a system. The truth of something that makes it knowledge must hold independently of its having been present for an instant or so as an element in a human's field of consciousness. Thus, knowledge is not created by us, but discovered.

As always, we must attend to exactly what Descartes says. He is going to 'seriously undertake' to get rid of all his former opinions. This is not the same as simply announcing that he will no longer believe them. This would be to disclaim the possibility of truth, not to enquire how to know that one has achieved it. What counts

3

is the form his new undertaking assumes. Doubting a belief, in Descartes' sense, may be regarded as a kind of critical assault upon it. If the belief is true, then, as he argues later, it has the possibility of being clearly and distinctly seen to be so. But what is clearly and distinctly seen to be true *cannot* be disbelieved. And insofar as to doubt a belief is to disbelieve it, however temporarily, doubt is not possible in the case of what we cannot bring ourselves to disbelieve.

It is this position from which he starts, and not simply from the position that he does not know to be true what he does not clearly and distinctly see to be so. That is a position he is not justified in taking up until he has discovered, independently, something he cannot but know to be indubitably true. Otherwise how can he know that what is claimed to be a test for something's being true in fact works? Therefore, assuming knowledge is possible at all, he can only know that he knows, if, when he takes himself to know, he then has no reason to suppose it even possible that he doesn't. But for this to be so, not only must he be quite certain that what is taken to be known is in fact so, but also that there is not, and could not conceivably be any possibility of its being false.

Therefore for Descartes nothing that is possibly false, however remote this possibility, can properly be regarded as knowledge. But when can something not be even possibly false? How can one be sure that somehow, somewhere, at some time, in some respect, something allegedly known to be true may not turn out to be false? Only if such falsity is inconceivable. But we cannot know that it is inconceivable that something should be false unless we first try to conceive it so. And trying to conceive something as false is one of the things Descartes means by 'doubting'. We can see from this at once that if there is anything that we do really know, it must be indubitable, i.e., the attempt to conceive it as false, or to see that about it in respect of which it is not immediately and finally seen to be true, necessarily fails. Thus, the 'method' of doubt is absolutely basic to Descartes' enterprise. Small wonder that Descartes placed so much importance upon the need for a thorough understanding of his First Meditation. Clearly then it is not surprising that he should have been so impatient with Gassendi, who seems not to have found more to

4

say about the method of doubt, in his First Objection to Descartes' Meditations, than this:

On one point only I am not clear; that is, why you should not have preferred to indicate simply and with few words that what you previously knew was uncertain, in order subsequently to choose what might be found to be true, rather than by regarding everything as false, not so much to dismiss an old prejudice, as to take up with a new one. Thus, for example, it became necessary to feign that God was a deceiver, or some evil spirit that mocks us, in order to convince yourself; whereas it would have seemed to be sufficient to ascribe that to the obscurity of the human mind and the weakness of its nature alone. (ii, 136)

One cannot *start* philosophizing by claiming to know that the human mind is both obscure and weak. Yet even so, all the more reason for a method whereby this obscurity (which the mind is not so obscure as not to recognise) and weakness (which the mind is not so weak as to be incapable of inventing a method for compensating) is overcome.

Our first concern is with Descartes' way of separating, from all that he takes himself to know, the things he finds himself able to doubt, and which, on that account, he is not entitled to claim to know. He does not expect that all he takes himself to know can actually be proved false, but only those things that really are. Things may be assumed false that are not; but the slightest dubiety excludes them, initially at least, from being considered suitable as a foundation for a 'firm and permanent structure in the sciences'. Descartes had discovered not that *all* his former opinions were false, but only that many were. Without knowing the intrinsic mark of truth he does not, now, know which (if, indeed, any) of the remaining and unexamined opinions may not also turn out to be false. In each one there might be some reason, however slight and hidden, for supposing it not entirely true.

On the other hand, an opinion might pass for true simply because the right question has not been asked, the right situation not invoked, or observation taken. If everything that might show an opinion to be false has not been done, then how can we claim to know it isn't? We can't, says Descartes. We logically cannot assert something to be true and also possibly false at the same time.

But inasmuch as reason already persuades me that I ought no less carefully to withhold my assent from matters which are not entirely certain and indubitable than from those which appear to me manifestly to be false, if I am able to find in each one some reason to doubt, this will suffice to justify my rejecting the whole. (i, 145)

If we are not entirely certain that a given opinion is true, then how can we claim to know that it is? But what would constitute 'entirely certain'? Not being able to find even one reason for doubting? But what is to count as a reason for doubting? Let us examine this question.

Any proposition conceivably false is so on account of its providing us with at least one reason for doubting. First, then, what sort of proposition is it that could not conceivably be false; or, what sort of proposition is it that we might know not only to be true, but necessarily so? It cannot be the sort of proposition that we ordinarily claim to know to be true. For ordinarily when I claim to know, I am prepared to withdraw my claim if I turn out to be wrong, since my claim to know does not entail the claim that my being wrong is logically inconceivable. For to know that nothing could falsify a claim to know some matter of fact about the world is to possess a kind of omniscience. And we do not claim omniscience whenever we claim to know something. In short, we are ordinarily allowed to claim that we know, without being called upon to guarantee that no future experience could impugn that claim. But not by Descartes. For if it is conceivable that some future experience could show that what we claim as knowledge could be false, then our claim cannot be to entire certainty, and therefore we do not have knowledge. It is not merely that unless we know that no future experience can invalidate our claim to knowledge we are not entitled, on Descartes' view, to claim to know; we have to know it to be impossible for such a contingency to arise in the future. Only then are we entitled to claim entire certainty, for only then will it be the case that if one knows one can't be wrong. And this will follow not merely from the meaning of the word 'know', but from the nature of knowledge itself.

Let us now recall that the intention of Descartes was to 'freely address myself to the general upheaval of all my former opinions' (i, 144). He had claimed at the outset that for this it 'is not necessary that I should show that all of these are false' (i, 145).

Yet he did, as we saw, seem to think it necessary to show that they could be. And the reason for this is connected with Descartes' way of bringing his method to bear upon all our 'former opinions', so that he should not need to go and somehow dig each one of them up for an endless inspection. There is no time for a procedure of this kind. A short cut is necessary; and it is with Descartes' method of short-cutting that we are here concerned.

Since the opinions he is going to examine date from a pre-reflective period of his life, they may be regarded as based upon no more than he has received from the senses. Now if there is any one reason to doubt the veracity of the senses, then all opinions based upon them become systematically infected by the same doubt.

All that up to the present time I have accepted as most true and certain I have learned either from the senses or through the senses; but it is sometimes proved to me that these senses are deceptive, and it is wiser not to trust entirely to anything by which we have once been deceived. (i, 145)

With all cases of such 'deception' Descartes is not concerned. Sometimes our senses cannot do their job properly, as when objects are too small, or too distant. They do not then so much deceive us as fail us. And if we do not recognise this then we deceive ourselves and cannot blame the senses.

But what about near things under optimum conditions, such, for instance, says Descartes, as his own body as he sits and writes? 'And how could I deny that these hands and this body are mine' (i, 145), he asks, some 250 years before G. E. Moore. But immediately he remembers that insane people are no less convinced of truths that seem to them to be as clear to them as Descartes' truths are to him. And often they are deluded. How can he be certain he isn't? Yet Descartes seems reluctant to pursue his search for certainty through the experiences of those whose condition by definition can provide no rational basis for the kind of science he is determined to build. And besides, he is committed to proceeding from his own consciousness rather than from anyone else's.

So he considers dreaming, his own dreaming. For here, he maintains, he is often as certain of things being so that aren't, as any insane person. Consequently in dreams we believe what at least in some sense is not the case, for otherwise why should we distinguish them from waking? But the point that impresses itself upon Descartes is that he can find no mark by which to distinguish a dream state from a waking one. Consequently he cannot be certain in any single case that what appears to be a waking state might not after all be a dream. Thus, in regard to knowledge by the senses, he now has, in *all* cases, some one 'reason to doubt' what his senses declare to him is the truth. He writes:

At this moment it does indeed seem to me that it is with eyes awake that I am looking at this paper; that this head which I move is not asleep, that it is deliberately and of set purpose that I extend my hand and perceive it; what happens in sleep does not appear so clear nor so distinct as does all this. But in thinking over this I remind myself that on many occasions I have in sleep been deceived by similar illusions, and in dwelling carefully on this reflection I see so manifestly that there are no certain indications by which we may clearly distinguish wakefulness from sleep that I am lost in astonishment. And my astonishment is such that it is almost capable of persuading me that I now dream. (i, 146)

The problem concerning the ontological status of dreams is introduced merely as a justification for regarding as suspect *all* claims to sense knowledge.

Descartes' master-thought now is that even if we do suppose that all sense knowledge is itself dreamed, we can still argue from the nature of much of that knowledge to the existence of a world that is not dreamed, but is constituted by the actual things about which we do dream. What he is aiming to show is this: not so much that there must be a waking world, as well as a dream one—though this is what he at first appears to intend—but that there are truths in human experience such that waking *or* dreaming, they cannot be impugned. Here there are two points to bear in mind. Firstly, Descartes has to assume that where there is a dream there must be a dreamer who is not himself part of that dream, but who can be part of the experience of another person—or at least dreamed by him. It is difficult to see how this assumption can be avoided at all, in talk about dreams. Even if we regard the dream as taking place within a larger dream the dreamer of the inner dream must be represented as being a constituent of the outer one. That he is only, in turn, a dreamed constituent is irrelevant; to talk about dreams is to imply entities whose experiences may be, but whose selves *qua* dreamers are not, parts of those dreams.

The second point depends upon Descartes' obvious use of the same model as for the first, namely, a dual standpoint; sometimes he takes his stand as if from within a dream, and sometimes (after pretending to be trapped within it) from a point external to it.

Now let us assume that we are asleep and that all these particulars, e.g. that we open our eyes, shake our head, extend our hands, and so on, are but false delusions; and let us reflect that possibly neither our hands nor our whole body are such as they appear to us to be. At the same time we must at least confess that the things which are represented to us in sleep are like painted representations which can only have been formed as the counterparts of something real and true, and that in this way those general things at least, i.e. eyes, a head, hands, and a whole body, are not imaginary things, but things really existent. (i, 146)

The only necessity for Descartes to make this confession arises from the fact that his model requires it. For from his external standpoint, of course, he sees 'real and true' things; and from his internal standpoint he sees the 'painted representations' of these— but not *as* representations. Only, Descartes' model assumes the very thing he has so far denied, namely, that he can tell simply by inspection whether or not a given experience is dream or waking. For presumably he recognises 'real and true' things as those of which painted representations are made in dreams. At least he seems to know which is the real and true thing, and which the painted representation. And this cannot be justified by saying that the real and true things have to be experienced before one can dream about them, since the point at issue is our right to say that what comes first cannot be a painted representation. And we prove nothing by calling a dream a 'painted *representation*'.

Here, perhaps, Descartes is unwittingly trying to do two jobs at once. He is seeking something ultimately certain. He has cast doubt upon every single sense experience he has ever had. His move has been to argue that we can never be sure that we are not dreaming. Well, at this point is he trying to prove that an external world after all exists? Or is he trying to prove that there is *something* we know which is unshakeably true? But he doesn't really need at this point to prove that there is a waking world. All he needs to prove is that even if the waking world is also a dream world of another order, and even if we can never be certain whether a given experience is of one order or another, providing only we can find experiences of such a kind that their truth will be unaffected whichever order they occupy, he has got rid of whatever reason for total doubt may be derived from the fact that we certainly sometimes dream.

Now in some ways Descartes is as empirical as Hume. He does not think that we can dream or imagine unless a minimum of basic components are given to us, not something we present to ourselves, as in a dream or flight of imagination, but presented to us in circumstances where in the last resort we are hardly at liberty to refuse acceptance. Unless something is given to us, surely Descartes is saying, we can neither dream nor imagine, any more than we can perceive, physical objects. And although in the following quotation Descartes mentions only the colour sense, it is easy to see that what he says applies as well to the other sense modalities.

For, as a matter of fact, painters, even when they study with the greatest skill to represent sirens and satyrs by forms the most strange and extraordinary, cannot give them natures which are entirely new, but merely make a certain medley of the members of different animals; or if their imagination is extravagant enough to invent something so novel that nothing similar has ever before been seen, and that then their work represents a thing purely fictitious and absolutely false, it is certain all the same that the colours of which this is composed are necessarily real. (i, 146)

It is, however, not only with secondary, but also with primary qualities that Descartes is concerned. More precisely, with primary quality, or 'corporeal nature in general'. Unless, he means to say, we have had an independent and prior experience of what, like colours when first observed, is 'necessarily real', e.g. the attributes of extension, we cannot produce these later ourselves. This is not to say that these are held by Descartes to have the same ontological status as the contents of the various sensory modalities, but only that they depend for being experienced upon something other than our nature as thinking substances—in other words they are not innate.

And for the same reason, although these general things, to wit, [a body], eyes, a head, hands, and such like, may be imaginary, we are bound at the same time to confess that there are at least some other objects yet more simple and more universal, which are real and true; and of these just in the same way as with certain real colours, all these images of things which dwell in our thoughts, whether true and real or false and fantastic, are formed. . . . To such a class of things pertains corporeal nature in general, and its extension, the figure of extended things, their quantity or magnitude and number, as also the place in which they are, the time which measures their duration, and so on. (i, 146)

At this place we are not in a position to deal with the relation between the 'objects yet more simple and more universal', or that 'corporeal nature in general' which pertains to them; yet it is already clear that Descartes is maintaining that these 'objects yet more simple and more universal' possess, on that very account, the intrinsic power of resisting our attempts to cast doubts upon the truths they purport to express.

And therefore the faculty by means of which we apprehend these truths constitutes a knowledge of 'real and true things', operating in accordance with its own laws. By examining these operations Descartes hopes to arrive eventually at indubitable truth, for they do not depend upon whether or not something or other is the case in the world as known through the senses. We can be right about the nature of corporeality, but wrong in any given statement about some actual corporeal state of affairs. For to be right about the world we certainly need to know something about corporeal nature as such. But corporeal nature as such is corporeal substance and can only be described (or formulated) in terms that 'are very simple and very general', i.e. in the language of Arithmetic, and Geometry 'and other sciences of that kind which only treat of things that are very simple and very general' (i, 147). The point of all this is precisely that statements in that language do not depend for their truth upon whether anyone is sleeping or awake, or whether the actual world of corporeal nature is in one rather than in another condition, or even, one might add, upon whether the sensible world itself be regarded as a modification of thinking substance or of corporeal substance. Speaking of these things that are very simple and general, Descartes says:

To such a class of things pertains corporeal nature in general, and its extension, the figure of extended things, their quantity or magnitude and number, as also the place in which they are, the time which measures their duration, and so on. (i, 146)

What Descartes needs to (and does) bring out here, is the point that truths about the nature of primary qualities depend upon a mode of apprehension that is no less reliable when we dream than when we are awake. Here, then, for him lies a higher degree of certainty than he has so far reached. The truths here possess an independence such that once we see them to be true we know they would continue so though not only the world of dreams, but the physical world itself should cease to exist.

That is possibly why our reasoning is not unjust when we conclude from this that Physics, Astronomy, Medicine and all other sciences which have as their end the consideration of composite things, are very dubious and uncertain; but that Arithmetic, Geometry and other sciences of that kind which only treat of things that are very simple and very general, without taking great trouble to ascertain whether they are actually existent or not, contain some measure of certainty and an element of the indubitable. For whether I am awake or asleep, two and three together always form five, and the square can never have more than four sides, and it does not seem possible that truths so clear and apparent can be suspected of any falsity [or uncertainty]. (i, 147)

Let us take note of the phrase 'an element of the indubitable'. It is clear from this alone, apart from other considerations, that Descartes does not take himself to have reached that complete indubitability which he seeks. And in the Latin version, his first, he did not feel able to close the above paragraph with the expression 'or uncertainty', as he did in the French. Let it be, Descartes in effect says, that there is no real difference between dreams and waking life (although he has all along assumed the opposite), still something is necessary to constitute the corporeality (dreamed or real) of physical objects (likewise dreamed or real).

What are these truths which are not less true in dreaming than waking life? They are, we may remember

objects yet more simple and more universal, which are real and true;

and of these just in the same way as with certain real colours, all these images of things which dwell in our thoughts, whether true and real or false and fantastic, are formed. (i, 146)

These are things which he has said possess an element of indubitability whether they are actually existent or not. They are not extended things, or they would not apply equally to dreaming and waking experiences. Yet they do apply to extended things. They are not themselves figured, yet they apply to figures. They themselves have no quantity, magnitude, or number, yet, as we have seen, they apply in such a way to all these things, that in terms of these we understand them. Descartes says again and again that there are many such truths if only we would not be too proud to attend to them. In imagination you can call up a circle, or a triangle, or a straight line, and then by thought you will know that their very essence entails the possession by them of certain properties. The part is less than the whole, two things equal to a third are equal to one another in the same respect, and so on.

And the point about these is that to see them at all, whether dreaming or waking, is to see that they *could* not be false. This has nothing to do with induction or deduction. They are seen as independent of any need for justification. It is our immediate knowledge of their intrinsic indisputability that constitutes our intuition of them. Descartes' 'simples', as he has called them, have three characteristics. They cannot be known save as necessarily true. They cannot be negated and remain intelligible. And their truth is simple in the sense that there cannot be anything simpler from which they can be derived. Now, does a knowledge of these simples constitute that kind of indubitable knowledge sought by Descartes? We do not, admittedly, see how they could be false. But does this entitle us to conclude that it is impossible that they could be? For, consider, is not the claim that since *we* do not see how something could possibly be false it cannot be, itself a claim to indubitable knowledge?

But what we now have to be concerned with, thinks Descartes, is the deeper question whether even the clearest human intuition of some given truth can be self-authenticating. Someone may be quite certain something is true, and unable even to conceive its being false; but how can it follow from this condition of someone's state of mind that he may not be wrong? Perhaps there is

13

a physical universe, and perhaps knowledge *is* possible. Perhaps, even, we know this because we possess an organ of knowledge. But how can we be sure this organ is in a healthy condition? Might it not be chronically diseased, giving us systematic distortion of the truth? Or perhaps our 'organ of knowledge' is healthy, but functions at its best *when* it is most successful in falsifying the world to us—or perhaps (it might even be) in suggesting that there is a world to falsify? *The* method of doubt, indeed. We may well begin, here, to wonder what sort of knowledge it can be that Descartes seeks, and whether it is a form of knowledge that should properly be classed as human or divine. In the upshot it is my purpose to show that for Descartes this disjunction is by no means as exclusive as it looks.

I have, here, been raising the question of whether there is a knowledge such that no conceivable hypothesis could render it dubitable. What we have now to consider is not whether we can, or might, be mistaken, but whether things are so arranged that we must be. And what Descartes has to show is that in some one respect at least this is impossible. This alone would save us from having to 'conclude' that even the concept of knowledge is a fictitious one. The cosy propositions that seemed no less true when they occurred in a dream than when they occurred in waking are not, at this stage, necessarily less suspect than the objects of sense perception themselves.

It is not enough, therefore, for Descartes, that we cannot think how we could possibly be so mistaken; *we must also have some reason for being unable to doubt that our thinking that we cannot possibly be mistaken about a given thing entails that we cannot be.* If we had such a reason then our knowledge would no longer have to rest upon a possibly conditioned ground, but upon something itself independent of any conceivable human limitation. In that case we would know that we could not have been primed to 'know' falsely. It would thereupon follow that in some matter, at least, we could have a knowledge as pure as that of God. And this would be a knowledge that no finite limitation could contaminate. Now what Descartes is asking is not whether we could get such knowledge, but whether, without realizing it, we do in fact have it, and can use it. For if we have not got it already we have not got anything at all upon which such a knowledge can be grounded, either. Without truth being somehow in us, we could have no ground whatsoever for supposing that we could recognize truth if presented with it. But if we have got it then there is some knowledge in our possession such that we could no more doubt it than God could doubt the knowledge he has. But if we do have such knowledge then it must be something, that very thing, that no conceivable hypothesis could shake.

Such, for instance, as the hypothesis not merely that our organ of knowledge is diseased (wires crossed, if you like) or happens to be designed to give as knowledge what is not, but that some being endowed with all that is necessary for the purpose, is deliberately seeking all the time actually to deceive us. From such a being there would appear to be no conceivable escape. For if even by chance we were to hit upon some loophole in his design he would be on the spot at once to close it and create even more sophisticated avenues of deception. Our being deceived would thus be the intentional action of a being presumably not less powerful for that purpose than God—but a *malin génie*, and a very personal one.

It is true that we could question the apparatus of deception that Descartes sets up. Is it more or less likely, we might ask, that two and two make four, than that there is a deceiver such as Descartes envisages possible? But this would be irrelevant; for there might be; and if there were, how could we ever know? Let us permit ourselves for a moment to glance at some of the speculative possibilities. Perhaps, indeed there is a world of the kind we take ourselves to have knowledge about, but it is not the same world. Perhaps there was once such a world, but not now. Perhaps there will eventually be a change in the present world so that it then becomes as we now think it is. Perhaps such a world will one day be created where no world of that kind, or perhaps indeed of any kind, existed before. Perhaps there never was or will be such a world. Perhaps there is nothing but what is in my mind when I think, but in such a way that before I can properly identify it I have forgotten what it was and think that what I remember is true, when in fact all memory is illusory. This is to say that memory is simply imagination of some state of affairs plus imagination of that state of affairs having once been actually a present state of affairs. Perhaps, in that case, there is no time as we now conceive it, either. For if nothing at all happens as I suppose it to, then there is no need for a past time for it to have happened in, nor for a future time, since there isn't going to be anything that would need time in order to happen after something else. And we can be deceived into even supposing something is happening now when it isn't. For we are not deceived unless we believe something to be true, and we cannot be said to believe something to be true if we do not feel sure that it is. But if we can feel sure that something has happened in the past, when it perhaps has not, how can we be sure that the feeling of being sure is not itself something that depends less than we think upon what we are sure about— and perhaps even not at all?

It should now be evident that the question before us has changed from whether we can be in error, to the question of whether we are fated never not to be in error. Suppose we had been so fated by a being with supernatural power. Suppose that in every respect in which we can be deceived he does his best to deceive us. The question is: must he succeed? If so then the power to gain even the minutest possible grain of knowledge *cannot* lie in us. We could not, on such an assumption, even know with certainty that something, at some time, is not something we know for certain. We could not, in that case, recognise as true something presented to us even as it might be presented to God and known by him to be so.

Knowledge would now appear to be infinitely removed from us. But Descartes, in searching for something true, first by his introduction of dreaming, and now by his introduction of the *malin génie*, seems to have ended by showing, not what is true, or how to tell that something is true, but by showing that even the concept of knowledge in its purest sense has no application whatsoever, and moreover *can* have no application whatsoever at least to himself, Descartes, a thinking being—perhaps! Can Descartes, Houdini-like, escape from this trap into which he has so tortuously led himself? If not, the Meditations should end here.

But they don't, and he begins to prepare his escape. He has stated those conditions under which it would be true to say he has no knowledge whatsoever. The conditions conceivably, even if not in fact, apply; therefore, conceivably, even if not in fact (something he cannot know) he has no knowledge whatsoever. But either he in fact does have knowledge, or he in fact does not. But even if he does, he doesn't really know this for a fact at all. For it rests upon a condition which is entirely hypothetical. He doesn't know whether he knows or not.

The next move is to give up, for strategic reasons, for the time being, the search for knowledge altogether. For it is only whilst I suppose that I know, that I can be wrong. If I refrain from supposing I know, then I cannot be wrong. But if I am not wrong I am not deceived; and if I cannot be wrong I cannot be deceived either—no matter by whom. The price of not being deceived, then, is to take nothing as true. Only obviously this cannot apply to practical matters, such as those of life and death, and so on, as Descartes has already made clear. Nor, in any case, will it be easy to disbelieve on principle what one has for long believed by habit. It will not be easy, either, to disbelieve things that though not entirely indubitable, are more rather than less indubitable. Here, unless we hold them to be entirely false, we are more likely to believe them entirely true than only very likely so. And whereas if we hold them true we are open again to be deceived, if we say not that they are false, but that we disbelieve that they are true, then we are not fulfilling one necessary condition for being deceived, namely believing that something is true, whether this something is a positive or a negative proposition.

But in taking up this position we are in effect refusing to allow our thinking to be dominated by those habits set up in us by our commerce with the sensible world. In this way it is clear that Descartes intends to make room for the autonomy of rational thought. It is true that for the moment all he wants to do is remove us from the dominating influence of sense experience. Instead of believing that nothing is true but what we know through the senses, we are learning to live with the possibility that if anything at all is true, it need not, and indeed cannot be what we know through the senses—at least if by 'true' we mean unquestionably true. We are also in this way learning to recognise not merely the autonomy of thought, but that in thought rather than in the senses we are more likely to find truth, if we are to find it anywhere. Nothing is more fundamental for understanding Descartes than to gain from him the insight that through thought, and not through sense experience is knowledge attainable—if it is attainable.

But it is not sufficient to have made these remarks, we must also be careful to keep them in mind. For these ancient and commonly held opinions still revert frequently to my mind, long and familiar custom having given them the right to occupy my mind against my inclination and rendered them almost masters of my belief; nor will I ever lose the habit of deferring to them or of placing my confidence in them, so long as I consider them as they really are, i.e. opinions in some measure doubtful, as I have just shown, and at the same time highly probable, so that there is much more reason to believe in than to deny them. That is why I consider that I shall not be acting amiss, if, taking of set purpose a contrary belief, I allow myself to be deceived, and for a certain time pretend that all these opinions are entirely false and imaginary, until at last, having thus balanced my former prejudices with my latter [so that they cannot divert my opinions more to one side than to the other], my judgment will no longer be dominated by bad usage or turned away from the right knowledge of the truth. For I am assured that there can be neither peril nor error in this course, and that I cannot at present yield too much to distrust, since I am not considering the question of action, but only of knowledge. (i, 148)

It can of course be argued that Descartes has here set up a dualism of thought and action which has had considerable ill effects. With this I am not now concerned. But whether, on the other hand, that is the way to avoid error, is another matter. If I have no beliefs I am not in error. If I have true beliefs I am not in error either. But 'not being in error' means something quite different in each case. For where there is no bid for truth there can be no risk of error. Or perhaps one should put it another way; in respect of theory, at least, that about which one has no beliefs cannot be that about which one is in error, whereas that about which one does have beliefs, may or may not be that about which one is in error. And not to be in error, because one believes nothing at all, is a condition of no value for Descartes' purpose, for in so far as one really believes nothing at all, one cannot by thought move to something one can believe without error, i.e. to knowledge—which is the goal of his efforts. From a purely sceptical position no advance whatsoever is possible. At some point, where Descartes begins to advance, there must be something that he must be prepared to say is true; and however obvious it must be to him that it is true, will he succeed in showing that it is also something that could not have been false? That is a question for the Second Meditation.

As Descartes approaches the end of his First Meditation, he gives his position an extra twist. For he now declares not just that he will not believe the sensible world to exist, nor therefore even his body with its sensory organs, but than he does in fact believe them to, only in believing it, he believes falsely. Thus he will regard himself as entertaining a false belief, though he no more knows for certain that this belief is false than he does that it is true. It is clear to me that his hope lies, at this juncture, in the possibility that in his review of beliefs, all of which he hypothetically regards as false, one will resist this treatment. In that case he will have taken the first step towards knowledge. If not, then, being undeceived, he is no worse off than before, and still in the most advantageous position for recognising the unfalsifiability of some view he may meet with, if it turns out to be such. Hence he writes:

I shall consider myself as having no hands, no eyes, no flesh, no blood, nor any senses, yet falsely believing myself to possess all these things; I shall remain obstinately attached to this idea, and if by this means it is not in my power to arrive at the knowledge of any truth, I may at least do what is in my power [i.e. suspend my judgment], and with firm purpose avoid giving credence to any false thing, or being imposed upon by this arch deceiver, however powerful and deceptive he may be. (i, 148)

This, indeed, is no natural human frame of mind. No wonder Descartes ends his Meditation in such sombre mood.

CHAPTER TWO

AT THE END of Meditation One we left an extremely bodiless Descartes. He had thought his body away, together with all other body, yet found himself still in being, if anything with a more accentuated self-consciousness than ever. Certainly thinking one's body away has not entailed, for Descartes, thinking one's mind away. Loss of body, then, seems no handicap to the existence of a thinking being. Being without perception is evidently not being without thought. So Descartes thinks. If his experiences are only the fictions of his mind, then he does not know that they have not been put there. Nor does he know that there is not something somewhere completely indubitable. So perhaps this something is that which has put the fictions in his mind.

But surely, Descartes supposes, a better candidate for this honour would be myself. For it is not clearer to me that a being unknown to me should have put those fictions in my mind than that I myself should have. So at least I am clear to myself; and it is equally clear to me that I am something. For otherwise how could I even have conceived myself as the cause, whether I am or not? And in my case I know there must be someone (namely myself) for whom all knowledge may be nothing but fiction. Thus, whether as producer of fictions, or receiver of them, Descartes finds his attention drawn to himself. But since he has to doubt all things, must he not also doubt his own existence? Perhaps here too he is being deceived into thinking he is someone when he isn't.

On the other hand, even if there are fictions, these fictions are not fictional. Whether or not he himself has produced them they exist in his consciousness. They are *his* fictions—which they could not be unless he existed. He for whom they are fictions can no more be part of those fictions than he who dreams can be part of his own dreams—in which case, of course, there would be no one to have dreamed them. To doubt requires that we postulate

20

fictions (since we cannot logically claim there is nothing at all).
But we can no more argue that the fictions themselves are not
anybody's, than that the real experiences which we should be
having if these were not fictions, are not. However problematic
the ontological or epistemological status of our experience-or-
fiction, there is nothing problematic about the observing being
whose existence is entailed equally by truth or fiction. If there is
no such being there is nothing at all.

At this point it is vital to remember Descartes' methodological
position. He will not take himself to know anything whatsoever
as long as he has the slightest reason to doubt. Nothing can be
counted as known unless no possibility remains conceivable by
which it might be shown that it is not (in the slightest conceivable
respect) what we suppose it to be. It is conceivable that whatever
we take to be a waking experience is in fact a dream, that whatever
we take ourselves to remember as having happened did not.
Therefore, so far, we have not found anything at all that can
count, for Descartes, as knowledge. And if it is also conceivable
that the being Descartes refers to as 'I' does not exist, then knowledge is absolutely ruled out if only because one of the necessary
conditions for it is missing, namely, someone to 'possess' it. Thus
Descartes asks whether it is conceivable that he, Descartes, not
the outwardly appearing figure who is for him conceivably as
unreal as all other physical objects, but the Descartes for whom
there may or may not really be physical objects at all, does not
exist.

But I was persuaded that there was nothing in all the world, that there
was no heaven, no earth, that there were no minds, nor any bodies:
was I not then likewise persuaded that I did not exist? Not at all; of a
surety I myself did exist since I persuaded myself of something [or
merely because I thought of something]. (i, 150)

It is not the fact that he thinks of this or that, but the fact that he
thinks at all that matters here. Thus to think wrongly is still to
think. There is at least a thinking. And thinking itself is inconceivable for Descartes (as he argues in other places) except as the
activity of a substance, i.e. a thinking thing—which he knows from
first hand, insofar as he is not conscious of a thinking that is not
his thinking, or, more properly, himself thinking.

There is still another possibility to be considered; perhaps a deceiver is at work here too. Is it conceivable that perhaps after all I am only deceived into supposing myself to exist? But if I am deceived into supposing I exist (as distinct from being deceived into supposing to exist what does not) then not only must I exist, in order to be deceived, but also, since outside a relationship with the *malin génie* (*ex hypothesi*) I have no existence, he must be understood as actually having caused me to exist in order for him to deceive me into supposing I do, when really I don't. If this is inconceivable, then nothing is gained by introducing the device of a *malin génie* here, and the last possible reason for doubting that I exist would seem to be rolled up. Illusory selves are inconceivable animals; where there is nobody at all to be taken in there are no illusions. As for deception, this requires not merely one intelligent being, but at least two. So that even (which is inconceivable) if I could conceive myself as being deceived in supposing myself to exist, the necessary condition for this would have to be that I suppose myself not to be deceived into supposing a *malin génie* to exist. But my only excuse for introducing him is to get rid of myself. And it can be argued that I have more reason to doubt his existence than my own. Moreover, to believe in his existence rather than my own, to deny knowledge of my own existence (which could conceivably lead me to further knowledge) when even if I accept that he exists I can never know this with the same certainty with which I know of my own existence, would on Descartes' principles, be to exchange the substance of knowledge for a distorted reflection of the shadow. It would be odd of Descartes to have wanted to show in this Meditation that the human mind 'is more easily known than the body', and end by concluding that nevertheless it is less easily known than the existence of the *malin génie*.

Certainly being capable of being deceived is enough for being someone, but the self we are considering is capable of more than that; he is also capable, as we have seen, of protecting himself against deceit in general, and now against being deceived into thinking that perhaps after all he doesn't exist. For in protecting himself against being deceived in thinking he does exist, he has to think himself into doubting everything. And now he is not only the one who is deceived, but he is also the one who pretends to himself that whatever might be false is. He is not only a conscious being, but also a thinking, i.e. a cogitating one. He can reject the mere evidence of his senses, and he only then discovers that his true nature is to think, for it is only without this thinking that he ceases to be a self, and with this thinking he does not essentially need anything else.

Descartes covers his argument in an important respect. The mere capability of being deceived, or of believing uncritically, is not enough to characterise a consciousness such as our own. The conception of a self is the concept of a thinker, and therefore of an actual or potential critic. The categories of true, false, valid, invalid, appear here, and it is, it seems to me, the active and critical, rather than the passive and gullible, self, who resists, by his thinking, his own theoretical annihilation, and in doing so affirms his own theoretical indestructibility. Which is all that, at this stage, Descartes requires.

But Descartes himself has not yet made use of the 'active-passive' kind of distinction just noted, since it is hidden rather than revealed in his exposition. Hence the self who emerges out of his first formulation of the argument from thinking to existing, is not yet the recognisable self characterised by awareness of its own self-identity:

But there is some deceiver or other, very powerful and very cunning, who ever employs his ingenuity in deceiving me. Then without doubt I exist also if he deceives me, and let him deceive me as much as he will, he can never cause me to be nothing so long as I think that I am something. So that after having reflected well and carefully examined all things, we must come to the definite conclusion that this proposition: I am, I exist, is necessarily true each time that I pronounce it, or that I mentally conceive it. (i, 150)

Whereas hitherto Descartes has argued that to think anything at all is to exist, he now argues, in effect, that to think of oneself as existing is as much a proof that one exists, as to think of anything else as existing. And indeed it is a double proof. For the self declares to exist not an illusory self, but itself. Since a self must exist to declare that it does, and the self that is declared to exist is also the self that declares itself to, the self that is declared to exist is meant to be the same self, and therefore to have the same 'truth and reality' as the self which makes the declaration.

C

23

Nevertheless, and this is relevant to the thesis of this book, the self so far 'demonstrated', however, real, is only an atomic pulse of our everyday self, without continuity between the self declared to exist on one occasion, and the self declared to exist at any other: 'I am, I exist, is necessarily true each time that I pronounce it, or that I mentally conceive it' (i, 150). But, so far, presumably not otherwise. What guarantee, for instance, have we that the self deceived is the one that now resists deception? Or that the self today is identical with the self of yesterday? Or even that the self that began to declare its own existence is identical with the self that finished it?

Descartes' next task must be to discover the unity that confers continuity upon the pulses of self which are all that he has so far shown (indubitably?) to exist. He is set here, however, to avoid including in the self what is not it. For in mistaking what is not himself for himself he would be taking as part of himself what is not. He wants to be as certain of what he is, as he now is that at least sometime it is true that a pulse of self exists. Thus:

But I do not yet know clearly enough what I am, I who am certain that I am; and hence I must be careful to see that I do not imprudently take some other object in place of myself, and thus that I do not go astray in respect of this knowledge that I hold to be the most certain and most evident of all that I have formerly learned. (i, 150)

In asking himself what he is, says Descartes, he is not concerned with definitions, for these lead away from himself, in the direction of the species and the genus, both directly and collaterally, without end, thereby raising more questions than are answered. It is not a classificatory system within which to place himself and so read what he is in terms of the system, that Descartes seeks, but an understanding of his own nature as it is in itself, and therefore in just those respects in which its explanation is in terms appropriate to itself only, and not to other things. Hence, indeed, the sub-title of Meditation Two, 'Of the Nature of the Human Mind; and that it is more easily known than the Body'. To understand this is to understand why Descartes does not regard himself as having lost anything of himself by supposing himself bodiless in a bodiless universe, but rather as more clearly exhibited in his true light. For now, in being bodiless etc., he is also without perception, and without feeling. If he can still identify himself, even for an instant, then this can only be by that which is closer to his essence than anything else. And, of course, it turns out to be thinking; for in the fact that he thinks (and that something— whether 'I' or self—thinks, is indubitable) is expressed the nature of a thinker.

It follows, firstly, that the thinker is not entitled to claim to exist when he is not thinking, nor even for the smallest period which he does not remember having endured. The question raised here does not concern our actual beliefs, but our justification for holding them. And just as the thinker cannot know himself to exist when not thinking, so he cannot, supposes Descartes, think without knowing himself as the subject thinking. Secondly, if there were some other activity which he could identify as an essential expression of the self, then in that activity he should find his self as the subject exactly as he does in thinking.

The problem for Descartes now is to identify, if he can, activities in which the self expresses its true nature no less than in thinking. That is to say activities in which the self no less reveals itself than in thinking. This rules out, at once, activities of a physical, or emotional kind, for instance, or whatever depends for its existence upon what falls in 'the sphere of the doubtful'.

Can I affirm that I possess the least of all those things which I have just said pertain to the nature of body? . . . I find none of which I can say that it pertains to me. . . . Let us pass to the attributes of soul and see if there is any one which is in me? What of nutrition or walking [the first mentioned]? But if it is so that I have no body it is also true that I can neither walk nor take nourishment. Another attribute is sensation. But one cannot feel without body, and besides I have thought I perceived many things during sleep that I recognised in my waking moments as not having been experienced at all. What of thinking? I find here that thought is an attribute that belongs to me; it alone cannot be separated from me. I am, I exist, that is certain. But how often? Just when I think; for it might possibly be the case if I ceased entirely to think, that I should likewise cease altogether to exist. I do not now admit anything which is not necessarily true: to speak accurately I am not more than a thing which thinks, that is to say a mind or a soul, or an understanding, or a reason, which are terms whose significance was formerly unknown to me. I am, however, a real thing and really exist; but what thing? I have answered: a thing which thinks. (i, 151)

So far, Descartes has not 'admitted' knowing anything other than his own existence as a finite thinking substance. In seeking the basis of his continuing self-identity he is after some clue to what else he may be besides a being that thinks. But to ask whether or not some of the things he can doubt, e.g. physical objects, may not after all be expressions of what he essentially is, is also to enquire into the limits of the nature of the self. And beyond these limits, if there is such a beyond, lies the not-self, i.e. that which is expressed by whatever is not an expression of his own nature. Now it is fundamental to Descartes' position never to move from less to more certainty, but always from that of which we are more sure than any other known position at the time. Thus we can understand why his very first move must be from the most certain of all positions conceivable. If the nature of the self were not to think then it would be hard to see how knowledge would be possible for it. But thinking is in its very essence a search after truth—after knowledge. Since, then, it is the nature of the self to know, it is from what the self knows, really knows, that we must begin; and what it knows most indubitably, Descartes has argued, is its own existence *qua* thinking substance. And this it does not have to infer (nor could it) from anything other than itself, for no premise could be more certain to the self, Descartes maintains, than the certainty it has of its own existence. But, also, the self cannot be held able to know something to be other than itself, unless it knows itself well enough to know what cannot be part of itself. In other words, the self must have complete knowledge of its own essence in order for it really to know that this or that thing is not part of itself.

Now on the one hand, as we saw, Descartes insists that the self cannot but know itself—at least in some measure. But on the other hand it does not follow from this that what the self does not know as part of itself cannot be part of itself, or that if anything is part of the self the self is necessitated to know this to be so. Descartes has not supposed that the self is transparent to the knowledge of itself, in the sense that we simply look and see instantly all that we are. Our access may be privileged, but is not necessarily gratis. It was not immediately obvious even to Descartes that we really exist; not to speak of his striving to discover the nature of his own soul. Descartes does not say that we must know all (or even anything) about our selves; but only that we can—if we reflect, hard. And that is what he does.

Well, the fact that I know that what I know about myself may not be all there is to know about myself does not alone entitle me to say that there is more to me than I now know. Though, of course, so far, there may be. Descartes has from the beginning been concerned with the question: how can I find something that I know, unless I know myself well enough to know that I know? From this point on he considers himself justified in claiming that he does know himself well enough to know this—but not, yet, more than this. It is clear that though Descartes does not yet know all that he is, he must not use statements about what he is not (since he can doubt them, and what he can successfully doubt cannot be a part of his own essence—that essence which by its nature we have seen he cannot doubt) as grounds for a conclusion about what he essentially is.

But it is very certain that the knowledge of my existence taken in its precise significance does not depend on things whose existence is not yet known to me; consequently it does not depend on those which I can feign in imagination. And indeed the very term *feign* in imagination ⟨form an image⟩ proves to me my error, for I really do this if I imagine myself a something, since to imagine is nothing else than to contemplate the figure or image of a corporeal thing. (i, 152)

It is absolutely vital to be clear at this point. The existence of any corporeal object, Descartes has argued, is dubitable. So images of any corporeal object are images of the dubitable. They have, therefore, no foundation in certainty. Moreover the activity of feigning, itself, is one that we know of, in the first instance, only in relation to corporal objects, i.e. to things we can doubt. Therefore this activity necessarily participates in the same dubiety that shrouds its objects. How, then, asks Descartes in effect, can things which are dubitable characterise an essential quality of things which are indubitable? And since they cannot, we must conclude that nothing that we can know by an activity of imagining can be an essential part of that substance whose nature is to think. Not to see this clearly is not to see the true basis of Descartes' dualism—an epistemic one. Whatever the self may turn out to be it must be something as indubitable as the self's existence as a thinking being: whatever is not as indubitable as that *cannot* be part of a self.

Since what Descartes is denying is that anything known by the imagination can be part of a thinking self, to suppose that imagination can help us to learn more about the self than thinking can, is to suppose that truth is more likely to be generated from dubitable than from indubitable grounds.

For this reason I see clearly that I have as little reason to say, 'I shall stimulate my imagination in order to know more distinctly what I am,' than if I were to say, 'I am now awake, and I perceive somewhat that is real and true: but because I do not yet perceive it distinctly enough, I shall go to sleep of express purpose, so that my dreams may represent the perception with greatest truth and evidence.'

No wonder Descartes then proceeds:

And, thus, I know for certain that nothing of all that I can understand by means of my imagination belongs to this knowledge which I have of myself, and that it is necessary to recall the mind from this mode of thought with the utmost diligence in order that it may be able to know its own nature with perfect distinctness. (i, 152-3)

It was his doubting that revealed to Descartes that he is a thing that thinks. But to doubt is to think not only in the sense that doubting is thinking, but also in the sense that doubting in Descartes' sense requires us to think. Descartes thinks not only when, but also because he doubts.

He desires to know the truth, is averse to being deceived, or even simply to being ignorant. And now Descartes proposes to unite his pulses of thinking substance into an intuitable and continuing self:

Am I not that being who now doubts nearly everything, who nevertheless understands certain things, who affirms that one only is true, who denies all the others, who desires to know more, is averse from being deceived, who imagines many things, sometimes indeed despite his will, and who perceives many likewise, as by the intervention of the bodily organs? (i, 153)

What can these 'mental acts' have in common? Not the same object, for some of their objects can be doubted whereas others cannot.

The only remaining thing they can have in common relates to

their origin. Each activity is *my* activity; and the self to which each activity 'belongs', whose activity it is, is *my* self. How do I know? Exactly in the way I know that I think. We may recall that for Descartes one is no less thinking when being deceived than when not. Thus that some activity of mine, such as imagining, for instance, cannot be relied upon to give me truth, is irrelevant to its being *my* activity. It is not self-contradictory to speak of invalid thinking. Therefore something's being invalid is not by itself sufficient to prevent it from being an instance of thinking. Therefore imagining would not fail to be considered thinking merely because it could be false in any claim it might make to be considered knowledge. Nor, if this is so, would perceiving, or even feeling. The sense of 'think' is here wider than it has been so far. But the relation between the two senses is perfectly clear. So far Descartes has contrasted the thinking that gives him indubitable knowledge with other kinds. And there is a kind of thinking, in the strict sense of the word, which gives him, and can give him, only truth. From this all other activities of the self are separated, for reasons we should by now comprehend. But there is another sense of thinking, as we have just seen, in which dubiety concerning the outcome is possible. And in this wider sense, thinking includes not only thinking as it is more strictly conceived, but also imagining, perceiving and feeling, in spite of their dubiety. Now, if he can establish between the self and these more dubitable activities of the self the same kind of relation as between the self and thinking in the more rigorous sense of that word, then might he not be justified in referring to them as 'thinking', to indicate no more than that they do share this relation?

What then is this relation? Firstly, they are related to me as acts (or activities) of mine. Roughly, this is the sense of 'mine' which guarantees my privileged access. But it is more than that. They are all equally modes, or forms, or maybe we should simply say 'ways', of my being conscious of whatever it is I am conscious of. Am I less certain that I perceive (whether truly or falsely) than that I think, even when I think truly? If not, then to perceive (or imagine, or feel) is just as much an expression of the essential nature of the self as to think, even in the strictest sense of that word. And just as Descartes maintains that thinking, in the strict sense, even in a dream (which he does not doubt possible) admits of as much validity as thinking outside it, at least as an activity of the self, so these other activities, even if dreamed, are none the less activities of the self. For to dream is to do something, to experience something, in short to undergo some form of conscious existence. And especially since I cannot be certain at any time that I am not dreaming, (even when thinking in the strict sense) the question of whether I am dreaming or not is irrelevant to the question of whether I am conscious or not. For whether what I am conscious of as existing, exists or not, my being conscious, in the way I am, is an inexpugnable fact about the nature of my (human) mind; and whether I can know the truth (if there is a truth) of what lies beyond consciousness, or not, I can know the truth about what occurs, so to say, 'within' consciousness itself—regarded as a modification (and no more) of the 'fabric' of consciousness.

It is one thing to claim that the objects of certain ways of being conscious, i.e. imagining, perceiving, etc., are part of my essential nature, a claim which, for Descartes, is false. It is another to claim that the various activities by which consciousness is spelled out are part of my nature, even my essential nature. In every activity of mind, Descartes seems to suppose, there is some element of thinking without which it could not be brought within that form of consciousness wherein it has the possibility not merely of being, but also of being understood.

Thus Descartes' own words are enormously significant:

Is there nothing in all this which is as true as it is certain that I exist, even though I should always sleep and though he who has given me being employed all his ingenuity in deceiving me? Is there likewise any one of these attributes which can be distinguished from my thought, or which might be said to be separated from myself? For it is so evident of itself that it is I who doubts, who understands, and who desires, that there is no reason here to add anything to explain it. . . . Finally, I am the same who feels, that is to say, who perceives certain things, as by the organs of sense, since in truth I see light, I hear noise, I feel heat. But it will be said that these phenomena are false and that I am dreaming. Let it be so; still it is at least quite certain that it seems to me that I see light, that I hear noise and that I feel heat. That cannot be false; properly speaking it is what is in me called feeling; and used in this precise sense that is no other thing than thinking. (i, 153)

By 'precise sense' then, Descartes clearly means regarded as an activity of the self, and without any reference whatsoever to whether or not the object of the activity is what it may appear to be to the self.

On the other hand we should bear in mind that even with regard to the objects of the mind's activities, these are not necessarily to be dismissed as false for being, in Descartes' sense, dubitable. We can point out that it is precisely because of *perceptions* he had that Descartes began to hold perceptions theoretically suspect. And so with feelings. We think some feelings must be false because others are true. For instance, the water could not have been cold a moment ago, when now it feels warm. Indeed, the very doubts we feel in these matters arise just because we find it incomprehensible that the senses cannot be trusted. This is not to suggest they are not dubitable, but only to remind ourselves that what is dubitable might none the less be true; and that in this sort of case it is hard to see how what appears to be true, isn't. However, what I imagine, or perceive, or feel to be true, may not be; but since it has been proved that I exist as a thinking thing, the activities we have been examining are no less mine, as we saw, whether what they purport to reveal to me is true or not. And so the same self that formerly perceived, and later imagined what it had perceived, and later still doubted that what it perceived was what it seemed to be, and that thereupon exercised its will in seeking to resolve its doubt, by all this and much more shows that the diversity of its forms of expression are not only not dissolved in its unity, but actually kept alive by it.

From this point Descartes takes himself to have demonstrated, with all the certainty it would be meaningful to expect, that he exists and that his nature is to be conscious in a variety of ways, or, we might say, by means of various activities such as those he has enumerated. But has he not burned his boats behind him? Fleeing from the sea of uncertainty he has at last found refuge upon the island of consciousness; but how does he propose now to return to the mainland of corporeal nature? If such a return is out of the question what becomes of his grandiose plans for a 'firm and permanent structure in the sciences'? If nothing, then what possible good is his precious certainty to him?

Descartes is for the time being confined within his own con-

31

sciousness. He does not yet know whether what his consciousness 'tells' him about the world outside himself is true or false. Nor can he even be certain that there is a world outside his consciousness. Thus he cannot be certain that those elements in his consciousness that appear to represent to him what lies outside consciousness do so. It is precisely the dubitability of the independent existence of what purports to be represented in consciousness (as for instance perceptual objects) that unfits it for being an essential part of the self. On the other hand, it does not follow from this that the activities by which the dubitable is grasped by the self (*as* dubitable, be it said) are themselves dubitable. As we have seen, it would be difficult to give sense to such a claim. Thus it is indisputable, for instance, that we imagine, but not indisputable that what we imagine is true. This brings out the queerness of the view that the self actually maintains itself (or rather is maintained) in existence by assimilating within its own consciousness what it *itself* (that of which it is most of all certain) cannot know to be equally certain. The self would appear on this view to have a kind of built-in indifference to truth, or at least a built-in capacity to get along without it. And this, I would say, frightened Descartes.

It is not surprising at this stage of his argument, therefore, that Descartes should suddenly become sensitive to the fact that his natural and his rational tendencies conflict. He still finds it natural to take as real that which does not seem so by the 'light of nature'—which is Descartes' expression for what we might call 'rational understanding'. If, however, the light of nature is what it appears to be, then it is by it that Descartes makes up his mind to understand why his natural bent here should so glaringly conflict with it. So at this point he grasps the nettle with a brave firmness; if it continues to sting he is adrift again and for ever. Hence his meditation upon the piece of wax.

From this time I begin to know what I am with a little more clearness and distinction than before; but nevertheless it still seems to me, and I cannot prevent myself from thinking, that corporeal things, whose images are framed by thought, which are tested by the senses, are much more distinctly known than that obscure part of me which does not come under the imagination. (i, 153)

In some sense, at least, Descartes could regard the self, the existence of which he is so sure about, and of whose thinking nature he is so certain, as obscure. Yet at the same time he can regard as 'much more distinctly known' that which he knows in fact to be much more obscure—or at least dubitable in precisely the way that the self is not.

Although really it is very strange to say that I know and understand more distinctly these things whose existence seems to be dubious, which are unknown to me, and which do not belong to me, than others of the truth of which I am convinced, which are known to me and which pertain to my real nature, in a word, than myself. But I see clearly how the case stands: my mind loves to wander, and cannot yet suffer itself to be retained within the just limits of truth. Very good, let us once more give it the freest rein, so that, when afterwards we seize the proper occassion for pulling up, it may the more easily be regulated and controlled. (i, 153-4)

He will give free rein to his ordinary common sense attitude. It is not as thinking substance that his mind loves to wander, but as will—something he discusses at length in Meditation Four. However his aim in letting it have its own way and follow its natural bent is to catch it so to say *in flagrante delicto*.

Well, one question common sense does not ask is what precisely it is about a given experience that makes it one of a physical object. It does not, for instance, ask whether the way we see something as a physical object is also the way we see it as the sort of physical object it is. We identify what kind of thing a physical object is by our senses; yet this, according to Descartes, is the kind of knowledge upon which least reliance can be placed. However, the real point of Descartes' concern is this: that we do not get our knowledge of something's being a physical object from the same source as we get our knowledge of what kind of physical object it is. The argument for this is that all the sensible properties of a physical object may change, without our supposing the physical object to. It is the same thing that changed. There was not a replacement of one physical object by another, but the replacement of one set of identifying properties in a physical object by another set of identifying properties in the same physical object.

In no single case is it causally impossible for the actual physical object itself to be replaced by another. Though I may think the change has only been one of properties, it might have been of the physical object as well. Only we seem necessarily to assume that this is not the case, unless there seems reason to suppose it is. This is certainly the most convenient assumption to make; but what certainty could we possibly have as to its validity? No certainty based simply on sense experience itself. And yet Descartes cannot bring himself to doubt that insofar as his experience is one of a physical object at all, and whether there is a physical object independent of his experience, or not, there must be something that remains the same however much its experienced qualities may be made to change in response to some external causal agency. That is to say, even if there is no physical object outside his consciousness he cannot think of something as a physical object without thinking of it as something known by some part of him which, so to say, stipulates the way he is to know it if he is to know it as a physical object at all. And, as Descartes makes clear when he later comes to discuss imagination, the way he has to know it turns out to be a complex of 'directives', only one of which specifies that it must be experienced as continuous through change of its experienced qualities.

Let us follow part of Descartes' meditation upon the piece of wax.

But notice that while I speak and approach the fire what remained of the taste is exhaled, the smell evaporates, the colour alters, the figure is destroyed, the size increases, it becomes liquid, it heats, scarcely can one handle it, and when one strikes it, no sound is emitted. Does the same wax remain after this change? We must confess that it remains; none would judge otherwise. What then did I know so distinctly in this piece of wax? It could certainly be nothing of all that the senses brought to my notice, since all these things which fall under taste, smell, sight, touch, and hearing, are found to be changed, and yet the same wax remains. (i, 154)

Descartes thus disposes more or less of the secondary qualities. Does the object considered in terms of primary qualities remain unchanged? If this were so, it would be our *imagination* that provided us with the need and power to postulate something that remains the same in a physical object no matter how numerous the changes it is caused to suffer. But is it so? Descartes continues.

Perhaps it was what I now think, viz. that this wax was not that sweetness of honey, nor that agreeable scent of flowers, nor that particular whiteness, nor that figure, nor that sound, but simply a body which a little while before appeared to me as perceptible under these forms, and which is now perceptible under others.

Is the changeless element then simply 'a body'? What could this be?

But what, precisely, is it that I imagine when I form such conceptions? Let us attentively consider this, and, abstracting from all that does not belong to the wax, let us see what remains.

That is to say, remains of the wax considered merely as a physical object.

Certainly nothing remains excepting a certain extended thing which is flexible and movable. But what is the meaning of flexible and movable? Is it not that I imagine that this piece of wax being round is capable of becoming square and of passing from a square to a triangular figure? No, certainly it is not that, since I imagine it admits of an infinitude of similar changes, and I nevertheless do not know how to compass the infinitude by my imagination, and consequently this conception which I have of the wax is not brought about by the faculty of imagination. (i, 154–5)

Thus it is not our imagination that induces in us the need to postulate a changeless somewhat to maintain the continuity of a physical object through change. It begins to look as if the source of our tendency to regard physical objects as more distinctly present to us than even our own selves could be something grounded in the very nature of the self itself as *thinking* substance, that is to say, grounded in a source so close to us, and easily known by us, that it could indeed serve to provide us with the confidence we have in the reality of physical objects. In this approach we may be said to *think* physical objects, as such, rather than know them in some more dubitable way.

What Descartes is doing here is not a kind of transcendental deduction. Unlike Kant, he is not concerned with objectivity as such; he is considering not corporeality in general, but a single piece of wax. As always he is guided by what he can, or thinks he can, most clearly and distinctly perceive. And general ideas, he says, 'are usually a little more confused' than particular ones. When he asks 'What is this extension?' he means the extension of that particular piece of wax.

What now is this extension? Is it not also unknown? For it becomes greater when the wax is melted, greater when it is boiled, and greater still when the heat increases; and I should not conceive [clearly] according to truth what wax is, if I did not think that even this piece that we are considering is capable of receiving more variations in extension than I have ever imagined. (i, 155)

Thus what characterises a particular piece of extended substance is not only its unity and self-identity through change, but also the endless and unimaginable various forms it can take. The wax, *qua* extended substance, contains, so to say, more possibilities of change, more diversity of form than I could either perceive or imagine. Or rather, that is how I am compelled to conceive it. In other words, my conception of extension is the conception of more than human experience could ever actually present me with. And more therefore than can be derived from it.

We must then grant that I could not even understand through the imagination what this piece of wax is, and that it is my mind alone which perceives it. I say this piece of wax in particular, for as to wax in general it is yet clearer.

It is not only the general idea of extended substance that is known through the thinking of Descartes' mind, but even the particular extended substance before him, namely the piece of wax, is (however surprising it may be) equally known not by imagination, or sensibility, but only by the thinking of his mind.

And now he becomes concerned to relate this thinking activity of the mind whereby it comes to perceive physical objects to the other activities involved.

But what is this piece of wax which cannot be understood excepting by the [understanding or] mind? It is certainly the same that I see, touch, imagine, and finally it is the same which I have always believed it to be from the beginning.

With one sweep Descartes restores to the particular piece of extension the qualities which make it not merely a piece of extension but also that particular piece of wax. Then he continues his main argument:

But what must particularly be observed is that its perception is neither an act of vision, nor of touch, nor of imagination, and has never been such although it may have appeared formerly to be so, but only an intuition of the mind, which may be imperfect and confused as it was formerly, or clear and distinct as it is at present, according as my attention is more or less directed to the elements which are found in it, and of which it is composed. (i, 155)

Analysis, in other words, has clarified the conception of what perception of physical objects is. Perception may be confused, as when we do not see a thing in such a way as to bring out the thinking involved in it; or clear and distinct, as when we do. Thus perception, strictly speaking, is, Descartes tries to show, an intuition of (or inspection by) the mind. This 'activity' does not automatically synthesize the other elements in perception; it can even be confused by them. But when not, we understand with the kind of clarity that makes us believe in the reality of corporeal nature despite the evident dubiety of the senses. Our belief, then, in the reality of physical objects is grounded in whatever it is that also prevents us from being able to sustain doubt as to our own reality as thinking things. Certainly, if Descartes is right, it is not by the senses that we perceive body as such, but by the mind.

Nevertheless, Descartes complains, his newly won knowledge seems to escape him from the moment he relaxes his attention; and the seeing of something (as he has seen the true nature of the piece of wax) clearly and distinctly, conflicts with his habitual verbalisings. The suggestion is that our speech habits mislead us when we use language for purposes of analysis, as distinct from the more practical purposes of everyday life. Clarity of thought, and perhaps especially distinctness of thought, is something not only possible without being verbally expressed, but would not be achievable at all if this were not so. The 'great feebleness of mind' he speaks about takes the form of relying upon words to provide us with concepts, and grammatical form to provide us with a description of the world: 'for although without giving expression to my thoughts I consider all this in my own mind, words often impede me and I am almost deceived by the terms of ordinary language' (i, 155). The application of this general view is not only important in connection with his analysis of the kind of activity that is involved in perceiving a physical object, but also with every other metaphysical point he touches, and especially when he comes to talk about the way we know the self, and know God. But meanwhile it is with physical objects in relation to our observation of their physical nature that we are still concerned.

Descartes' point is this: we use the language of secondary qualities when we see something as a physical object, although the language of thought would be, as he has in fact argued, more *logically* appropriate. For it is by secondary qualities that we most effectively distinguish one physical object from another; and it is with particular objects that we have to deal, on a practical level, rather than with their physical nature as such, i.e. as pure extended substances. We have already made the point that from the secondary qualities alone we cannot construct our concept of a physical object. Now we can add that by no activity of the senses can we perceive a physical object, and therefore that no description of a sensing activity can be the proper description (as distinct from perhaps the most useful one) of the activity by means of which we claim to perceive a physical object. All this lies behind the following passage:

For we say that we see the same wax, if it is present, and not that we simply judge that it is the same from its having the same colour and figure. From this I should conclude that I knew the wax by means of vision and not simply by the intuition of the mind; unless by chance I remember that, when looking from a window and saying I see men who pass in the street, I really do not see them, but infer that what I see is men, just as I say that I see wax. (i, 155)

The comparison between seeing the wax, and seeing men passing in the street below is intrinsically misleading. We do not judge there are men wearing the hats and cloaks in the way that we would judge something to be a piece of wax. For we could be brought to see that what we supposed to be men were machines, but not that what we have the same reason to suppose a physical object is really not. For Descartes, seeing physical objects is not an inference, but an intuition of the mind, as he repeats again and again, a kind of mental seeing, or inspecting; and it is still this intuiting that Descartes would have had to engage in for him to recognise a man or a machine, if he had gone down into the street to look at close quarters. Indeed, just as he might have mistaken machines for men, so might he have mistaken putty, or clay, for wax. But he could not, in either case, have mistaken a mere combination of sensible qualities for a physical object. Which is why it was misleading for Descartes to have given this example. Indeed, the translators Haldane and Ross were misled into using the word 'infer'.[1]

So far, then, Descartes has been careful to examine his problem without allowing himself to be seduced by the ordinary ways of speaking about things, into supposing that a logical analysis of what 'body' is will be bound to give us the results that the linguistic forms we use to speak about 'things' suggest. When the philosopher is less careful than this we cannot blame ordinary language. In what way are the vulgar wrong? *Don't* they see physical objects? Never? Would Descartes have recommended that we should never make an existential statement by using the word 'see', or 'hear', etc., but rather by using the word 'judge'? One can imagine the following conversation: 'I judge that to be a house.' 'Why, doesn't it look like one?' Presumably nobody ever sees a physical object. But if so, we could not then even claim that we judge what we see to be a physical object. If there *is* anything to *be* seen (as we claim when we claim to see), do we also have to add the claim that something is *there* to be seen? Descartes would surely not be recommending that the word 'see' (for instance) should only be used so that no statement of the form 'I see X' entails that X exists as a physical object. (It should not follow from the linguistic fact that the word 'see' has a wide spread of sense that it should never be used. For if, to simplify the sense, we are going to lay down that it is wrong for me to say that I see my hands when I am looking at them, why are we not equally bound to lay down that it is wrong to say I see stars when I bang my head? In the first case, presumably, it is wrong to say 'see' because my hands are really there to be seen; and in the second, because the stars are not.)

Would we then say that the only thing not to be seen is body? But no ordinary discussion would have any concern at all with this. I have seen the men who sometimes do and sometimes do not wear hats and coats; but not the bodies that sometimes do and sometimes do not wear the properties of wax. When we ordinarily talk about seeing physical objects it is, as I suggested above, not

[1] Descartes' Latin is 'judico homines esse' and the French translation has 'je juge que ce sont de [vrais] hommes'.

the bodiness of things we are interested in, but their kind. It would be just as absurd to suppose that since people are not attending to corporeality, they must be attending to sensible qualities. In these matters people are surprisingly unconfused. Philosophers tend to distinguish between the pre-reflective and reflective levels of human existence. But it is philosophical conceit to suppose that where there is no theoretical reflection there is no practical reflection; and that where there is no reflection upon how we experience there is no reflection upon experience. However, Descartes was concerned with his own distinctions, not these. And this is of the greatest importance to him here. For he is concerned with the problem of ultimate knowledge, and this for him is also the problem of ultimate clarity and distinctness. For him, only the mind thinks, and not the body; and for him, only a special kind of thinking by the mind is that which will bring him to the ultimate form of knowledge he seeks. In relation to this all other forms of experience are confused. Indeed he seems himself to make no qualitative distinction between ordinary human experience and that of an animal: for him they are both confused—whether equally so or not. But his reasons for this are plain. Just as Kant, in his *Groundwork of the Metaphysic of Morals*, is seeking only for the pure element of the moral as such, so Descartes, in the Meditations, is seeking only for the purely knowable as such.

And it is in this light that we should read:

A man who makes it his aim to raise knowledge above the common should be ashamed to derive the occasion for doubting from the forms of speech invented by the vulgar; I prefer to pass on and consider whether I had a more evident and perfect conception of what the wax was when I first perceived it, and when I believed I knew it by means of the external senses or at least by the common sense ⟨*sensus communis*—about which much will be said in the final chapter⟩ as it is called, that is to say by the imaginative faculty, or whether my present conception is clearer now that I have most carefully examined what it is, and in what way it can be known. It would certainly be absurd to doubt as to this. For what was there in this first perception which was distinct? What was there which might not as well have been perceived by any of the animals? But when I distinguish the wax from its external forms, and when, just as if I had taken from it its vestments, I consider it quite naked, it is certain that although some error may still be found in my judgment, I can nevertheless not perceive it thus without a human mind. (i, 156)

Now Descartes doesn't want to be thought of as basing his conclusions on 'linguistic analysis'. It is one thing to notice how language used uncritically can lead us systematically into error. It is another thing altogether to discover in one's new found state (linguistically naked—almost—Descartes might have said) the new guide to knowledge. The one thing this new guide cannot be is simply a new language. It must be something itself not a form of language, since it is that by means of which the adequacy or otherwise of our language is judged—as by Descartes in the passages quoted above. What Descartes is concerned to explicate is not language, but insight—intuition, as he calls it—that by which we judge the existence of body. What he is concerned with here is his 'present conception' of what the wax is. And this is not just another word, but something in knowing which he knows whether a given word is or is not a fit name for it. You can 'see' how much more clearly we have this knowledge now than formerly. Our knowledge now is not merely clear; it is also distinct, for what can be separated in what we know of the piece of wax, has been separated and has been examined separately, as well as in its place in the whole. Whether or not animals can frame ideas and use them in constructing 'body', or not, Descartes need only show that *we* can, and do. We come upon the pure element of corporeality which cannot be known otherwise than by an activity of the mind—whether or not a necessary condition for that activity is also some activity of the senses as such. And here at last we reach the point where by its own operation the mind achieves for us that great certainty as to the existence of physical objects, which it has been Descartes' purpose to understand. The certainty can now be seen to be grounded in the mind's certainty of its own existence as a thinking thing. And yet it is still only the certainty of the existence of a piece of wax, and not that certainty which alone, as Descartes had previously demonstrated, should attach to our knowledge of the self.

His next move is now prepared completely, and speaks for itself.

What then, I who seem to perceive this piece of wax so distinctly, do I not know myself, not only with much more truth and certainty, but also with much more distinctness and clearness? For if I judge that the wax is or exists from the fact that I see it, it certainly follows much more clearly that I am or that I exist myself from the fact that I see it. For it may be that what I see is not really wax, it may also be that I do not possess eyes with which to see anything; but it cannot be that when I see, or (for I no longer take account of the distinction) when I think I see, that I myself who think am nought. (i, 156)

There are two points to note. The first concerns certainty, and the second spontaneity.

Descartes says that the existence of nothing can be more certain than his own. For if he sees clearly that physical objects exist, then he who is aware of this can exist no less. And if physical objects don't exist (since, as he says, he doesn't at this point take account of the distinction), and he only thinks they do, then it is at least true that somebody, namely Descartes, thinks they do—which he couldn't unless he existed. Now there is a link between the certainty that knowledge brings, and the spontaneity with which knowledge is achieved. To explain: secondary qualities, it is true, are also elements in human consciousness, i.e. elements within mental experience, or, we might say, qualities of thinking substance. But we are passive in respect of them. They happen to us, and there is nothing to say about them unless they become ordered into physical objects standing to each other in relations such as those described by causal laws, which they could not be understood as doing, if we had been unable to grasp them as physical objects. It is therefore, in respect of that activity by means of which sensible qualities are grasped as physical objects that we have to look for a spontaneity of the mind, awareness of which constitutes that self-certainty for which Descartes seeks. To say the mind is passive to sensible qualities is to say that the causes of those qualities are alien to mind. There is nothing here for mind to do. Consequently we are not, so far, active as mind. For the mind to be spontaneous, however, is for it to become active with regard to sensible qualities in a way that will organise them into physical objects, i.e. provide them with a body. When the mind is passive we are at the stage where we know only that we are, but not what. To know what we are the mind itself must announce its own nature to us by its behaviour. It is in what is given by the self to what is given to it, that Descartes finds the spontaneity, i.e. the self-expressing nature of mind. And it is when this activity receives closest attention, and our picture of the corporeal nature of that which we perceive is at its clearest, that we come to realise that this activity is of something that we, as minds, are. Thus, corresponding to this stage, we find Descartes throwing emphasis not merely upon our knowledge that we are, but also upon our knowledge of what we are. Only when mind has, by thinking, made itself most at home in the world of corporeal objects is it in a position to attain the greatest peak of certainty as to its own nature, as well as to the truth of its own existence. But though our greatest certainty is generated by the self in its most spontaneous form of self-expression, this cannot be that form of spontaneity by which it 'judges' something to be a physical object. For the latter requires, as a necessary condition, the stimulus of sensible experience, whereas the most spontaneous form of the mind's activity must be that in which having separated its own activity from the passive elements in experience it is moved to attend to this as an expression of its own nature—it must be, in other words, self-knowledge.

The piece of wax, then, is not 'in' the mind, since extended substance, cannot be 'in' that which it makes no sense to regard as extended. Nevertheless it is only by mind that we know it. Hence, though we cannot learn about the nature of mind by what we know about physical objects, we can learn about the nature of mind by what we know about the way we know physical objects. So Descartes sums up a large part of what he has been doing.

since it is now manifest to me that even bodies are not properly speaking known by the senses or by the faculty of imagination, but by the understanding only, and since they are not known from the fact that they are seen or touched, but only because they are understood, I see clearly that there is nothing which is easier for me to know than my mind. (i, 157)

The very arguments by which Descartes has advanced to this position have been such as to deprive us of any right to suppose that for all the certainty we might now have as to some part of our minds, we have or can possibly have any certainty at all, that anything exists other than our own minds. Certainly, so far, we possess no obvious grounds for hope that if something else does exist we can know it. Descartes is still a long way from his goal of placing all human knowledge upon a basis of indubitability, and seems to have drawn a magic circle round his own mind; within this circle the arch deceiver is powerless, now, but outside he remains as invincible as ever.

What Descartes set out to do, by the Second Meditation, was to show that whatever else may by his method be brought within the sphere of the doubtful, the human mind cannot. In the process he also learnt that it is no less indubitable that the nature of the mind is to think, than that it exists. Now, what he claims to know for certain is, so far, only that he is a thinking thing. For, suppose he were a corporeal object: he would then have no less reason to doubt his own corporeal existence than to doubt any other corporeal existence. He would hence have to forego the certainty he has so far won. He denies he is a body only because he is not able to affirm it with absolute certainty. We should recall what he undertook in the First Meditation:

But inasmuch as reason already persuades me that I ought no less carefully to withhold my assent from matters which are not entirely certain and indubitable than from those which appear to me manifestly to be false, if I am able to find in each one some reason to doubt, this will suffice to justify my rejecting the whole. (i 145)

This is the key passage to the Second as well as to the First Meditation.

Now there can hardly be a more significant question than whether Descartes is essentially a corporeal substance which, among its various accomplishments, also thinks, or another kind of substance, namely one that is substantial only in the way necessary for it to think. Yet here Descartes' critics seem hardly to have understood his purpose—though this is certainly less true in the case of M. Arnauld than in that of anyone else—especially Gassendi. Basically, what bothered Arnauld was this: how can it possibly be proved from the fact that I can doubt the existence of body (any body) that body does not exist? For, by this argument of Descartes, since (as our key passage reminds us) I can doubt the existence of my own body, I can deny its existence too. However, Descartes doesn't need to deny the existence of body, or even to be able to doubt the existence of body, to make his main point, which is also part of Arnauld's worry, namely that even if it does exist it is not that substance of which thinking is a characterising activity. For even if the fact of the existence of his own body were indubitable for Descartes, it would still not follow from this that he was not essentially a thinking thing. I shall discuss this shortly in some detail, but make the point now to show that for all his subtlety Arnauld had not fully thought out which of his objections to Descartes were and which were not necessary for his main contention, namely, that Descartes had not shown that the essence of the 'I' is its power of thinking, and nothing else.

Perhaps the best statement of Arnauld's worry is the one he himself takes from the Meditation's Preface to the Reader, where Descartes is concerned with the two objections to the Meditations which he takes seriously. 'But I shall show hereafter how from the fact that I know no other thing which pertains to my essence, it follows that there really is no other thing which really does belong to it' (i, 138). Let us quote Descartes' preceding statement:

The first objection is that it does not follow from the fact that the human mind reflecting on itself does not perceive itself to be other than a thing that thinks, that its nature or its essence consists only in its being a thing that thinks, in the sense that this word *only* excludes all other things which might also be supposed to pertain to the nature of the soul. To this objection I reply that it was not my intention in that place to exclude these in accordance with the order that looks to the truth of the matter (as to which I was not then dealing), but only in accordance with the order of my thought [perception]; thus my meaning was that so far as I was aware, I knew nothing clearly as belonging to my essence, excepting that I was a thing that thinks, or a thing that has in itself the faculty of thinking. (i, 137–8)

Now, Descartes makes a distinction between the order of truth and the order of his thought, and claims to be concerned in the Second (as indeed he is in the First) Meditation with the order of thought rather than with the order of truth. The reason for this is simply that he is not yet in a position to know whether what seems to be true, by the deliverance of thought, is in fact so. Moreover this knowledge of truth, i.e. of whether the world, in truth, is what the human mind says it is, cannot come up for discussion until Descartes has been able to demonstrate beyond conceivable doubt that where no reason remains for us to doubt that the truths we find are as we suppose them to be, so they must be. Within the magic circle indubitability is not impossible, but outside it, as remarked, the arch deceiver is invincible—if he exists. So that until Descartes can demonstrate that no such creature can exist the spectre of such a being will continue to haunt us, and the possibility of knowledge remain elusive. How Descartes attempts this I hope soon to be able to show; but meanwhile it should be clear enough why he cannot on his own principles make any claims whatsoever about a corporeal world, nor therefore any claim as to how body (the existence of which is dubitable—and which is therefore of one type) could be related to the human mind (the existence of which is indubitable—and which is therefore of a quite different type). Thus when Arnauld makes his fundamental criticism that since Descartes' argument is relative only to the order of thought 'the argument is exactly where it was, and . . . therefore the problem which he promises to solve remains entirely untouched' (ii, 81), the plausibility of his claim depends firstly upon our forgetting the key passage I re-stated above, and secondly upon the fact that Descartes had not up to the end of the Second Meditation constructed the chain of argument which by the Sixth Meditation was ready to cope with those problems relating to matter and mind which lie at the heart of all the criticisms levelled against him in this area. Since in Meditation Two there is no proof of the existence of anything at all other than the human mind, Descartes, as I argued, could not yet claim knowledge of anything but what he could be certain of as characterising it, namely that it thinks. And Arnauld is simply saying that it doesn't follow from the fact it thinks, that it doesn't do any thing else, or that something else might not be true about it, such for instance as that it is also a body. How can you be certain that you know something so completely that no more can belong to its essence?

We shall return to this question in our discussion of the Sixth Meditation, but meanwhile certain things can be said. In his Reply to Objections IV, Descartes writes: 'For in my opinion nothing without which a thing can still exist is comprised in its essence, and although mind belongs to the essence of man, to be united to a human body is in the proper sense no part of the essence of mind' (ii, 97). Presumably the latter is true because we can conceive of ourselves as disembodied but not as unthinking. In other words we can conceive ourselves as being able to think without at the same time having to conceive ourselves as embodied. And since, claims Descartes, being a body is not, whereas thinking is, enough to constitute a self, it follows that thinking is the essence of mind. This might be held to be true independently of whether or not possession of a body is a necessary condition for the actual functioning of such a mind. That is Descartes' point. Yet Descartes isn't arguing that because there isn't to his certain knowledge more to his essence than thinking, there might not be more 'in me of which I am not yet conscious . . .' He holds that there might. This would, presumably, *give* him more than he has simply in thinking. But what he doubts, because he has no reason to suppose it true—as distinct from possible—is that this would also *make* him more. Thus he concludes: 'Hence it was that those additional attributes were judged not to belong to the *essence* ⟨my italics⟩ of the mind' (ii 97).

Now of course one cannot tell what is the essence of X unless all of X is known. A short way is to define X in terms only of what is known, as Arnauld criticises Descartes for doing. Yet Descartes sometimes appears to be saying that there may be more to mind than thinking, i.e. that the nature of mind may be more extensive than he has yet discovered. But the question is whether anything else would add to the essence of that whose already-known essence is expressed in thought, or would merely enrich what is, in all its essence, already given. However, Descartes also maintains that since nothing more is requisite, as he puts it, for him to have a mind, than that he should be able to think, the essence of his mind lies in its thinking. The debate here between Descartes and Arnauld is quite fascinating. Arnauld observes:

And certainly, some one will say it is no marvel if, in deducing my existence from the fact that I think, the idea that I form of the self, which is in this way an object of thought, represent me to my mind as merely a thinking being, since it has been derived from my thinking alone. And hence from this idea, no argument can be drawn to prove that nothing more belongs to my essence than what the idea contains. (ii, 84)

Arnauld's trouble is that he did not try to show, as he should have done to make his own point properly, that perhaps it cannot be true of any being that it can think and can do nothing else. Descartes himself remarks that in the very passage that Arnauld was criticising: 'I did, as a fact, assume that I was not yet aware that my mind had the power of moving the body, and that it was substantially united with it' (ii, 97). But this assumption requires justification. Can thinking, at any rate in the sense of cognition, be as independent of awareness of a body as Descartes thinks he is entitled to assume? And to say that he can in fact conceive himself as thinking without awareness of a body is not to answer this question. Could a being with no history of sensible experience, or of moving sensible objects, think? What reason has Descartes to suppose it could? It might well be argued that the essence of mind is to enable action to take place, perhaps even moral action, and that thinking is only a necessary condition for this, in the way that having a body may be for thinking. The reason why this possibility seems alien to the atmosphere of Descartes was clear enough to Descartes who himself tells us, before embarking upon his course of hyperbolic doubt wherein he conjures up the evil genius (who might conceivably release him from all moral obligations) that there is no danger in his undertaking (the undertaking we are studying in this book): 'For I am assured that there can be neither peril nor error in this course, and that I cannot at present yield too much to distrust, since *I am not considering the question of action*, but only of knowledge' (i, 148).[1]

What are we to deduce from Descartes' first two Meditations? This: that unless acting, that is, bringing about changes in the world, is part of thinking (which Descartes must deny, since acting requires a body and a body cannot be entailed, on his theory, by thought) the essence of man, whatever else it may be, is not action. Could Descartes really have wanted to maintain that it is not part of man's essential nature to be an agent? Could he even have wanted to maintain that it is doubtful whether man is an agent? Yet however broadly we interpret Descartes' *cogito*, it is difficult to see how we can pass from the claim to be aware, to the claim to do. Our knowledge of our own agency must somehow stand

[1] My italics.

on its own feet, if it in fact is to be knowledge at all. That we are active in respect of our thinking Descartes has no doubt. Indeed it is precisely by our activity in this sense that we come to know for certain that we exist as thinking beings. But this is not the sense of agency required by the expression 'man (not just 'mind') is an agent'. Mind can only find out, whereas man can change what there is for mind to find out.

CHAPTER THREE

PART 1

DESCARTES ended his Second Meditation believing himself to have established

that even bodies are not properly speaking known by the senses or by the faculty of imagination, but by the understanding only, and since they are not known from the fact that they are seen or touched, but only because they are understood, I see clearly that there is nothing which is easier for me to know than my mind. (i, 157)

This suggests that Descartes regards understanding as somehow closer to the nature of mind than any other of its equally indubitable activities. For it is by the understanding that all the other activities themselves, as well as their 'objects', are understood, i.e. achieve that intelligibility without which we could not properly be said to be conscious of them. Descartes appears to suppose that the only way to understand what the mind is, is to understand how it understands—remembering, of course that unless what is understood constitutes knowledge, there can have been no proper understanding either. But if we can discover how the mind understands we shall thereby have discovered how knowledge is attained. We shall also have discovered more precisely what the mind itself is. Our knowledge about how we know will then be as indubitable as our knowledge of our own existence.

The foregoing considerations possibly throw some light upon Descartes' opening moves in Meditation Three:

I shall now close my eyes, I shall stop my ears, I shall call away all my senses, I shall efface even from my thoughts all the images of corporeal things, or at least (for that is hardly possible) I shall esteem them as vain and false; and thus holding converse only with myself and considering my own nature, I shall try little by little to reach a better knowledge of and a more familiar acquaintanceship with myself. I am a thing that thinks, that is to say, that doubts, affirms, denies, that knows a few things, that is ignorant of many [that loves, that hates], that wills, that desires, that also imagines and perceives; for as I remarked before, although the things which I perceive and imagine are perhaps nothing at all apart from me and in themselves, I am nevertheless assured that these modes of thought that I call perceptions and imaginations, inasmuch only as they are modes of thought, certainly reside [and are met with] in me.

And in the little that I have just said, I think I have summed up all that I really know, or at least all that hitherto I was aware that I knew. In order to try to extend my knowledge further, I shall now look around more carefully and see whether I cannot still discover in myself some other things which I have not hitherto perceived. (i, 157–8)

Now, Descartes claims to know that thinking is his essential nature. This he cannot doubt. But if it is his essential nature because he cannot doubt it, then nothing else can really be part of himself in the way that thinking is, or his thoughts are, unless these are equally indubitable. But if they are, why has he not yet discovered them? Perhaps they are there on a level that requires more sophistication for their discovery, as with Plato's slave boy in the *Meno*. But how can he tell that what he takes to be part of himself really is so, in the case where it isn't something the truth of which is unavoidable the moment he begins to reflect at all? He can't, unless he has a method which commends itself to him as true with no less certainty than does his own existence as a thinking thing. This, however, is not to suggest that Descartes thinks he can become familiar with, or indeed, even get to know himself as a pure spiritual substance. He is acquainted with himself already only insofar as he knows himself in his actual thinking, that is to say, as an activity of his own substance. The substance is revealed only in the activity. Indeed, that is why he had difficulty in establishing even *that* he existed when not thinking. In seeking 'a more familiar' acquaintanceship, he is not seeking to get beyond his own self-expressing activities to the pure substance of the self, but to discover himself as engaged in more kinds of activities likewise identifiable as expressing himself as a self.

Descartes' task now is to 'look around more carefully and see whether I cannot still discover in myself some other things which I have not hitherto perceived'. To discover in himself things he hasn't hitherto perceived is, in this context, not to discover concepts, but to discover other parts of the self, or to discover 'more' of what the self is, more, that is, of the self. The only problem will be to isolate in consciousness what is indubitably the self, from what is not, or is something in its own independent right. Now there is at least one thing he knows indubitably:

I am certain that I am a thing which thinks; but do I not then likewise know what is requisite to render me certain of a truth? Certainly in this first knowledge there is nothing that assures me of its truth, excepting the clear and distinct perception of that which I state, which would not indeed suffice to assure me that what I say is true, if it could ever happen that a thing which I conceived so clearly and distinctly could be false; and accordingly it seems to me that already I can establish as a general rule that all things which I perceive very clearly and very distinctly are true. (i, 158)

In that specimen of truth which has rejected every effort even to question it, he has what he calls 'this first knowledge'. It is not certain because clear and distinct; but because it could not be otherwise. The clear and distinct perception of anything at all is reliable only because it *cannot* happen that a thing so conceived should turn out to be false. We only conceive something very clearly and very distinctly when we discover that trying to negate it fails in the sense that we are then left with something we cannot understand and cannot even see how to begin to. Thus Descartes defines a 'clear and distinct perception' so that it is logically impossible for it to be mistaken. This alone entitles him to argue from this one case to all cases; but in the order of discovery there is one case which, though logically no truer, was easier for us to discern than any other could be. And it was not by looking for what we could perceive clearly and distinctly, but by the method of doubt that we arrived at that first knowledge.

Is there not a parallel here with perception? There is a quality of experience in actual waking life that we find impossible to discount when we then look around and ask ourselves if we are dreaming. Such predicates as 'vivid', 'lively', for instance, do not appear to have satisfied Hume as marking the difference between impression and idea. There is something terribly elusive yet unmistakable that makes us feel a bit foolish in asking ourselves whether we are really awake. And so thinkers have sought to distinguish between waking perceptual experiences and, for instance, dreaming, not by some intrinsic mark, but by some such thing as the way these experiences are related to each other. So Berkeley, and so Descartes himself. It is simply that to determine unquestionably the objective validity of an experience it seems to have been felt to be logically safer to go outside the experience itself and demonstrate it to be a member of some structure, such as a system of complex relationships, membership of which determines the ontological status of the experience.

Is this not analogous to the case of Descartes' test of truth? Certainly there is something about the feeling of certainty that we have when we contemplate a logical argument, or our own existence as thinking beings, that makes it seem silly to question further what we see so clearly and distinctly. Descartes himself speaks of perceiving very clearly, and very distinctly, yet he must have been aware of the absurdity in supposing clarity and distinctness, for *his* purpose, to be merely a matter of degree. When he says that if something seen clearly and distinctly could once be shown to be false, we could never again trust this test of truth, is it not like saying that if it could be shown that something we saw as 'clearly and distinctly' as we do waking experiences should turn out after all to be a dream, we could never again trust the peculiar vividness of this kind of experience? Descartes is saying here that there is a kind of clarity and distinctness which is in fact as peculiar to our apprehension of an indubitable truth, as the experience of actuality in our receptivity of physical objects is peculiar to us in that condition only. And what needs to be made clear now is this: if his criterion for testing truth is itself universally valid, then another fact about mind is that under certain conditions, also known to it, what it takes to be true, is. And if this truth is as indubitable as that a mind's essence is to think, then thinking and discovering truth together constitute the essence of mind. If, therefore, thinking should turn out, under those conditions, to point beyond consciousness, its deliverances must be accepted—logically must. If true, this is clearly a very important advance for Descartes.

Therefore it is not surprising that in his next step he seems less concerned to argue that we do not perceive 'external' objects, than with testing out the criterion for testing truth that he has just discovered. His argument that he does not in fact perceive outside objects has been stated more fully for him by Hume in the opening sections of 'Scepticism with regard to the Senses' in his *Treatise*. Nevertheless, he too is concerned with the question of how we can know that corresponding to ideas we have in the mind there must be something outside the mind. For if he can have clear and distinct ideas that point to an external world that turns out not to exist, might we not find ourselves with an idea of God, also very clearly and very distinctly conceived in our mind, but no more existent outside it than are physical objects? To repeat, it is necessary to test out his new found criterion, especially to make sure that there aren't any exceptions to it. If I then turn out to have a clear and distinct idea of a necessarily existing Creator, who is also a perfect Being, that perfect Being cannot but exist. And it is precisely with this issue more than with any other that Descartes is concerned.

The question before him now is whether or not he clearly and distinctly perceives that physical objects exist. Speaking of physical objects, he says:

But what did I clearly [and distinctly] perceive in them? Nothing more than that the ideas or thoughts of these things were presented to my mind. And not even now do I deny that these ideas are met with in me. But there was yet another thing which I affirmed, and which, owing to the habit which I had formed of believing it, I thought I perceived very clearly, although in truth I did not perceive it at all, to wit, that there were objects outside of me from which these ideas proceeded, and to which they were entirely similar. And it was in this that I erred, or, if perchance my judgment was correct, this was not due to any knowledge arising from my perception. (i, 158)

We may note at once that whereas Descartes still describes the ideas present in his mind as clearly and *distinctly* perceived, it is only as very *clearly* perceived, and not as *distinctly* perceived at all, that he describes the experience of what he takes to be the objects duplicating externally the ideas in his mind. For him, to see these duplicates distinctly as well as clearly is in fact not something that can make logical sense unless one knows the sign of something's being external to one's mind. And this poses further logical problems, as Hume pointed out, concerning how one can know something to be outside one's mind when one is confined within it by the very conditions for human experience. Descartes doesn't, be it noted, here deny that there may be something outside his mind resembling his mind's ideas of physical objects. Only, he insists he does not clearly and distinctly perceive it—another matter.

Descartes has said that he cannot take an idea's being clear and distinct as guaranteeing its truth should he ever turn out to be mistaken. But he does not seem to have a distinct as well as a clear idea of external objects. If, nevertheless, there are such objects, then my judgment that there are could still not constitute knowledge; for my perception, being necessarily only of ideas, gives no knowledge of what, by definition, causes those ideas. Body is understood by thought, and not seen by eyes; for eyes do not think, any more than thought visualises. The impossibility of my seeing a physical object thus turns out to be a conceptual impossibility. At any rate, upon reflection, I discover that though I may have thought that I clearly and distinctly see physical objects, I do not, and I could not have done so; and the very conception of an entity which is at once in my mind (for it to be seen by me) and also outside my mind (thus making it impossible for it to be seen by me) is logically unacceptable. Thus, for Descartes, not only is clearness *and* distinctness the criterion for something's being knowledge, but the conceptual impossibility of a conceivable contradictory is the criterion for something's being clear and distinct. It is no wonder that when Descartes comes to discuss the way in which these criteria are applied, he looks for his examples to arithmetic and geometry.

The *malin génie* is useful to Descartes in two ways at least. The mere possibility of his existence provides us with sufficient ground to suspect that things may not be as they appear, and so to examine them more closely. But unless we presuppose that after examining the matter we are in a stronger position to assess the weight of our suspicion, such an examination is pretty pointless. Also, the mere possibility of a *malin génie* ensures that however extensive our examination, we can never be absolutely certain we are not being tricked. If it is alleged that unless we can specify how we are tricked we can give no real meaning to the statement that we are, the *malin génie* provides a reply. His power ensures that despite all our precautions he can get the better of us. And since he is not impossible, it is not impossible that we live in a state of constant and fantastic deception. Now, Descartes does suppose it possible he might be deceived even in such matters as that two and three make five. He admits that he doesn't see *how* this could be possible, but he is entitled to expect us to go along with him to see what use he makes of this possibility. This doubt he calls a metaphysical doubt. It might almost be put another way, namely, that one cannot (and indeed how could one be entitled to?) suppose that one's relation to the world is such that being made the way one is, or the world being what it is, we can in fact have knowledge, as distinct from having the idea of having it. Doubt of this sort doesn't make sense unless it is applied precisely to what we cannot understand to be doubtful in any other sense.

But Descartes lets go, for a moment, of this position.

Let who will deceive me, He can never cause me to be nothing while I think that I am, or some day cause it to be true to say that I have never been, it being true now to say that I am, or that two and three make more or less than five, or any such thing in which I see a manifest contradiction.

As we have seen, however, these challenges do not all present the same logical problems; the first still remains a special case. When he says, for instance, 'He can never cause me to be nothing while I think that I am', is not this an absolute claim? If Descartes thinks that he exists, then not even God can unmake the fact that Descartes exists; he certainly cannot unmake it on the spot, nor perhaps ever unmake it. Nevertheless, Descartes knows just what he is doing. He continues:

And, certainly, since I have no reason to believe that there is a God who is a deceiver, and as I have not yet satisfied myself that there is a God at all, the reason for doubt which depends on this opinion alone is very slight, and so to speak metaphysical. But in order to be able altogether to remove it, I must enquire whether there is a God as soon as the occasion presents itself; and if I find that there is a God, I must also enquire whether He may be a deceiver; for without a knowledge of these two truths I do not see that I can ever be certain of anything. (i, 158–9)

Thus, provided only that he can find an affirmative answer to the first of these questions, and a negative one to the second, there is nothing left standing between him and the *possibility* of his being able to establish an absolute claim on an unassailable foundation. In view of their importance, then, he prepares the ground with great care.

Consider, for instance, one sentence in the above quotation. He says that God can never cause him to be nothing while he thinks he is (and he could have added, or might be) something. Therefore it emerges unconditionally (not merely seems to), that in this, God, even God, cannot deceive him. In order to deceive him, God must give him the capacity to be deceived, and, therefore, to believe certain things to be true. And from that alone man's rationality could be derived. But in the next assertion, that God cannot cause it to be true that Descartes has never been, notice the conditional 'it being true now to say that I am'. That is, if Descartes exists, then this fact confers an absolute right to affirm as true the statement that he does. But is the proposition that two and three make five in the same category? Is it not precisely because he cannot be as sure of this that he institutes the method of metaphysical doubt?

Now God, we claim, is a person, and persons know what it is to deceive. We know that God, if he exists, could deceive us if he wanted to. But could he want to? The metaphysical doubt is Descartes' answer to a God who would want to deceive us. For, as long as we can maintain that doubt, even God can no more deceive us than he could make us think that we don't exist at the very moment that we think we do. Unless we thought that there might be something in which God could not deceive us even if he wanted to, we would have no rational justification for beginning the Cartesian journey.

The only thing, then, that stands in the way of Descartes' claim that knowledge is possible, is the mere possibility of the existence of a power who could deceive us if he wished. And of course one of the very signs of his success, as we saw, is that we should be deceived, and deceived in those very respects in which we are certain that deception is even inconceivable. Descartes therefore has to show that God does exist, but could not be properly conceived as deceiving or (presumably) permitting the deception of his own creatures. He thus undertakes to find out whether God exists; but in his search he is for the moment restricted to his own mind, and therefore begins by attempting to get together some sort of inventory of its 'contents', in order to familiarize himself with his self.

In whatever other senses he may elsewhere use the term 'idea', it is reasonably clear what he means by it here. Ideas are representations. One might say that ideas are always 'of' something, and that which they are of is, or is described in the same terms as, that which they represent. This doesn't entail that there must always be an external object represented by the idea. We can, within limits, form our own ideas. But they would still have to be ideas of something, for how else would they be ideas?

Descartes mentions two more classes of thought: that of volitions or affections, and that of judgments. As to the former it is clear that, to take a few examples, in the case of fearing, or approving, or denying, and in the case of intending, or loving or hating, or suspecting, and so on and on, an object is required. Each one has to do whatever it is that it does, to *something*. These thoughts cannot stand alone, then, but require ideas. Alone they would be like functions without arguments, unable to operate, and therefore not happening, i.e. not really being even thoughts— unless possibly the thoughts of operations which for lack of an object they fail to perform.

It is, however, with the class of thoughts known as judgments that Descartes is really concerned. For it is only when ideas as such are linked with judgment that they may properly be described as true or false. Otherwise they are merely suppositions, and a supposition as such cannot itself be true or false, any more than a desire, or a hate, or a fear can. A volition or an affection may be misguided or morally wrong; it is none the less a fact for that. An idea (a propositional idea, we might say) that carries with it no judgment as to its applicability or otherwise beyond itself cannot be true or false either, for in the bare idea there is nothing asserted with regard to it that could bring it into the class of what is true or false. 'Thus there remains no more than the judgments which we make, in which I must take the greatest care not to deceive myself' (i, 159-60).

Among the contents of his mind, then, Descartes has narrowed down his search to judgments. For him, ideas without judgments are like propositions without truth values, and it is only when an idea is asserted to hold beyond itself as, for instance, when I say not simply that I have an idea of an apple, but that I see one, that I risk the penalty of being wrong because I have judged something to be what it might not.

This last point is for Descartes a matter of much concern, for he has to enquire here, not whether the idea of God exists, but whether God himself does. He thus is compelled to start by examining his ideas in those cases where they are coupled with claims that they actually do represent something external to themselves, since God, if he exists, must somehow be more than just the idea I have of him, if indeed that. And so far none of the ideas claiming to have objective counterparts have had their claims confirmed. But we must now notice they are not constrained from within themselves to assert anything at all. We do the asserting for them. The claims themselves could be true or false. They are not necessitated to be either. Those ideas we judge to be of external objects Descartes calls adventitious; they are thought by us to come from 'outside' ourselves, so are neither innate, nor innovated, for then we would regard them as imaginings and not as of external objects.

Suppose, then, that we find an idea of God. Mightn't that too be false of the world? Hence we must try to find what it is that lets us suppose something to be what it isn't, especially that lets us suppose something in our mind to be the effect of something outside it, when there may be no such external thing—and perhaps no 'outside' either.

He writes: 'And my principal task in this place is to consider, in respect to those ideas which appear to me to proceed from certain objects that are outside me, what are the reasons which cause me to think them similar to these objects' (i, 160). And of course he is as intent on considering whether objects which appear to proceed from outside his consciousness really do, as he is on considering why they should appear to if they don't. There is no point in stating here Descartes' arguments for the non-existence, or the possible non-existence of external objects. He does not always indicate which of these he has proved, but he doesn't need to. His reason for wanting to prove the existence of God is that unless he proves, not that God probably exists, but that he necessarily does, he cannot establish a claim to knowledge. In this respect he would be no better off with a probable God than he believes the atheist to be with none.

He begins by contrasting judgments based upon natural inclinations, in which he says we are instructed by nature, and which are sometimes mistaken, with judgments based upon the natural light, in which we cannot be mistaken. 'When I say that I am so instructed by nature, I merely mean a certain spontaneous inclination which impels me to believe in this connection, and not a natural light which makes me recognise that it is true' (i, 160). One does not recognise as true what nature instructs; one merely believes it. One does not merely believe what the natural light shows: one *recognises* it as necessarily true. And, argues Descartes, our belief in the separate existence of an external world is not the result of a natural light. If it had been, we could never have been brought to doubt it.

for I cannot doubt that which the natural light causes me to believe to be true, as, for example, it has shown me that I am from the fact that I doubt, or other facts of the same kind. And I possess no other faculty whereby to distinguish truth from falsehood, which can teach me that what this light shows me to be true is not really true, and no other faculty that is equally trustworthy. (i, 160–1)

Whatever it is in us that tells us the truth, cannot (logically cannot) have to refer to something else for guidance as to whether its judgment in this respect is true. For in that case the regress would be infinite—and knowledge would again become problematic. By this argument Descartes stakes, at this strategic point, a claim to the sovereignty of reason. If reason had assured him that the external world exists, he would have had to believe in it, since, as he says, 'the natural light *causes* me to believe'.

So far, Descartes has been more concerned with whether there can be anything external at all to ideas, than with whether this or that external thing would, or could, resemble the idea of it. His basic argument concerning the impossibility of knowing that something *like* our ideas is external to them is a slight variant upon that used in Meditation One. Since it is admitted that I *can* produce from myself the sense of something's being existent as part of a world external to me, as I do in dreams, perhaps I do the same even when I take myself to be awake. Up to this point

Descartes has supposed himself not to know all there might be to know about himself. What proportion his knowledge may form of all there is to know he has not even tried to assess. It is therefore just possible that there is a faculty in him that produces his waking experiences (whether or not—which he doesn't discuss—it is the same faculty which produces dreams). Thus it is not yet possible to prove there is anything external to himself. He is forced to conclude that by no method that depends upon a discerned difference between a thing being in the mind and a thing being outside it can we show that anything is outside it. And if there were no other methods he would have to give up, for he really is committed, as the next, and inescapable step, to proving that *God* necessarily exists. There is, however, another tack, and the infinitely resourceful Descartes pursues it.

Let us, he says, assume that all ideas have the same status, and drop all questioning as to which do and which do not have external counterparts. It is to ideas merely as modes of thought that he now turns. It is at any rate certain that he has these ideas. But it is equally certain that they differ among themselves. There is not only a multiplicity of ideas, but also a diversity.

But yet substance cannot be first discovered merely from the fact that it is a thing that exists, for that fact alone is not observed by us. We may, however, easily discover it by means of any one of its attributes because it is a common notion that nothing is possessed of no attributes, properties, or qualities. For this reason, when we perceive any attribute, we therefore conclude that some existing thing or substance to which it may be attributed, is necessarily present. (*Principles of Philosophy*, i, 240)

We do not, however, meet with these attributes neat, but as manifested in a variety of qualities, or properties. Those diverse manifestations experienced as finite particulars, Descartes, following a long tradition, calls 'modes'.

Though we can conceive of extension, which is the attribute of corporeal substance, without having to conceive its modes, we cannot conceive its modes without conceiving extension. This holds, too, for individual thoughts, modes of thinking, in relation to the attribute of thought. This, he believes, entitles him to claim that whatever we can think about independently of what cannot be thought about independently of it, has more being, or, as he says (also following a long tradition) a greater degree of reality than it. I am not arguing for this position here, and indeed Descartes doesn't really argue this point in the Meditations; he merely states it as obvious, which as a *logical* point it really is. Within a logical system the formulae which do not depend upon other formulae within the system may be regarded as more fundamental to the system than those that do so depend. One might say, the less conditioned, the more basic. And this is simply to say that more follows, given the formation rules and rules of inference of the system, from the basic formulae than from the others. It is easy to see that if the world is regarded as such a system then to say of something A that more follows from it than from B is to say that it is more real, i.e. generative of more facts (true propositions) than B. And for Descartes God is the most real of all substances for they are all generated (created) by Him; not he by them.

Descartes opens:

But there is yet another method of enquiring whether any of the objects of which I have ideas within me exist outside of me. If ideas are only taken as certain modes of thought, I recognise amongst them no difference or inequality, and all appear to proceed from me in the same manner; but when we consider them as images, one representing one thing and the other another, it is clear that they are very different one from the other. There is no doubt that those which represent to me substances are something more, and contain so to speak more objective reality within them [that is to say, by representation participate in a higher degree of being or perfection] than those that simply represent modes or accidents; and that idea again by which I understand a supreme God, eternal, infinite [immutable], omniscient, omnipotent, and Creator of all things which are outside of Himself, has certainly more objective reality in itself than those ideas by which finite substances are represented. (i, 161–2)

He is no longer going to suppose that every idea in his mind must have an external cause. The light of reason has shown him that in case after case where he has supposed that it has, this was merely 'by a blind impulse'. Henceforth he will accept nothing as true but by the light of nature. Though the causes of ideas may not be open for our inspection, the ideas themselves are. To have an idea in one's mind is to know what the idea is, i.e. is an idea of. The question of whether the cause of an idea, and what the idea is an idea of, are identical, is not one Descartes finds necessary to raise at this point. To know an idea is indubitably to know what it is an idea of, or, what it represents. We should watch this word 'represent' here, for it is ambiguous as between 'means' and 'is the effect of'. We should also remember that Descartes is still within the charmed circle and is only entitled to speak, so far, about meaning. Yet Descartes does not suppose that because something is in the mind it can be there without a cause. To state the case at its weakest, he does not suppose that without the sufficient conditions for it we could 'have' any idea at all. These conditions, at the present stage of his enquiry, are not located externally to mind, but within it. The question whether and at what point the sufficient conditions themselves, being ideas, cannot be further explained except by what is *outside* the mind, is not now up for discussion.

Here Descartes would remain trapped were it not for his one possibly redeeming idea—that of God. He can, however, no more suppose that causal relationships don't exist, than that logical relationships don't. Nothing comes from nothing. And that there cannot be in the effect more than is contained in the cause is simply a particular instance of the dictum *ex nihilo nihil fit*. Certainly if causality is like logic, then just as nothing can appear as a term in the conclusion which was not in a premise of that conclusion, so nothing can appear in an effect that was not an element in the cause. And that the greater degree of reality, or the more perfect, cannot proceed from the less is for Descartes clearly and distinctly true in the light of nature. Hence the significance of his observations here: 'And this is not only evidently true of those effects which possess actual or formal reality' (i, 162). By 'formal reality', Descartes means that which is not itself an idea, but what an idea represents.

Let us observe Descartes move from the one use of causality to another. He begins by thinking of causality between physical objects, then applies his results in considering the relationship between physical objects and ideas, thus taking this as if it were really a special case of the former.

Now it is manifest by the natural light that there must at least be as much reality in the efficient and total cause as in its effect. For, pray, whence can the effect derive its reality, if not from its cause? And in what way can this cause communicate this reality to it, unless it possessed it in itself? And from this it follows, not only that something cannot proceed from nothing, but likewise that what is more perfect—that is to say, which has more reality within itself—cannot proceed from the less perfect. And this is not only evidently true of those effects which possess actual or formal reality, but also of the ideas in which we consider merely what is termed objective reality. To take an example, the stone which has not yet existed not only cannot now commence to be unless it has been produced by something which possesses within itself, either formally or eminently, all that enters into the composition of the stone [i.e. it must possess the same things or other more excellent things than those which exist in the stone] and heat can only be produced in a subject in which it did not previously exist by a cause that is of an order [degree or kind] at least as perfect as heat, and so in all other cases. (i, 162)

It is in the very next passage that he extends this type of causal relation still further so as to include minds as well.

But further, the idea of heat, or of a stone, cannot exist in me unless it has been placed within me by some cause which possesses within it at least as much reality as that which I conceive to exist in the heat or the stone. For although this cause does not transmit anything of its actual or formal reality to my idea, we must not for that reason imagine that it is necessarily a less real cause. (i, 162)

It is clear now, that having extended his causal notion to mind and realised that, on his definition of mind as being all that extension is not (or, perhaps better, nothing that extension is), this cannot be done without contradiction, he has to decide whether to withdraw his concept of mental phenomena as a class of effects of physical causal processes, or to be left with 'uncaused' mental phenomena which thus become autonomous, imprisoned, and inexplicable. He decides to have it both ways, and is not lost for a word with which to effect this. Just as ideas 'participate' in formal reality, so ideas 'borrow' their own formal reality from that 'thinking substance' we discussed earlier, and whose application we now observe. A modification has taken place in myself as a finite thinking substance, and indeed had to, for the idea to gain entry. But of course it didn't gain entry from the external world, for it was never there. In some sense, therefore, it must have been produced within the finite thinking substance, and if the effect of anything at all, is at least as much its effect as anything else's. The weird position is therefore reached that the idea is of one thing, but caused by another.

We may perhaps put the matter in a slightly different way. There are three possible types of causal relationship: first, between ideas, second, between things, and third, between ideas and things (or things and ideas). Descartes' special interest lies in the latter. Before he can prove that this sort of relation is even possible, however, must he not show that there *are* things that are not ideas?—whereas what he would appear to be aiming at is to show that in the supposed fact of such a relation there is necessitated an acceptance of the truth that there are things outside the thoughts claiming to represent things. Otherwise the argument would be no stronger than the argument that ideas cannot represent unless they represent something; and since they represent, there must be something they represent. But this is a statement about the word 'represent' and not about reality. Descartes has given as one example of cause the first sort.

To take an example, the stone which has not yet existed not only cannot now commence to be unless it has been produced by something which possesses within itself, either formally or eminently, all that enters into the composition of the stone [i.e. it must possess the same things or other more excellent things than those which exist in the stone] and heat can only be produced in a subject in which it did not previously exist by a cause that is of an order [degree or kind] at least as perfect as heat, and so in all other cases. (i, 162)

He then follows with the example already quoted which he seems to imagine must be of our third sort. 'But further, the idea of heat, or of a stone, cannot exist in me unless it has been placed within me by some cause which possesses within it at least as much reality as that which I conceive to exist in the heat or the stone.' Well, *if* there are hot objects, stones, i.e. corporeal substances with the qualities of heat and stoniness, and *if* I am brought into physical contact with them (near or far), an effect upon me will be caused by them. But suppose there are no physical objects, then what? Descartes has not at all proved that this case might not just as well come under our second type of causal relation, namely, that between idea and idea. His examples, it must be admitted, seem ideally chosen to skate over the ambiguity, for they are ideas of objects which we normally take it for granted *do* have external existence.

Perhaps all he is entitled to argue is that on no occasion could he have had the idea (not sensation?) of heat, unless *he* had always had (formally or eminently) 'all that enters into the composition of' the idea of heat. Why should not this situation meet with Descartes' requirement that 'the idea of heat, or of a stone, cannot exist in me unless it has been placed within me by some cause which possesses within it at least as much reality as that which I conceive to exist in the heat or the stone'? The things that entered into the composition of the ideas are themselves, before they so enter, part of the total cause of the ideas; but they are not, on our hypothesis, external. And Descartes does not appear to me to have succeeded in excluding this possibility. The independent existent of which something is the idea, that which it represents, may itself be simply another idea. Independence must be shown to belong to independently existing things which are not ideas, representations, at all, but are things that really are the thing represented in (or by) ideas.

And although it may be the case that one idea gives birth to another idea, that cannot continue to be so indefinitely; for in the end we must reach an idea whose cause shall be so to speak an archetype, in which the whole reality [or perfection] which is so to speak objectively [or by representation] in these ideas is contained formally [and really]. (i, 163)

Why cannot one idea continue to give birth to another indefinitely? Why should not this process go on eternally, then, within the 'field' of thinking substance? It is no argument that ideas have only an objective reality and therefore there must be somewhere a formal reality of which they are the objective reality, but a conclusion to be demonstrated.

Thus Descartes continues: 'the ideas in me are like [pictures or] images which can, in truth, easily fall short of the perfection of the objects from which they have been derived, but which can never contain anything greater or more perfect' (i, 163). The idea depends for its being, or, we might say, its intelligibility to a finite thinking substance, upon the nature of that finite thinking substance. It cannot be anything more or other than it is possible for a finite thinking substance to contain. It cannot, for instance, be a finite extended substance. There is this much truth to be found in what Descartes says. But the idea itself does not therefore have to be some form of embryonic resemblance to an actual thing that is present. And it is only because in the case of the idea of God Descartes does not find such an actual thing in himself that he looks outside for the original model.

Therefore, when Descartes says: 'Thus the light of nature causes me to know clearly that the ideas in me are like pictures or images etc.' he is not so much following 'the light of nature' as a certain interpretation of it. Descartes sees a certain conceptual necessity, namely, that if one thing is an original, and another is a copy, the copy can fall short of the original (though not too short if it is to be a copy), but cannot (logically cannot) copy more than there is in the original. But does the light of nature tell us that ideas in us are derived from objects which are not themselves ideas? For that is what he is really needing to read in its light.

The point about Descartes' conception of cause as he has so far used it, is that an actual cause does have actual effects. The real stone exists because really constitutive elements are really powered into really producing it. The action of the sea is still present in the fineness of the sand. They have something in common, the cause and the effect, by which one is the actual effect of the actual nature of the other, and possesses in itself, therefore, something of the same actual nature, or corresponding specifically to it. In this sense the cause can be seen as giving something of itself to the effect. But the concept of cause used now at this crucial point is not the concept of something that loses by giving. The sun uses itself up by giving off heat, but not by my feeling that heat. The stone loses nothing by my seeing it. There-fore, the effect must, in a sense, have *nothing* in common with the cause. When the effect is an idea, in a sense it has nothing the cause had. This is the point raised by Caterus in the First Set of Objections.

In this sense an idea can be the effect of another idea, but not of a thing. The idea may be said to take on the *character* of a thing without the thing having to give away either itself or its character to the idea. The character of the thing, as idea, qualifies a mental substance, but is seen *as* qualifying a physical substance. How otherwise would I ever have an idea of a physical substance?

How, as Gassendi asked, can extension be represented in mind when mind is not extended? or colour, when mind is not coloured? Descartes writes: 'For although this cause does not transmit anything of its actual or formal reality to my idea, we must not for that reason imagine that it is necessarily a less real cause' (i, 162). A cause, however, there is, namely the conditions determining the effect. Therefore there is a 'real' cause. In this case, as we have seen, none of the formal (actual) reality can be the same, since the substances concerned in the transaction are entirely distinct. And yet what is represented in the mental substance claims to be like the cause in such a way that surely *if* you could have direct knowledge of that cause you could not distinguish your experience from your experience of the effect. And though ideas are modifications of spiritual substance, something in its own right, and of its own kind, and therefore not fitted to substantialise shape, or the other properties of *extended* substance, this spiritual substance does have the characteristic property of being able so to relate to extended things that it can be used as a kind of medium by means of which the otherwise alien qualities of extended substance can get themselves represented in a mind. In this way, Descartes holds, extended things are represented in minds; and the alternatives are not simply self-contradictory but quite mad, as for instance that the thing itself is in the mind, or that since this cannot be, we cannot know anything at all—when we certainly do, as witness for instance the fact that ideas do manage to refer to beyond the knowing mind. So with a certain amount of what Samuel Alexander might call 'natural piety', Descartes simply accepts the point of view he does as the only hypothesis on the basis of which knowledge of spatial entities makes sense.

It is therefore not perhaps surprising that at this point it is not so obvious that Descartes gets the better of Gassendi, who on this particular topic, despite in my opinion missing the entire point, manages to be not only plausible but even impressive. In his Objections Relative to Meditation Six he writes (and I think he is worth quoting here at length) as follows:

But since you make that assertion and certainly treat only of that solid body, from which you maintain that you are separable and distinct, I do not on that account so much deny that you have an idea of yourself, as maintain that you could not possess it if you were really an unextended thing. For, I ask you, how do you think that you, an un-extended subject, could receive into yourself the semblance or idea of a body which is extended? For, if such a semblance proceeds from the body, it is certainly corporeal and has parts outside of other parts, and consequently is corporeal. Or alternatively, whether or not its impression is due to some other source, since necessarily it always represents an extended body, it must still have parts and, consequently, be extended. Otherwise, if it has no parts, how will it represent parts? If it has no extension how will it represent extension? If devoid of figure, how represent an object possessing figure? If it has no position, how can it represent a thing which has upper and lower, right and left, and intermediate parts? If without variation, how represent the various colours, etc.? Therefore an idea appears not to lack extension utterly. But unless it is devoid of extension how can you, if unextended, be its subject? How will you unite it to you? How lay hold of it? How will you be able to feel it gradually fade and finally vanish away? (ii, 196–7)

To this Descartes replies with a most inappropriate weariness:

Here you ask, *how I think that I, an unextended subject, can receive into myself the resemblance or idea of a thing which is extended.* I reply that no corporeal resemblance can be received in the mind, but that what occurs there is the pure thinking of a thing, whether it be corporeal or equally whether it be one that is incorporeal and lacking any corporeal semblance. But as to imagination, which can only be exercised in reference to corporeal things, my opinion is that it requires the presence of a semblance which is truly corporeal, and to which the mind applies itself, without, however, its being received in the mind. (ii, 231)

But he might have reminded Gassendi (again!) of the argument from which he concluded that the wax, as extended, was understood by thought, rather than experienced by the senses. And if extension is grasped by an act of thinking the latter itself logically cannot also be extended. He could, that is, have argued that all the problems raised by Gassendi proceed entirely from an assumption which in fact begs the question, namely that external objects possess in themselves, and in total independence of the activity of mind, the properties which characterise them from within the experience through which we learn about them. Descartes has in Meditation Two made it plain that he only has knowledge of extension after he has formed a clear and distinct idea of it, and this takes place only in the light of nature, i.e. in the process of intellection. All this is wrapped up in Descartes' remark that what occurs in the mind in the presence of an extended thing, as of an unextended one, is the pure thinking of it. That Descartes knows that Gassendi never really got the point is shown, too, in his reply to Gassendi's criticism that if Descartes is really, as Gassendi puts it, 'not yet convinced of the existence of earth, sky, stars, and other objects', why does he walk about on the earth, or sit down to a meal when he is hungry? 'But this', replies Descartes, 'manifestly involves a begging of the question; for you assume what has to be *proved*, viz, that it is so certain that I walk on the earth that I can have no doubt on the matter' (ii, 215).[1] But this whole matter is discussed on a much higher level in the debate between Descartes and Caterus. The latter realises all the time that Descartes is only concerned with a scientific system of metaphysical knowledge. Thus in the debate between these two thinkers there is a detailed discussion of the kind of relation that may be envisaged as possible between ideas and 'external objects' such that the former may be said to *be* the idea *of* the latter.

A world of things is possible provided the field of ideas is not logically self-contained.

For just as this mode of objective existence pertains to ideas by their proper nature, so does the mode of formal existence pertain to the causes of those ideas (this is at least true of the first and principal) by the nature peculiar to them.

Our question, of course, must be whether 'the mode of formal existence' couldn't do its job of acting as a cause, and even the right kind of cause, just as well if it were itself an idea as if it were an external object.

This is Descartes' problem too, and that explains the parenthesis in the sentence I have just quoted. So now, having prepared the ground, he is going to try to break out of the circle of ideas. When he makes his next move we shall also have his reason for believing the circle incomplete.

And although it may be the case that one idea gives birth to another idea, that cannot continue to be so indefinitely; for in the end we must reach an idea whose cause shall be so to speak an archetype, in which

[1] My italics.

the whole reality [or perfection] which is so to speak objectively [or by representation] in these ideas is contained formally [and really]. (i, 163)

The question is, why must we reach a cause of the kind Descartes says we must? Not, as far as I can see, because of any reason that Descartes gives.

The power of a cause must itself be an effect of something with such power; but the power to enable things to cause other things can originate only in a cause whose power is not simply to transmit causal power that has been given to it, but which itself is the origin of that very causal power—not merely the first cause, but the only real cause, i.e. the only cause which itself has active and not merely passive causal power. Since whatever is, is caused, then whatever is, is caused (really caused) by such a first cause. Therefore the cause of my ideas, as well as the cause of everyone else's, past, present and to come, is grounded in this one something.

This argument form holds of things as well as of ideas, if there are things. Descartes has still not succeeded in proving there are, but only (if his premises are right) that there is an originating cause of whatever is; he has not yet demonstrated that the substantial nature of this cause is other than the substantial nature of mind. His argument is compatible with the view that only minds exist, and that what he calls formal reality may be only a different kind of pattern of spiritual substance. Ideas *are* sometimes 'of' ideas—so why might they not always be so? Descartes has indeed already told us that ideas can 'borrow' their formal reality from spiritual substance.

But there is more to Descartes' argument than this. When we speak of things having their archetypes, we have gone beyond a causal manner of speaking. We are saying that ideas, and indeed things, whether ideas or not, are copies; they may be copies of copies, and so on, according to the point in time, or they may even be only first order copies, but they are copies of something which itself cannot be a copy, because there just isn't anything else for it to be a copy of. This ultimate somewhat must then be not only the cause of things, but also the cause of their being what they are, and the cause of their being like the original.

Thus there is not merely change, but change regulated so as to result at every step in entities copying, with more or less detail and accuracy, the original, the archetype. If this is so, the causal laws are subordinate to that archetype and are what they are only insofar as they bring about the type and order and perhaps development of the copies (such development, presumably, being towards something ever nearer the original).

The original must be perfect in the sense that there just isn't any possibility of something's becoming better than it. This is a logical truth really, and Descartes introduces it into his attempt to prove the existence of an external world.

Thus the light of nature causes me to know clearly that the ideas in me are like [pictures or] images which can, in truth, easily fall short of the perfection of the objects from which they have been derived, but which can never contain anything greater or more perfect. (i, 163)

He is now treating the 'formal reality' of what is expressed in an idea in terms of perfection. The possibility that there could be more perfection in the thought than in the thing, in the objective reality of a thing than in its formal reality, is abandoned by a series of moves that Descartes seems to think also justify his claim that there are things that are not thoughts as well as things that are. At last, then, for him, it makes sense to look for what there is in thought that not only enables us, but even forces us, to go beyond it.

PART 2

But what am I to conclude from it all in the end? It is this, that if the objective reality of any one of my ideas is of such a nature as clearly to make me recognize that it is not in me either formally or eminently, and that consequently I cannot myself be the cause of it, it follows of necessity that I am not alone in the world, but that there is another being which exists, or which is the cause of this idea. On the other hand, had no such an idea existed in me, I should have had no sufficient argument to convince me of the existence of any being beyond myself; for I have made very careful investigation everywhere and up to the present time have been able to find no other ground. (i, 163)

This is an important statement on more than one count, and it is worth taking notice of one of them at this point though not at length, since the relevant development does not occur until we reach the Fifth Meditation. Whether he argues, as he here does, that since only God himself can be the cause of the idea of God, and we do have such an idea, therefore God must exist: or whether he argues, as he does in the Fifth Meditation, that the very idea of a perfect Being entails the necessary existence of such a Being (this is only a partially true formulation, as we shall see), in either case unless it is granted that we do in fact have such an idea, the existence of God is not demonstrable. But it is on another point of the statement that we now concentrate our attention.

Descartes can only be deceived if God deceives him. If no God exists hyperbolic doubt cannot be justified since its meaningless-ness then, so to say, takes charge, and it ceases to *be* doubt. But if God does exist, then since he must be perfect he couldn't deceive (this being logically impossible for a perfect Being to do), and hence a necessary condition for the possibility of hyperbolic doubt becomes logically impossible. However, the argument that since Descartes cannot be the cause of the idea of God, something else must be the cause, does entail minimally that at least something other than Descartes exists, something that is not simply a bit of furnishing lurking in the recesses of his own consciousness and with no claim whatsoever to an existence independent of the existence of Descartes himself. At this point therefore, he would be entitled to claim to know that something exists other than himself, even if he were not also entitled to claim to know just what. But it is the peculiarity of this case that the very considerations which alone entitle him, on his account, to infer the existence of something beyond himself, also by their very nature entitle him to infer its character.

It can be seen, therefore, that everything depends upon whether Descartes can demonstrate beyond all possibility of doubt that in his mind there is at least one idea such that he himself could not have produced it; and this is what he now undertakes to do. He starts by offering a kind of inventory of what seem to him the significant classes of ideas he finds within himself.

But of my ideas, beyond that which represents me to myself, as to which there can here be no difficulty, there is another which represents a God, and there are others representing corporeal and inanimate things, others angels, others animals, and others again which represent to me men similar to myself.

It is among the sorts of items here inventoried that he now has to rummage, and it is obviously quite necessary to follow him in his own words as he meditates, for if he is mistaken here, the basis for the Sixth Meditation which he is still busily laying is pretty worthless. He continues:

And in regard to the ideas of corporeal objects, I do not recognise in them anything so great or so excellent that they might not have possibly proceeded from myself; for if I consider them more closely, and examine them individually, as I yesterday examined the idea of wax, I find that there is very little in them which I perceive clearly and distinctly. Magnitude or extension in length, breadth, or depth, I do so perceive; also figure which results from a termination of this extension, the situation which bodies of different figure preserve in relation to one another, and movement or change of situation; to which we may also add substance, duration and number. (i, 164)

There are really two kinds of idea here that concern Descartes, the idea of a particular body as known through sense experience; and the idea of corporeal nature as such. Our ideas of the first type, as for instance our pre-reflective knowledge of the piece of wax discussed in the Second Meditation, are not clear and distinct, since no knowledge attained by the senses can be. And it is in order to examine this point thoroughly that Descartes does not immediately examine our idea of the second kind, which concerns the clear and distinct kind of knowledge of corporeal characteristics such as those dealt with by mathematics and understood by the categories appropriate to extension.

Now one thing helpful to grasp at this point (though not at this point demonstrated) is the fact that for Descartes it is only in respect of the cognitive syntheses that are produced by the nature of thought alone that true clarity and distinctness are to be attained. Thus whatever is not clear and distinct can only result from what is not essentially thought activity, and therefore not essentially of his nature, And in this respect what is not clearly and distinctly perceived lacks reality to the same degree. This is the central thought behind the following quotation:

As to other things such as light, colours, sounds, scents, tastes, heat, cold and the other tactile qualities, they are thought by me with so much obscurity and confusion that I do not even know if they are true or false, i.e. whether the ideas which I form of these qualities are actually the ideas of real objects or not [or whether they only represent chimeras which cannot exist in fact]. (i, 164)

If these, then, are necessarily present in any perception we can have of particular corporeal objects, then the latter can be no more clearly and distinctly perceived, *qua* corporeal objects, than the obscure and confused elements will permit. Our understanding of them can be clear and distinct, but only insofar as they are understood, and not insofar as they have to be known also through the senses.

Descartes reasons that the various sensory qualities he mentions are obscure and confused, and 'represent what is nothing as though it were something'. This claim has far-reaching consequences for Descartes' thought. If he could feel that in some other sense of clear and distinct than that in which our mathematical knowledge, for instance, is so described, we could describe our sense perception of corporeal objects as clear and distinct, then he could grant that our knowledge of them is good enough for them to have been produced in us by a perfect Being, if there were one.

What he means, he tells us in effect, by saying that these sensory ideas are confused and obscure, is that they possess what he calls 'material falsity'. This is a conception he distinguishes from formal falsity, which he regards as false 'properly speaking', and is the falsity we may meaningfully attribute to judgments. What is it for an idea to be materially false? It is for that idea to represent as something what is really nothing, or really something else; or even to represent an alleged something which cannot exist because it is endowed with contradictory properties. The water feels warm and then cold, but since it cannot be both, it is neither. The fact that the conditions under which the water is felt are different in each case are irrelevant. What is felt of the water is in the one case one thing, and in the other its contrary.

But sensory ideas may be obscure and confused, insofar as one is not sure whether to describe their objects as, say, very hot or (sometimes this is true for a short period) very cold. Here, we don't know *what* to think. We seem unable, not merely to give the right name, but to decide what we feel. This is frequently so with such things as sweet and sour in taste, pleasant or unpleasant in smell, or in sound; and there are times when we are not sure whether we feel one thing or quite the opposite, especially in the case of our emotions. It is not at all inconceivable that we might have an experience we don't know how to describe because we cannot decide between actually contradictory descriptions.

However, Descartes' choice of illustration is by no means random. And using the contrast of heat and cold he is able to argue as if what applies so clearly in this kind of sense experience, applies similarly to other kinds. 'For example, the ideas which I have of cold and heat are so far from clear and distinct that by their means I cannot tell whether cold is merely a privation of heat, or heat a privation of cold, or whether both are real qualities, or are not such' (i, 164). But it is with the concept of privation that he is really concerned, not with questions of naming. He doesn't know whether something we call 'cold' is not really the (felt, presumably) absence of something we call 'heat'. Now he has already told us that all ideas represent, or copy, or image, something other than the idea itself. But, we don't seem to know whether cold is a privation of heat, or heat a privation of cold. Whichever we say, the other may be correct. We can never be sure it isn't. But we have been told to treat what we are not entirely sure about as if it were false. Moreover, for example, since in asserting something to be cold, we are presenting that thing as something it is not (since the idea of cold is really the idea of the not-hot), the idea of cold is false, for it pretends that cold is something when in fact it is only the (felt?) absence of its contrary. But it claims it to be the felt presence of a specific thing, not the felt absence of something else. Therefore it is false—it may perhaps be accused of false pretences.

Descartes wants to say, I think, either that in the case of heat and cold we can have an idea without the existence of a sensation that the idea can be of, or that there is a sensation, but without a precise sensory definition. In particular, he wonders whether feeling something as cold is really feeling it as not hot; or the converse. But does this really mean anything? What is the *absence* of cold? Is Descartes denying that it is one thing to be aware that something is not cold, and quite another to feel it as warm? Do we also *feel* it as not-cold? Sometimes a taste will appear sweetish, sometimes sourish. Do I therefore ask whether sweet is the absence of sour? or sour the absence of sweet? Why should we say that because something tastes, or feels, other than you had reason to expect it would (or even might) what you do experience must be the absence of the other thing? And anyhow, if each is only the absence of the other, there isn't anything to *be* absent, or to be felt. (Unless, of course, it is maintained that one experiences literally an absence, and that one absence is experienced as different from other absences.) Failing to experience what you had expected to, is not actually experiencing what you had not expected to.

The point might be clearer from the illustration of the drawing of a cube. The drawing isn't false, and when I see it directed towards me, I do not argue that, since a moment ago it had been directed away from me, it follows that what I now see as directed towards me is really my now seeing the absence of its being directed away from me; or conversely. But whatever you choose to say about this particular experience it would be as wrong to insist that there is nothing at all drawn on the paper as to insist that because one doesn't know whether something feels hot or warm or cool etc., there is nothing to be felt at all. The assumption underlying this particular example is that sensations are simple. They may, however, be complex enough to contain elements of each other. After all there are sour-sweet things, just as there are bitter-sweet; and there is the kind of sensation which at first seems neither, and then both hot and cold. The very hot and the very cold, for instance, as we surely all know to our cost, are not always immediately distinguishable from one another. What Descartes is really saying is that if we don't even know whether a sensation is or is not what we say it is, then we cannot even claim to (know that we) have it. Apart from not being able to claim knowledge of an external cause for a doubtful effect, there is certainly nothing clear and distinct here. But if in thought we have to learn skill, why not in sensibility too? Many experiences are confused only because we lack the skill to clarify them. And if by 'obscure and confused' Descartes really means 'what is not such as to be capable of being mathematically handled' he could have said so. But he doesn't. Having argued that certain sensory ideas cannot properly be said to represent things, he has continued as if all sensory ideas were equally infected with the falsity which in fact he has been able to discern in very few; and he now has to answer the question of what they can be properly attributed to as their cause. He cannot, after all, bring himself to deny that there are sensory ideas, even false ones. And whatever exists, can only do so by virtue of some substance 'in' which it does so. But since sensory ideas cannot meaningfully be said to qualify corporeal substance, they can only qualify an incorporeal substance, in this case mind.

First of all, insofar as sensory ideas are said not be of anything that exists in corporeal substance, though they confusedly appear to be, they lack that clarity and distinctness which they would have if they had been produced in us by God. But if sensory ideas are not attributable to corporeal substance, how do we know they are attributable to a thinking substance either? Somehow Descartes has to dislodge sensory ideas altogether. He has to do something that in a way is so out of keeping with the whole tradition relating to substance and qualities, ever since Aristotle, that it is easy to miss it. The sensory ideas *are going to turn out to be illusory in the sense that they are modifications that appear to inhere in a substance—when in fact they don't*. The *malin génie* may be forgotten by the reader, but never by Descartes.

The next step of this strange argument will be made clearer if we remember that according to Descartes, the standard conception of God requires that nothing deceitful, or false can issue from him insofar as he is a perfect Being, the highest reality. For falsity, in representing that which is not as if it were, might almost be said (though not by Descartes) to introduce unreality into reality, i.e. to produce a destruction of being. Now reality as such cannot introduce unreality; only a being himself lacking reality, and therefore imperfect, can. Hence, I can represent as real what in fact is unreal only in so far as I am imperfect. Thus what I produce insofar as I am imperfect cannot itself be true.

What would seem to follow is that what is not true or real could not have been produced even by a finite thing. But Descartes, having got away from the idea that whatever is must be in a substance, for long enough to establish that something might not be, almost scurries back under the protective shadow of those ancient wings. He is not going to say that sensory ideas inhere in no substance, since he is not certain of that either. Nor can he ever be, since his whole system of thought is based upon the principle that nothing can be that is not either a substance or a mode (or quality) of a substance. Thus since Descartes is not sure that there might not after all be a sensory idea that does have sufficient definition to be regarded as a real quality of some sort, he says in effect that even if there is, it cannot have been produced by God, and therefore can have been only by himself.

To these ⟨sensory ideas⟩ it is certainly not necessary that I should attribute any author other than myself. For if they are false, i.e. if they represent things which do not exist, the light of nature shows me that they issue from nought, that is to say, that they are only in me in so far as something is lacking to the perfection of my nature. But if they are true, nevertheless because they exhibit so little reality to me that I cannot even clearly distinguish the thing represented from non-being, I do not see any reason why they should not be produced by myself. (i, 165)

I remain baffled by the conception of something which represents nothing and therefore itself issues from nought. The light of nature has always been represented as telling Descartes that nothing can come from nought. And though it may make sense to say that what is *represented* by what represents nothing, comes from nought, it doesn't to say that what *represents* nought, must also come from nought.

So far, then, says Descartes, it is conceivable that I myself might have produced my sensory ideas. But might I not also, he asks, have produced some of the clear and distinct ideas which I have of corporeal things'? For instance consider the ideas 'substance', 'duration', and 'number'. Now even if I consider myself as a finite *thinking* substance, I do take myself to be a thinking *substance*, am aware of enduring through time, and of being able to number my thoughts. In these respects I can from my own experience of myself derive these concepts, and could therefore have used them to construct the idea I find within myself of corporeal substance.

I cannot, however, from my experience of myself as a thinking substance also derive the other clear and distinct ideas which go to constitute the conception of corporeal substance. Extension, figure, situation, motion, cannot be meaningfully attributed to a thinking substance. We recollect that Descartes does not believe in a pure substance, whether of extension, or of thought. Always there is something that is extended, or something that is thought. It would therefore prove difficult to distinguish between either substance, extended or thinking, as such. What they may both be said to have in common is that they enable certain things (however different in kind these things may be in the case of each substance) to form a continuing structure through change. For obviously substance permits change as well as continuity.

However, since unqualified substances are not, as such, mutually exclusive, they might not (though certainly Descartes does not say this) be as different as we think; and perhaps (who knows?) not different at all—as indeed Descartes somewhere suggests. In that case it could be that I produce the very properties that are supposed to be the distinguishing characteristics of extended substance. Certainly I am not aware of doing this, and I am aware that I cannot conceive how these could possibly characterise me. I can therefore be certain they are not in me formally. That is to say, insofar as I am a *thinking* substance, *I* cannot provide the formal reality of attributes that are clearly and distinctly what they are only as attributes of extended substance.

But there is another possibility. Firstly I do not yet know clearly and distinctly all that I am, and secondly, there is the familiar distinction Descartes makes between formal cause and eminent cause. The more perfect is sometimes a cause of the less. And within the depths of the so-far unknown self may lie hitherto unsuspected depths of perfection. It has not yet been proved that God exists, nor that if he does, Descartes might not be he. And perhaps the attributes of extended substances represent some activity of God's in which, for reasons we cannot hope to know, he represents himself in a limited way. The mere possibility of this is sufficient for Descartes' purpose. He writes:

But as to all the other qualities of which the ideas of corporeal things are composed, to wit, extension, figure, situation and motion, it is true that they are not formally in me, since I am only a thing that thinks; but because they are merely certain modes of substance [and so to speak the vestments under which corporeal substance appears to us] and because I myself am also a substance, it would seem that they might be contained in me eminently. (i, 165)

In brief this analysis is held to have shown Descartes unable to scotch the doubt concerning the possibility that he himself may be the source of corporeal objects. Since he doesn't yet know fully what they are he cannot claim to know that he himself has not produced them. As Descartes said at the beginning of this section of his enquiry: 'And in regard to the ideas of corporeal objects, I do not recognise in them anything so great or so excellent that they might not have possibly proceeded from myself.' Viewed as a conclusion from the foregoing, successful or not, Descartes has argued his case, and comes finally to his last remaining idea, that which at least purports to be of God.

Now, Descartes never pretends that to have a clear and distinct idea is always an easy thing. Sometimes it might be, but at other times one only has the idea because one engages in thought. Descartes, as we shall see, in fact holds that if you think the matter through you will find that you cannot doubt unless you have reason to doubt, and behind that reason must lie another, namely, what it is that makes something a reason for doubt. That, for Descartes, is the power that makes him doubt because it cannot tolerate the absence of knowledge. This presupposes the power to recognise what is not knowledge, and therefore, however hard to attain under the tutelage of nature, the very power of knowledge itself. Nothing else, for Descartes, can make sense, and the very fact of doubting is the best argument in its favour. Under the human condition how can reason not compel doubt? The clear and distinct idea of God is thus a most complex idea, and the evidence for our having it consists not least in this, that if we don't have it then doubting, and therefore thinking, just could not happen; for how could they in the absence of that intelligibility without which there is no understanding—of anything? And in this sense God must guarantee the truth of ideas that are clear and distinct, for otherwise we could not doubt at all. We doubt because we know not to be satisfied with what is not clear and distinct. If we didn't know this we couldn't doubt. But we couldn't doubt, without a knowledge guiding our doubt. I don't mean the shadow of doubt, but that doubt which is grounded upon the quest for the kind of certainty we could not even conceive if we were not involved at the same time in an operation that seeks to project its own absolute nature upon the pattern of our doubt in order to resolve that doubt absolutely. Knowledge does not only depend on God because without God's existence there is no guarantee that our clear and distinct ideas are reliable. For we couldn't even have had any such ideas (not simply that of God) if God didn't exist. And how would one *demonstrate* that nobody does have such ideas? However, with one possible exception, this is not a direction Descartes pursues very thoroughly, and as we shall see, he prefers to concentrate upon another argument to gain his case. The point I want to make here is that for Descartes doubting in its fullest sense, and having a clear and distinct idea of God are not all that far removed from one another.

Descartes has given us his definition of God. The various attributes he mentions as characterising God are attributed to a substance. Even God has to be a substance. As we have allowed that we may be familiar with what corporeal substance is from our own nature as substance, it is not too big a step to maintain that we can understand God too, insofar as he is substance—like ourselves. But he is infinite, and I am not. I could not have provided the formal reality for that idea I have which is characterized, as far as is possible for a finite mode, by the objective reality I recognize as that of God. It follows that insofar as my idea is of an infinite substance it must have proceeded from (been caused by) something other than myself. In brief my very knowledge of myself as a thinking thing presupposes a knowledge of the possibility of something forever more than my own limited self can contain; my idea of God is given (obliquely, as it were) with my idea of myself.

Descartes writes:

Hence there remains only the idea of God, concerning which we must consider whether it is something which cannot have proceeded from me myself. By the name God I understand a substance that is infinite [eternal, immutable], independent, all-knowing, all-powerful, and by which I myself and everything else, if anything else does exist, have been created. (i, 165)

We, however, must take Descartes up on the question of having an idea of God, as well, later, as on his claim to be more certain of this than of anything else at all.

When do I have this idea? Descartes answers, when I doubt, for then I presuppose the possibility of knowledge. The knowledge that I lack something, i.e. that I am deficient in this or that respect presupposes that I have the idea of a being who suffers no such lack, or suffers no lack at all, and lacking nothing is perfect. In view of the particular importance this point has for the thesis I shall be interested in advancing, I quote Descartes' own words:

Nor should I imagine that I do not perceive the infinite by a true idea, but only by the negation of the finite, just as I perceive repose and darkness by the negation of movement and of light; for, on the contrary, I see that there is manifestly more reality in infinite substance than in finite, and therefore that in some way I have in me the notion of the infinite earlier than the finite—to wit, the notion of God before that of myself. For how would it be possible that I should know that I doubt and desire, that is to say, that something is lacking to me, and that I am not quite perfect, unless I had within me some idea of a Being more perfect than myself, in comparison with which I should recognise the deficiencies of my nature? (i, 166)

When I argued earlier that even a confused idea can be ascribed to a substance, I was speaking of finite substances. Now, however, I speak of an infinite substance. And the question is whether, assuming it makes sense at all to speak of an infinite substance, who is God, one can ascribe to him a confused idea, especially one he puts into a mind he has made capable of seeking only clear and distinct ideas. As for the idea being an idea of God, well how could a confused idea, an idea aborted to the point where one is neither sure what it is or is not, and even whether it is or is not, be the representation in objective reality of the formal reality of an infinite and divine Being?

It might, of course, be argued that in no other way would an idea representing such a Being appear to a human creature. But in fact the idea of God could not differ more than it does from a confused, or obscure idea:

And we cannot say that this idea of God is perhaps materially false and that consequently I can derive it from nought [i.e. that possibly it exists in me because I am imperfect], as I have just said is the case with ideas of heat, cold and other such things; for, on the contrary, as this idea is very clear and distinct and contains within it more objective reality than any other, there can be none which is of itself more true, nor any in which there can be less suspicion of falsehood. (i, 166)

It does not, however, follow from this that my idea of God is adequate to him in the same sense as my idea of a triangle may be said to be adequate to it. The idea of God is the idea of something more than I can possibly conceive, since it is the idea of an infinite Being. Possibly in God, Descartes tells us, there are an infinitude of things which I cannot 'reach in any way by thought'. For I am not only a finite thinking substance, but also, as a person, a finite corporeal substance. This limits what I can hope to know of the world, and of God. But it is quite simple to build this fact also into the idea we have of God. The element of inconceivability in our conception of God is not an obscure, or vague, or confused idea, lying like a blot on the otherwise spotless lineaments of God, but a clearly conceived and intelligible limitation easily seen to follow from the contrast between God's nature and ours. It offers no ground for the view that the idea of God suffers from material falsity.

In Meditation Six Descartes will give all his attention to the problem of how, if at all, thinking substance and extended substance may be defined with absolute clearness and distinctness in relation to each other. Until then, therefore, he cannot be quite certain of all that may be involved in either. He is certain, he says, of what there is in each that is not involved in the other; but he is not certain that there may not be more in each than he is now certain there is. And may he not have brooded over the possibility that there might somewhere be an element that does not easily disclose itself? This possibility applies to extension no less than to mind, but the indications are that Descartes' main concern was with the latent elements yet to be found within mind. For whatever anyone might say about Cartesian Dualism, it remains impossible to read the Meditations without seeing that for Descartes there is an order of priority in which mind is unquestionably (and should we not perhaps say necessarily?) prior.

Since Descartes takes himself to know himself to be a thinking substance, and on the present evidence finite, he considers that he does not yet know certainly that he might not be more than he knows:

But possibly I am something more than I suppose myself to be, and perhaps all those perfections which I attribute to God are in some way potentially in me, although they do not yet disclose themselves, or issue in action.

84

He is not actually saying that God may inhabit the depths of his consciousness; but he cannot be sure that some (if not all) of those Perfections which make him argue to the existence of God, may not indeed linger within his own (*possibly* infinite) depths. And, being potential, their essential natures remain as yet unactualized.

As a matter of fact I am already sensible that my knowledge increases [and perfects itself] little by little, and I see nothing which can prevent it from increasing more and more into infinitude; nor do I see, after it has thus been increased [or perfected], anything to prevent my being able to acquire by its means all the other perfections of the Divine nature; nor finally why the power I have of acquiring these perfections, if it really exists in me, shall not suffice to produce the ideas of them. (i, 167)

Thus not only may Descartes become formally perfect; he may—with such power at his disposal—himself be the source of his ideas of perfection. Notice how Descartes tends to speak as if of a process that goes on independently of his direction. It isn't so much that he increases his knowledge, as that his knowledge increases. And as he doesn't see why it shouldn't continue to increase, it might increase to infinity. He seems to suggest that it is a power of acquiring perfections (rather than Descartes himself) that produces the ideas of those perfections as a kind of blueprint for itself. It bears considering what the impact of such a possibility must have been on many minds turning from contemplating the revealed Lord to contemplating the opening vistas within, full of dark and magical possibilities.

But Descartes rejects this view of the self as replete with the possibility of being God. The idea I have of God is of a being who actually is all he can be. Indeed, Descartes could hardly have forgotten St Anselm's insistence that not merely is God actual, but he is actual in his entire and infinite unity always and everywhere. To think of God, therefore, as potential in any single respect, would be to destroy the idea of his infinite Perfection. God may hide from me, but not from himself, nor therefore within me either; for within me, as Descartes has insisted, the sustaining power is in fact the very presence of God. Also, if our knowledge grows, it is imperfect. Hence doubt, and error. Precisely this sense of lack of knowledge demonstrates for Descartes his own imperfection. The idea of a perfect Being is the idea of a being who does not lack total actuality. Existence being a perfection, how could such a Being choose not to be in actuality exactly what he in essence must be? Thus Descartes states his third argument: 'And finally I perceive that the objective being of an idea cannot be produced by a being that exists potentially only, which properly speaking is nothing, but only by a being which is formal or actual' (i, 167). During the course of the Meditations Descartes has referred to the close relationship between his idea of himself, and his idea of God. But the idea of God seems almost to possess an inward power to necessitate the formal existence of its object. Hence Descartes is sometimes almost in greater danger of not being able to prove that *he* is not God, than of not being able to prove that God exists. However, to exist potentially is not, as Descartes says it is, to be 'properly speaking nothing'. To say that something exists potentially is indeed to say that it does not exist, but it is also to say that something else that does exist points to its possibility.

What Descartes is getting at is simply that, since even if God existed in him, he could only do so potentially, and since the nature of God cannot be conceived as limited to potentiality, God could not exist in him, and so he cannot be, or become, God.

What Descartes may be taken to have shown up to this stage is that he himself exists, that he is a being the nature of which is to think, that there exists also corporeal substance (for which he finds in himself no reason to claim responsibility) *if* he is not deceived, that he cannot be deceived *if* God exists, that he has an idea of such a Being, and, finally, that he, Descartes, cannot himself be the cause of that idea.

He has not, so far, attempted to prove that this idea must have been put into his mind by a perfect Being. This he soon tries to put right:

when I slightly relax my attention, my mind, finding its vision somewhat obscured and so to speak blinded by the images of sensible objects, I do not easily recollect the reason why the idea that I possess of a being more perfect than I, must necessarily have been placed in me by a being which is really more perfect; and this is why I wish here to go on to inquire whether I, who have this idea, can exist if no such being exists. (i, 167)

If I didn't exist I couldn't have the idea. But I do have the idea. Therefore I must exist.

What Descartes proposes is to enquire whether, granted that he has the idea, he could nevertheless exist if a Being answering to the idea did not exist. If he is able to show that he cannot exist unless there is such a Being, it will follow that the existence of such a Being is a necessary condition for his own.

What, then, or who, can be the necessary condition of Descartes' existence? Can we say he is self-caused? Did he produce himself? The implications of this question are made clear early. If he could have made himself at all, then he could have made himself God, since to make oneself from nothing, Descartes argues, is a greater accomplishment than to make himself into God from what he now is. Then could he have made himself? But since he has argued that it is more difficult to make yourself from nothing than to make yourself God from what you are, i.e. from something, he is able to argue that *if* he had made himself, he might just as easily (and therefore would) have made himself God right away. In which case he would not be the limited being he is; and nothing, as he says, would be lacking to him. He being finite, however, could not have made himself; and this in short is most of his argument.

But suppose he has not been made at all, nor therefore been made by God either, and thus has never been non-existent. The model of 'made' naturally turns our thought to an act in time, and therefore a point of time in which that act begins. Presumably we do not think of God as needing to take up a stretch of time in order to accomplish anything. For a perfect (and therefore omnipotent) Being to will something to be is also for him to have accomplished it. However, if Descartes has existed since eternity, God cannot have existed before him, nor therefore have been in a position to make him. But this presupposes the model just referred to, namely, one in which a thing is made once and for all from the moment it has been made.

This, however, assumes that there is no problem about how existence in time is possible, and that once a thing actually exists, or is brought into existence (which may or may not be a problem) it just remains there until something else is done to it, as if by a kind of existential inertia. But for Descartes it is no more evident than it is for Hume that what exists must continue. For neither of these philosophers is it obvious that things promote their own continuance, since for neither of them do 'matters of fact' necessitate any other matters of fact, even when the latter seem only later phases of the former, i.e., identical through time with them. It should not surprise us that Descartes is so sensitive to the contingency of whatever we learn to be so from the senses—those apparently ineradicable sources of illusion, the sphere where nothing is safe from doubt, and where therefore knowledge, and knowledge of necessity, is so far out of our reach. And it is this, it seems to me, and not a theory of time he has in mind when he writes:

it is as a matter of fact perfectly clear and evident to all those who consider with attention the nature of time, that, in order to be conserved in each moment in which it endures, a substance has need of the same power and action as would be necessary to produce and create it anew, supposing it did not yet exist, so that the light of nature shows us clearly that the distinction between creation and conservation is solely a distinction of the reason. (i, 168)

Not only can we not detect in any existent thing the power by which it brings about changes in other things, but neither can we detect within it the means by which it itself changes, nor, above all, for Descartes' immediate purpose, even that in it in respect of which we know it to maintain even its own non-changing existence. Neither our reason nor our senses inform us how all these things are so. And yet, as I hope will emerge from this work, indirectly, for Descartes, reason, by putting the existence of a sustaining God beyond all doubt, is made by him to do precisely the sort of job Hume insisted it could not.

Since, then, we do not find in anything the power to sustain itself in being, and since things which lack the power to sustain themselves cannot be conceived as having the power to sustain other things either, no member of the class of things that exist in time can be regarded as that which sustains any other thing. On the contrary, each thing is itself in need of power to exist. Therefore the cause of continuing existence of the world of temporal reality cannot be located within that world. What else can it be but that same something to which each thing owes its existence at *any* moment. Power, that is to say, is not lateral, but vertical, not from thing to thing, but always from God to thing. And the same God who gives things the existence they have at any instant, is the only possible Being who could possibly be conceived as giving them existence from instant to instant. And whatever power is requisite for giving existence to a given thing at one instant could clearly not be less or more than the power necessary for giving the same thing existence an instant later. Things are conceived as independent of one another, but never as independent of God.

This conception of producing, or making, is one in which collateral and not merely initiatory power is regarded as being exercised. If this is so, then the distinction between creation and conservation is not one of reason at all, but of imagination, and a confused imagination at that. For it is an imagination that confuses creation in the temporal sense of being precedent to the existence of the created thing, on the analogy with human production, with creation in another sense. Here, God is not regarded as otiose in respect of what he has created. Since nothing but God exists necessarily there is nothing else that could exist of its own nature. And since to exist is to exist for as long as the thing exists, for *as long as it exists* it exists not of its own nature but because of God's. And the latter is certainly the only sense Descartes has, or indeed logically can have in mind. In view of this it is immaterial to Descartes whether he considers himself as having been created in the beginning, as imagination would suggest, by God, and then left to exist on, or whether he considers himself as having existed from all eternity, uncreated; for in either case he, a finite and dependent creature, would never be free from the need for God's constant intervention to rescue him from annihilation, moment by moment. Thus his dependence upon God for his powers of existence, as for being what he is, and of becoming what he does, all ground his being inescapably in God's.

We have seen that whether created by God initially, or uncreated, a power must still be exercised collaterally with his existence in order for him to exist. But if there lies in him such a power, a power to conserve his self, a finite thinking substance, in being, then since this power must be that source of which he could no more fail to be conscious than God can of *his* power, he could not fail to be conscious of it. As a necessitating power, a power that necessitates his very being, he would grasp it not by the senses, but by thought, since only thought can grasp necessitation. For this grasping how could he be better equipped than he is? Having set out the position he answers briefly, but to the point: 'But I am conscious of nothing of the kind, and by this I know clearly that I depend on some being different from myself' (i, 169).

It might appear that Descartes has overlooked one possible argument against the view that God's creation is necessarily collateral with the existence of his creature. God is omnipotent, hence whatever is not self-contradictory or inconceivable in conceivable, he can bring about. Now consider the members of a series constituting some continuing object. It might be asked: 'Did God lack the power to confer upon the first member the power to confer upon the second member, and in turn all subsequent members, the power each required to maintain itself in being? How can he be omnipotent if he can never delegate power, but must always so to say stand by in person to administer it?' This possibility is surely, one might think, quite conceivable, clearly and distinctly, and there is nothing one can find self-contradictory about it. This, however, is not the case. To delegate power of autonomous existence, plus the power of granting to itself, or another, further autonomous existence would be to grant it what logically amounts to necessary existence. And the concept of a necessarily existing finite being is certainly one that Descartes regards, and must regard, as self-contradictory. Moreover, if, *per impossibile*, one could exist, God would no longer be the only necessarily existing being. In brief we should have a situation which we should have to regard either as one consisting of two perfect Beings, or, which seems the more logically consistent, none at all. But, by definition of a perfect Being, he logically could not act so as to encompass his own destruction, for this would be to give a practical demonstration that his existence was, after all, just *not* necessary.

On the other hand another possible objection to Descartes, here, might be regarded as more formidable. He has argued that if the power that conserves us were within ourselves we ought to be able to detect it, since as long as we have the possibility of a future it must be within us, and though everything within us is

evidently not known to us, that which must be constantly opera-
tive for us to exist at all, must, therefore, constantly be accessible
to a reflecting self, just as God, the power that does conserve us, is.
If he were that power, or possessed it, he could know that in
exactly the same way. The objection to Descartes is as follows. By
hypothesis the power within myself capable of keeping me existing
for ever would be a power the existence of which was not contingent, and so requiring to be conserved, but necessary. In that
case if I 'enter into myself' what I shall discover there is a necessarily existing being. In that case I shall not discover myself to be
the limited, dependent being I now do, but the very being that
I am now aware of only in my experience of myself as sustained
despite my limitations. In other words, it seems most likely that
I would discover myself to be God. If it is argued back that I
could not be the self-created and autonomous Being we name
God, without knowing it, the answer is that this is not entirely
obvious. For though Descartes does argue that God must be
actual and not merely potential, he need not concede that for a
being not to know that it is God is the same as for that being to be
God only potentially—which let us agree with Descartes, for
the sake of the argument, is conceptually impossible. Specula-
tion in these areas is dark and hazardous at best, but perhaps, taken
in conjunction with what may be less so, could be significant in
ways not immediately obvious.

Allowing, then, that God is omniscient, must this entail that
like some super Brains Truster he knows everything, all the time,
as if he dare not let anything out of his ken for fear of losing it?
And would such a concept of knowledge be intelligible? In any
sense of 'know' which is meaningful, something cannot be said
to be known unless it is selected, is the figure to some *unstated*
ground, the focus of a *selective* attention. Where all is in focus
nothing is. Thus, firstly, God's omniscience is not incompatible
with there being something which does not command God's
attention. But secondly, why may not that something be himself,
at some moment, somewhere, or in some respect? I do not take
myself to have been reborn each time I become self-conscious,
as distinct from conscious of other things; nor indeed when, as
after a dreamless sleep during which I have not been conscious of
anything, I come to. And if my self-identity is held safe during

such occasions, how can God's not be? Thirdly, however, is it inconceivable that in some pre-set way God might set limits of the most diverse kind upon himself, and in this remain, by his own will, as subject to his own limitations on his knowledge of himself, as by his own will, in his creations, he is subject to his own laws? Indeed, an understanding of just this point is vital to an understanding of the Sixth Meditation.

The argument that Descartes depends for his existence upon a being other than himself and with the power to confer existence would not also, by itself be an argument for its being 'that which I call God'. For God has not simply the power to exist of himself, but possesses all other possible perfections as well. Thus Descartes' idea of God is the idea of that which possesses them. And since the formal reality (containing all perfections), of which this idea is the objective reality, cannot be in Descartes—or he could not but know it—it must lie elsewhere; namely, in that from which he draws (whether he knows it or not) his power to exist.

and thus since I am a thinking thing, and possess an idea of God within me, whatever in the end be the cause assigned to my existence, it must be allowed that it is likewise a thinking thing and that it possesses in itself the idea of all the perfections which I attribute to God. (i, 169)

But this cause of my existence must itself have (or be) being. How otherwise could it be a cause? Why, then, it might be asked, doesn't the argument for this cause also prove that it too has a cause, and so on? Descartes answers, because this cause is God. Possessing all perfection it is self-completing as well as self-generating. Its nature requires nothing external to itself—for *any* of its perfection—nor to sustain the eternalness of its perfections. Otherwise, it would not be God.

Descartes' opponents are unable to accept that God requires a cause—even from himself. Says Arnauld in the Fourth Set of Objections: '*God can be self-derived not* in the positive sense, *but only* negatively, *i.e., in the sense of* not proceeding from anything else' (ii, 90). And the reason given is simply that an eternal being, having on before or after, exists eternally at any moment. Therefore, he cannot require something to cause him to be what he is, for he is what he is, at any moment, because he is that which, being eternal, *always* is, and thus requires no additional help—even (and indeed *especially*) from himself.

Therefore, just as the reply to the question why the triangle has its three angles equal to two right angles should not be in terms of an efficient cause, but the reason assigned should be the eternal and immutable nature of the triangle; so when we ask why God exists, or continues in existence, we must seek for no efficient cause, either within God or without Him, and for nothing similar to an efficient cause (for my contention touches the thing not the name for it): we should state as our reason this alone, 'because such is the nature of a supremely perfect being.' (ii, 91)

But further along:

And if our interrogator plies us with the question why no efficient cause is required, we must answer 'because He is an infinite Being, and in such a case existence and essence are identical'; for only those things, the actual existence of which can be distinguished from their essence, require an efficient cause. (ii, 92)

However, it is not only from the concept of God but also from that of cause that the objector argues. Having already made the point that a cause must precede its effect, he now makes the point that 'nothing can in any way be so related to itself as is an efficient cause towards its effect'. To which Descartes replies at once that he agrees with Arnauld insofar as Arnauld's argument is directed against the view that God needs an efficient cause for himself, even if from himself. But he insists on keeping the term 'cause'. What he stresses is that self-causation follows from what he calls 'the inexhaustible power of God' that belongs to God's essence. This is 'cause' in the most positive sense of that word—not cause by transmission, but by origination. Whatever God does he does absolutely from and by himself. Since this applies only to God, if there is anything at all, other than God, for which an efficient cause cannot be given, this can only be because it isn't known, and not because there isn't any. Thus, using Aristotle's system of classifying causes, Descartes claims his position to be that the formal cause (essential nature) of God is such that he—though he alone— has neither need nor use for an efficient cause as well. Moreover Descartes makes the interesting point that insofar as God may be regarded as standing to finite things in a relation by which they are conserved, it would be meaningless to say (and therefore he didn't say) that God stands in the same relation to himself—a Being of a type relevantly different in that, as we saw, its nature lacks the imperfection which alone would enable a thing to stand in that relation. A healthy man cannot stand in the relation of 'being cured by' to anybody.

Descartes' further defence, in his reply to Arnauld, of this use of the word 'cause' should be noted by those devoted to the 'ontological argument'.

But I think that it is manifest to all, that to consider the efficient cause is the primary and principal, not to say the only means of proving the existence of God. We shall not be able to pursue this proof with accuracy, if we do not grant our mind the liberty of asking for an efficient cause in every case, even in that of God; for with what right should we exclude God, before we have proved that He exists? (ii, 109)

This should be pondered over especially by those interested in the concept of cause, in view of Descartes' following observations. 'For those who follow the guidance of the light of nature alone, spontaneously form here a concept common to efficient and formal cause alike.' But here there is only space to note Descartes' explanation of what he takes to be the mistaken view to which he is opposed.

Consider the distinction between efficient cause and formal cause. The nature of a thing is said to be determined by its formal cause—its essence; in this sense it is self-derived. But the actual existence of the thing is said to be determined by an efficient cause; in this sense it cannot be called self-derived. If a thing is caused to exist its nature is self-derived. But it didn't have to exist. Therefore, efficient causes are not necessary causes. But, granted existence, the nature of the thing has to be what its essence proclaims in it. Therefore formal causes are necessary causes. Now Descartes maintains that people who think in terms only of Aristotle's classification suppose that if something is self-derived it cannot also be the effect of an efficient cause. And (since we are here considering efficient causes and formal causes exclusively) since this rules out causes except in the sense of formal cause—which is supposed not to account for existence— the existence of the thing is supposed not to require a cause at all.

But against this Descartes urges grave objections, since its outcome would be to make it impossible to use the complicated chain of causal arguments with which Descartes proves God's existence, and without which, he maintains, we cannot prove it.

The argument depends upon a distinction I stressed above between something's being self-caused, and its being God. If existence is a perfection, whatever can give itself one perfection would have the power also to give itself all. But if there is merely something that happens to be (but to be no more than) merely there eternally, it would not follow that it must also be God. That eternal something is no more God than a non-existent God could be. This is perhaps enough to show that at this point Descartes is fighting for his life. No wonder that in his reply to Arnauld on this matter he says: 'But if this ⟨Arnauld's, and the orthodox⟩ interpretation of *self-derived* were admitted, there would be no reason by which to prove God's existence from His effects, as was shown correctly by the author of the first Objections; hence we must on no account sanction it.' (ii, 110). In brief we should then have no reason to believe God exists. In which case, also, no foundation, as we shall see, for the ontological argument. We, however, are entitled to draw our own conclusions. Descartes frankly owns to being unable to define a precise sense of cause applicable to God's causality of himself. One of the conditions for A being the cause of B, namely that it should be simultaneous with it (a point Hume rejected), Descartes regards as fulfilled in the sense in which this applies to God; but not the other condition, namely, that A and B must be different entities— God not being different from himself. So God is only to some extent the efficient cause of himself—which in this context means not at all. A full and illuminating discussion of all this is to be found in the discussion between Descartes and Arnauld in the Objections and Replies. There, reluctantly, I must leave the matter.

Let us now turn to another of the less familiar of Descartes' arguments. He maintains that the idea of God is not a patchwork of perfections drawn from a variety of causes which have concurred to produce the thinker. The various perfections, and indeed all the properties I discern to be God's, cannot be drawn from a diversity of sources, since I not only discern them individually, but also in a unity, the overall quality of which is in turn a kind of simplicity in all his perfections, itself 'one of the principal perfections I conceive to be in Him'. And Descartes' point is that the nature of this unity is such that the different elements, which I am able to conceive in it, cannot exist apart, nor therefore have separate causes. Furthermore, the relation between this unity and its elements is such that he could only have received *them* each from the same source that he, as thinker, received *it*; for the unity is conceived as the unity of perfections, and therefore to conceive the unity is to conceive them. Hence, Descartes says, the cause of my perceiving the unity is also the cause of my perceiving the perfections which could not have been seen as united unless they were also seen for what they are in themselves—and, we may presume, the converse.

In Meditation Five Descartes will produce the most famous, and some think the most unconvincing, argument for the existence of God. As it is there stated it is taken up and confuted by almost everybody. But the ontological argument is part of a metaphysical system, and depends for certain of its assumptions upon that system. One of those assumptions, as we have already noted, is that we do have an idea of a perfect Being. Another is that there is something very special about the ontological status of that Being. Now the argument of Descartes we have just been discussing contributes something on behalf of both assumptions. For do we have to suppose that wherever the word 'existence' occurs it must be identical in meaning? Descartes does not think that 'idea' when applied to God, means exactly what it does when applied in any other case; nor that 'existence' does. And his argument in the paragraph under discussion is connected with this. He does not have to depend for his argument on existence being a 'predicate', but upon its being a perfection. If it is better to exist than not to exist, and if some things may be said to exist more than others, in that they entail the existence of more things than other things do, then we may be said to have the idea of something existing which entails the existence of more things than anything else can, and which therefore may be said to have more existence than anything else can. So if existence is better than non-existence, we have the conception of something more perfect than any other thing in respect of existence.

Descartes is seriously insisting that God's perfections are such that we cannot conceive any one of them to hold of him, without also conceiving the others to. And this conception is not something simply in our heads. If it is sufficiently clear and distinct it gives us, indeed, a vision of reality. This is one of the things that

Descartes means when he speaks of God guaranteeing the truth of our clear and distinct ideas; and it is what Spinoza meant when he spoke of that way of knowing which he calls *Scientia Intuitiva*, and partly what Hegel meant when he spoke of the objectivity, or 'Truth', of the categories of thought. In knowledge we escape the limitations of our corporeal being in a perfectly unmystical way—by the power of thought through which we achieve unity with the reality beyond as well as within ourselves.

Hence we must look closely at what Descartes has to say about the unity of God's perfections, since through one of these, namely the power of thought, we may ourselves come to know the 'truth' of the others:

Nor can we suppose that several causes may have concurred in my production, and that from one I have received the idea of one of the perfections which I attribute to God, and from another the idea of some other, so that all these perfections indeed exist somewhere in the universe, but not as complete in one unity which is God. On the contrary, the unity, the simplicity or the inseparability of all things which are in God is one of the principal perfections which I conceive to be in Him. And certainly the idea of this unity of all Divine perfections cannot have been placed in me by any cause from which I have not likewise received the ideas of all the other perfections; for this cause could not make me able to comprehend them as joined together in an inseparable unity without having at the same time caused me in some measure to know what they are [and in some way to recognise each one of them]. (i, 169–70)

Descartes may just as well be said to be arguing to the existence of God, from the idea of any one of his perfections, as from the idea of any other. The question, indeed, may not be whether we can predicate existence of these perfections, but of whether we could refuse to do so without contradiction. But to this subject we shall return when we discuss Meditation Five. Thus Descartes has ruled out any possible causes of himself other than God, and he now reminds us that it is both from the fact that he, indubitably a mind, exists, and the fact that in his mind he as indubitably finds the idea of God, that he knows God to exist. Yet is not this too pat? God not only creates him, but signs the work. And by means of the signature we identify the creator. We know, then, both that the self cannot create itself, and, through the signature, the Being that did, and indeed, it seems, the only Being that could.

However, the point of chief importance here is that I do discover that signature, and in the form of my idea of God. And the next question must be not how I know it for what it is, but how I discover it at all. For one like Descartes, who dwelt so much upon the problem of how any knowledge is possible (he did not have to wait for Kant) what could have been more likely to exercise his attention than the question of how, of all things, a knowledge of God himself is possible, whether we interpret this as knowledge by acquaintance of some sort, or by representation. His own words sum up much of his thinking so far:

It only remains to me to examine into the manner in which I have acquired this idea from God; for I have not received it through the senses, and it is never presented to me unexpectedly, as is usual with the ideas of sensible things when these things present themselves, or seem to present themselves, to the external organs of my senses; nor is it likewise a fiction of my mind, for it is not in my power to take from or to add anything to it; and consequently the only alternative is that it is innate in me, just as the idea of myself is innate in me. (i, 170)

We find here prefigured the argument of the Fifth Meditation that the idea of God possesses no less objectivity than any other idea, and is therefore no less necessitating as to the truths drawn from it. And one of these truths states that since I have the idea, God must have being; yet since I have the idea, God must necessitate that too. As we shall see when we come to discuss the Fifth Meditation, the so-called ontological argument need not be regarded as standing alone, for the causal argument, carefully considered, is shown to be its true parent. If it is the case that I could not have the idea of God unless he had caused me to, and if it is also the case that I cannot consider, not merely the idea of my own nature, but even my nature itself, without discovering that idea, not simply as the idea of that which conserves me and sets up for me a standard of truth and goodness, but also as the original of any such idea, then the existence of the original is inescapably presupposed.

For from the sole fact that God created me it is most probable that in some way he has placed his image and similitude upon me, and that I perceive this similitude (in which the idea of God is contained) by means of the same faculty by which I perceive myself—that is to say, when I reflect on myself I not only know that I am something [imperfect], incomplete and dependent on another, which incessantly aspires after something which is better and greater than myself, but I also know that He on whom I depend possesses in Himself all the great things towards which I aspire [and the ideas of which I find within myself], and that not indefinitely or potentially alone, but really, actually and infinitely; and that thus He is God. (i, 170)

This perhaps is the clearest statement anywhere in Descartes of the unity of the ground of his idea of God and his idea of himself. He knows God in knowing more of what he, Descartes, is. This is a complex dialectical conception. Descartes knows himself most certainly when he finds he cannot expunge by any doubt the fact of his doubt. In doubting he is most certain of his own existence in the very idea he has of himself. And in that same idea he discovers no less the existence of God. Again, I have made the point that the dichotomy between idea and thing is clearly not absolute for Descartes. The idea Descartes has of himself may be regarded as distinguishable from all other ideas, with one exception, by being both the idea and that which it is an idea of. And, allowing for the difference occasioned between a finite and an infinite thinking substance, that other idea is the idea of God, insofar as it can be adequate in the mind of a finite being.

This last point is one his critics seem not to have grasped. For instance Caterus, in the First Set of Objections, asks whether we do (or can) apprehend clearly and distinctly an infinite being. He certainly takes himself to be representing the religious point of view. How can man actually *know* God? Certainly not to know *something* of God is not to be able to be religious. And faith is a kind of knowledge. But to know God in the discursive mode, clearly and distinctly, is inconceivable unless either we ourselves are infinite, or God himself is finite—an equally unthinkable proposition. Indeed, since there are finite objects that I am incapable of thinking clearly and distinctly, 'shall I not be asked,—how can the infinite be thought of distinctly and not confusedly, if the infinite perfections of which it is composed cannot be perceived clearly, and, as it were, with true distinctness of vision?' (ii, 5). Descartes answers that of course we cannot grasp the infinite in all its totality, i.e. so that nothing of that which we grasp remains absent from our actual knowledge of what we grasp. Knowledge of what is infinite as infinite, is knowledge that it is infinite—a knowledge that can come only from our thinking clearly and distinctly that its nature presents us with no knowledge of how it could be limited. Thus the concept of infinity is meaningful to thought. But as compared with the thought of what is infinite in this or that respect (as with Spinoza's attributes) there is the thought of something limited in no respect whatsoever, as, for instance, Spinoza's conception of Substance. It is this universally comprehensive infinite that Descartes tells us he regards as truly infinite, and nothing else. This infinite is God. Whatever is limited in no respect by anything conceivable, is necessarily conceived as universally embracing—which is clear and distinct to thought, though unimaginable. But then, Descartes could never suppose a perfect Being to be a possible object of imagination. Indeed this would be as meaningless as it would be to speak of thinking what one hears, or sees, or smells, or tastes.

And the whole strength of the argument which I have here made use of to prove the existence of God consists in this, that I recognise that it is not possible that my nature should be what it is, and indeed that I should have in myself the idea of a God, if God did not veritably exist— a God, I say, whose idea is in me, i.e. who possesses all those supreme perfections of which our mind may indeed have some idea but without understanding them all, who is liable to no errors or defect [and who has none of all those marks which denote imperfection]. From this it is manifest that He cannot be a deceiver, since the light of nature teaches us that fraud and deception necessarily proceed from some defect. (i, 170–1)

CHAPTER FOUR

In Meditation Three Descartes took himself to have proved that God exists. And since God is regarded as being as incapable of deceit as of any other limitation, no serious doubt should remain that knowledge is possible. Yet we do fall into error. Indeed it is because Descartes originally found himself with beliefs that turned out to be false that he was moved to distrust them all. Whatever a conceptual analysis of God may reveal, the human race is not merely prone to error, but riddled with it.

It is not enough to urge that this is simply our own fault, that if we only use our minds properly we will make no mistakes; or that mistakes, as contingent, are not a necessary part of human nature. For we are finite creatures, and therefore 'as I find myself subject to an infinitude of imperfections, I ought not to be astonished if I should fall into error'. Error here, then, has a metaphysical basis. And that is a far more serious matter for Descartes. In this sense, how can it ever be eradicated? Yet God must have made our faculties of knowing perfect. This is the central problem of the present Meditation, which might be described as an attempt to square the *a priori* necessity of God's being morally unable to deceive us, with the empirical fact that we do err. It would, however, be truer to set the problem at a deeper level, as one in which it is not the empirical fact of human error, but the apparent necessity of it, that has to be squared with God's truthfulness. In one direction man reaches out to God; but in the other finds himself rooted in a kind of nothingness.

The problem grows out of man's dual nature as a thinking and an extended being. Hence Descartes begins Meditation Four by recalling this to us, and relating to it, as directly as he can, the difference between the reliability of our knowledge insofar as we are the one, and its unreliability insofar as we are the other. The sub-title of this Meditation is 'Of the True and the False'.

It starts:

I have been well accustomed these past days to detach my mind from my senses, and I have accurately observed that there are very few things that one knows with certainty respecting corporeal objects, that there are many more which are known to us respecting the human mind, and yet more still regarding God Himself; so that I shall now without any difficulty abstract my thoughts from the consideration of [sensible or] imaginable objects, and carry them to those which, being withdrawn from all contact with matter, are purely intelligible. And certainly the idea which I possess of the human mind inasmuch as it is a thinking thing, and not extended in length, width and depth, nor participating in anything pertaining to body, is incomparably more distinct than is the idea of any corporeal thing. (i, 171)

The mind, not being an extended thing, grasps most clearly what is also, like it, unextended. In the case of a thinking substance, the idea of that substance, as itself 'part' of that very same substance, does in fact have a privileged access to whatever else is a mode, or attribute, of that substance. Indeed, what is 'having an idea of the human mind' but the human mind thinking about itself? If the human mind is more distinct to the human mind than 'body' can be, then for a knowledge of what goes on in our own minds, we do not require to put our trust in an intermediary such as our senses.

Thus Descartes accustoms himself to 'detaching' his mind from his senses. Mind, though by nature at home only with itself, is, by the time we have begun to reflect, almost lost in the sensory consciousness that is our customary manner of knowing. Descartes' effort to suspend belief about the world has given his thinking a certain autonomy. He can consider his thoughts, now, in themselves, without having to ask himself whether they are also applicable to a world in regard to which his claim to knowledge must always be problematic.

Perhaps it *is* because God would never deceive us, Descartes seems to think, that we doubt. To doubt is to be unwilling to believe what is false. But doubt is itself something of the mind, not of corporeal substance: it is a way of seeing something purporting to be true, and wondering whether it really is.

And when I consider that I doubt, that is to say, that I am an incomplete and dependent being, the idea of a being that is complete and independent, that is of God, presents itself to my mind with so much distinctness and clearness—and from the fact alone that this idea is found in me, or that I who possess this idea exist, I conclude so certainly that God exists, and that my existence depends entirely on Him in every moment of my life—that I do not think that the human mind is capable of knowing anything with more evidence and certitude. And it seems to me that I now have before me a road which will lead us from the contemplation of the true God (in whom all the treasures of science and wisdom are contained) to the knowledge of the other objects of the universe. (i, 171–2)

Thus Descartes discovers in the very heart of his doubt something such that he does 'not think the human mind is capable of knowing anything with more evidence and certitude'.

Let us here remind ourselves of Descartes' argument for constant creation by God of whatever exists. Clearly, if we exist, the argument applies to us. But in this case, as in no other, I can know myself as in constant process of being redeemed from extinction by God. That is, I can know God, can myself experience him as the Being upon whom my being depends. This is not to say that I can have knowledge of God as he is in himself, but that I can have a knowledge of him as he sustains me. But what sort of knowledge could this be? A mystical knowledge? No, for by definition that is not clear and distinct. The answer is that my knowledge of God as my sustainer is nothing other than my awareness of myself as doubting. Look again at Descartes' words: 'And when I consider that I doubt, that is to say, that I am an incomplete and dependent being, the idea of a being that is complete and independent, that is of God, presents itself to my mind.' But consider just what the doubt is that in the earlier Meditations always brings Descartes to an awareness of God. It is the doubt of his own existence. He cannot doubt his own existence, because and only because he immediately becomes aware of himself being sustained by God. To be unable to deny one's own existence is to be unable to do the impossible, for insofar as a necessarily existing being sustains one, he thereby necessitates whatever is most essential to oneself—such as one's rational doubt. To be unable to deny one's own existence, is in effect like being unable to deny God's existence as this makes itself known to us by the fact of our being *unable*, so to say, to suppress our own being. Following the method of doubt, I deny that I exist. But what I then examine is not my denial, but the facts, namely my existence. Whereupon I discover that my own existence doesn't seem to depend upon me, any more than many other independently existing things do. From this point of view, whatever reason I may have for judging that the existence of corporeal objects does not depend upon me, also compels me to judge that even my own existence doesn't. Now what is this 'me' that also seems independent of me? If it were not independent, then could I not cease to exist if I willed so? For even if I did not originate myself, but nevertheless now maintain my own existence, I ought now to be able to end it. We should ponder carefully over Descartes' description of himself as a thing that thinks. For it is this thinking that he finds so to say pumped into existence through, and in the identity of, himself.

But what, precisely, is this thinking, and how does it show itself? By its questioning, surely. It wants to know, and thinks in order to find out. And in one respect it is true (is it not?) that we do not have to begin by setting ourselves to think, but observe ourselves already at it. Our cognitive processes have a life of their own. There is no conflict between 'I think' and 'It thinks in me'. Insofar as I think, and insofar as it thinks in me, I and it are identical. But 'it' is not God himself, but that appearance of him which, minimal though it may be, is necessary for the possibility of my existence. From the moment that I begin to be able to detach myself from the pressures of my corporeal existence I become especially aware of my self as a thinking thing, preoccupied now with the question of truth, instead of survival. Measured against this, as we have seen, old beliefs become subject to doubt. For doubt is perhaps the means by which the thinking subject shakes off the effect of having to inhabit a body unthinkingly, and achieves that kind of unclouded knowledge proper to thinking substance.

Still, this account of man as a thinking substance shows the importance for Descartes of being able to explain error. A purely thinking being might never be mistaken; but his thinking about the world requires information, reliance upon the senses, and risk of error. Should we then not think about the world, but only about thought? This is to despair. Could the perfect Being have placed us in a corporeal world, given us what to us are instruments for discovering truths there, together with the certainty that we do discover them, while in fact we don't? Would not the refusal to accept ourselves as ever being able to have knowledge of the corporeal world, amount to a distrust of God? Of course it would. And that is why Descartes touches this very point: 'And it seems to me that I now have before me a road which will lead us from the contemplation of the true God . . . to the knowledge of the other objects of the universe' (i, 172). So Descartes seeks for a method by which he can import into the concerns of everyday life, at least something of that certainty which can never fail him so long as he does not depart from 'the contemplation of the true God.'

Thus Descartes is committed now not only to the view that our faculty of pure thinking is perfect in its nature, but that so are all our other faculties for gaining knowledge:

In the next place I experienced in myself a certain capacity for judging which I have doubtless received from God, like all the other things that I possess; and as He could not desire to deceive me, it is clear that He has not given me a faculty that will lead me to err if I use it aright. (i, 172)

Only, God does not also appear to have given me a faculty by which to ensure that I use this faculty (whichever it be) aright. For perhaps that would have initiated an infinite regress taxing even omnipotence. The point here has nothing to do with Descartes' conclusion, but with the propriety of his introducing it to solve a problem that need not have arisen if he had not minded using the concept of 'arightness' earlier. Only then it would all have been philosophically of little account. The position is this: if God has given us the means of knowing our way around this corporeal world, can he escape responsibility if those means are of such a delicacy, or intricacy, that for ordinary people, i.e. all of us, error is practically inevitable?

And no doubt respecting this matter could remain, if it were not that the consequence would seem to follow that I can thus never be deceived; ⟨i.e. provided only that I use my faculty aright⟩ for if I hold all that I possess from God, and if He has not placed in me the capacity for error, it seems as though I could never fall into error. (i, 172)

Using 'my faculty aright', there would be no problem about squaring God's goodness with our lack of infallibility since it might even be shown that the latter itself had the function of making us aware of the need for thinking well enough to do justice to God's work in us. The really important consideration would be that God has given us the power of actualising that possibility of knowledge which our faculty presents us with. And though I have been speaking (following the text from which I quoted) of 'faculty', since we are here concerned not only with the 'contemplation of God', but also with 'the knowledge of the other objects of the universe', it is 'faculties' rather than 'faculty' that I should be considering.

We must now examine the continuation of Descartes' thought after he has explained that he cannot err in contemplating the idea of God.

yet directly afterwards, when recurring to myself, experience shows me that I am nevertheless subject to an infinitude of errors, as to which, when we come to investigate them more closely, I notice that not only is there a real and positive idea of God or of a Being of supreme perfection present to my mind, but also, so to speak, a certain negative idea of nothing, that is, of that which is infinitely removed from any kind of perfection; and that I am in a sense something intermediate between God and nought, i.e. placed in such a manner between the supreme Being and non-being, that there is in truth nothing in me that can lead to error in so far as a sovereign Being has formed me; but that, as I in some degree participate likewise in nought or in non-being, i.e. in so far as I am not myself the supreme Being, and as I find myself subject to an infinitude of imperfections, I ought not to be astonished if I should fall into error. (i, 172–3)

The picture is not simply of the corporeal world as one in which we are subject to error. It is of a state of affairs we find within ourselves, and in consideration of which 'I ought not to be astonished if I should fall into error'. For within myself I find 'a certain idea of nothing, that is, of that which is infinitely removed from any kind of perfection'. And this is not contingent. Nothing I could do would remove this nothingness, and as long as it is there, I can never be as certain of being able to use my faculties as effectively when I am not contemplating God, as when I am. For I am 'a thing that doubts', a thing that desires, hopes, aspires, and above all proves its passionate yearning for that perfection, the possibility of which speaks as if from within itself, by its refusal to believe what it clearly and distinctly sees to be false. But I am also a being that, though able to conceive what sort of language is least removed from adequacy in describing a perfect Being, cannot pretend to a knowledge of what it is to be supremely perfect.

The non-contingency of this negative element within us is shown by Descartes when he points out that 'I in some degree participate in nought, or in non-being, i.e. in so far as I am not myself the supreme Being'. It is not a contingent matter that I am not God, I necessarily am not, for my being so would be incompatible with his being perfect. And since, as Descartes has argued, and will argue again, God's non-existence is inconceivable, so must be the non-contingency of my nature, or any nature similar to mine. Whatever is not God must be 'infinitely removed from any kind of perfection'. It would seem then, that since it is inconceivable that God should cease to be, or, cease to be exactly what he necessarily is, it is also inconceivable that he himself could end his own existence, or, therefore, that he could do anything that would be tantamount to ending his existence, such, for instance, as creating another being as perfect as he is. Human error, therefore, is metaphysically enclosed, so to say, and something we should gratefully accept as the price of our existence. To blame God for not having made us perfect is to blame him for not having made us Gods as well.

Descartes has argued that God cannot have made man faulty since it would have been the gravest possible fault in God to have permitted (not to say created) a state in which man lives in continued deception. Hence error in man cannot proceed from a faulty constitution, nor from the objects judged. Moreover, it cannot proceed from God either. It is a defect, but not a defect in a person. We cannot even say that it is an imperfection in a person, such as would arise by virtue of an imperfection in a faculty of that person. Error is not an imperfect thing, or a defective thing, because it is not a thing at all. If it were it would depend on God. Therefore there is no need for any special faculty to relate us to such a thing. So apart from God's being too perfect to have created us with a self-deception mechanism, in fact he could not have created us with one because there isn't a *thing* called error. I commit an error because of what I do wrongly that there was no reason to do. I commit an error because something in itself not a defective part of me, operates in a way that stems from something accidental and not essential to its own nature. Descartes' own summary of his position reads:

Thus do I recognise that error, in so far as it is such, is not a real thing depending on God, but simply a defect; and therefore, in order to fall into it, that I have no need to possess a special faculty given me by God for this very purpose, but that I fall into error from the fact that the power given by God for the purpose of distinguishing truth from error is not infinite. (i, 173)

But this is not a defect in God. Nor, since I cannot ever hope to escape it, being a created thing, is it a defect in me. Nor, since God is a perfect Being, can it be regarded as a defect in some faculty God has placed in me. Error is a privation, perhaps, but not a defect, since it is not a thing to be defective.

So Descartes takes the next step:

Nevertheless this does not quite satisfy me; for error is not a pure negation [i.e. is not the simple defect or want of some perfection which ought not to be mine], but it is a lack of some knowledge which it seems that I ought to possess. . . . And certainly there is no doubt that God could have created me so that I could never have been subject to error; it is also certain that He ever wills what is best; is it then better that I should be subject to err than that I should not? (i, 173)

His argument runs: God wills what is best for us. We err. Therefore it is best that we should be subject to error.

Perhaps in some sense of 'best' it is best. But Descartes has been frantically trying to show that the nature of God is such that He could not have willed us to err. Now confronted by the facts he seems to give in at once. Since we err, it must be best. He should, of course, have continued 'Therefore that we are liable to err follows from the will (nature) of God.' But he doesn't, and can't.

The reason for Descartes' sudden and unexpected capitulation at this point is to be found in the first half of the second section of the quotation. 'And certainly there is no doubt that God could have created me so that I could never have been subject to error.' But there is more than doubt here. He has barely finished demonstrating that the nature of God is such that he *could* not have done what he now says there is no doubt that he could. Yet Descartes still insists that we cannot err in so far as we contemplate God. What he perhaps meant was that God could have created a being not subject to error. And in a sense God has. He has created insects, for instance, that—we are told—depend solely upon instincts to determine their movements for them, under the given conditions. But I cannot make sense of the notion of such a creature having made a mistake, or even of being aware of some other thing to do at the time it does any one thing. Given perfect conditions for the application of its instinct such a creature need never make a move which is not the right one. There would be no error, but neither would there be truth; there would be no mistake, but neither would there be knowledge. Such a creature, however, could not be 'me', a thing that thinks. My thinking, under conditions of contingency, exposes me to the possibility of error. If God modifies me to make it true of me that I should never err, the result would not be me.

Descartes has told us he is not satisfied with the way he has so far treated the problem of error, since it is not a pure negation, nor a 'simple defect'. I have already discussed the metaphysical considerations underlying this new turn in Descartes, but now concern myself with the application of these considerations to Descartes' developing thought about error in relation to the conception of 'defect'. Why does Descartes say that error is not pure negation? If there is a faculty it is not your nature to possess, then what you lack through the non-possession of that faculty, cannot be regarded as a privation. You cannot be said to be deprived of what it was never your nature to possess, nor can we be regarded as ignorant in respect of what our very nature precludes us from knowing—unless we wish to hold that Everest is ignorant of Einstein. Now for Descartes, 'pure negation' would be a description of that ignorance. The contrary, knowledge, does not, and could not, here exist. It is pure negation. And in respect of such knowledge it would be as meaningless to say that Everest could be in error, as to say that it is ignorant,

The very conception of error, we have seen, does imply, if not deception, an absence of God's unwillingness that a finite thinking substance should fall into error. And is not this out of character with the nature of a Divine Being? And here, having already said that God knows what is best for us, and that therefore we have no right to complain about his permitting us to err, Descartes realises that if a principle results in such a conclusion it may well itself come under suspicion. How can God know best if he permits what he does? Well, having only a short while ago said that we should not be astonished if we make mistakes, he now tells us not to be astonished if we cannot understand why God acts as he does, not in this regard only, but perhaps in an infinite number of matters.

One wonders here at what point Descartes would begin to suspect that there could be something wrong with his concept of a supreme Being. How much astonishment are we expected to repress? For that matter he could have said at the very start that even if God deceives us we have no business to be astonished for he may well have ends far beyond finite comprehension. But Descartes did not do that. He was certain simply that God would not, and indeed could not, deceive. The evidence seemed, at first, as if it could be made to lie the other way. But Descartes had no intention of resigning himself to the possibility that in some fashion beyond the power of finite comprehension, deception and perfection are not as incompatible as they appear.

The reason for Descartes' lapse here is not far away. For what he wants to follow from his claim that we have no right to question God's actions, is that no occurrence whatsoever can count as evidence against God's existence. We can never know God to be wrong: 'and this reason suffices to convince me that the species of cause termed final, finds no useful employment in physical [or natural] things; for it does not appear to me that I can without temerity seek to investigate the [inscrutable] ends of God' (i, 173). What he should be arguing against is the view that God is behaving unjustly to human beings. And this is not a questioning of God's ends in so far as they concern 'physical or natural things'. Moreover it is actually as one arguing *against* those who would doubt the existence of God that he expels teleological concepts from nature! We must not attempt to understand God's work in terms of our own values. Descartes does not advise us to question our capacity for understanding God's intentions, etc. when he does things that we admire, but only when he does things we don't. I do not see what answer he could have given to a possible suggestion that since we cannot understand why God does what he does, then for all we know, the things he does that seem to us good are really bad, and that even if we knew them to be so, we still should not criticise God; for we should not be astonished if God does things that seem bad, for we cannot hope to understand what he means by what he does—even if we could understand what he does.

It is difficult, in any case, to follow Descartes' argument that because there are an infinity of things that God does, or that are in God's power to do, which are not humanly comprehensible, there is nothing at all of his work that we can comprehend. If we take Descartes at his word and conclude that we cannot understand at all what God does, or means by what he does, then must not our conception of God be very different from what it would otherwise be? Can we suppose that God's ends don't concern us? And if we are not able to suppose this then how can we suppose ourselves unable to understand them? Even so Descartes hedges his position by arguing what in effect amounts to this: even if we do find an imperfection somewhere, we have no right to conclude from it that God is imperfect, since we can only say of something that it is so if we know it in relation to the entire universe; and this knowledge is of course ruled out for anyone but God. But Descartes shows an impressive faith not only in the knowability of things, but also in their rightness. And what Descartes takes himself to have done here is to have blocked any argument against the existence of a perfect Being grounded upon the existence of evil. In fact he has so arranged his position that no empirical evidence of human cognitive, or moral, limitations, or human ignorance, or human suffering, can count towards an argument against the existence of God.

How then is error possible if God is both good and omnipotent? His goodness is a guarantee that he would not deceive us, his omnipotence that he knows how to make us so that we need not deceive ourselves. We know he has not made us so that we cannot deceive ourselves, for we are often deceived. We know too that God could not deceive us, and that error is not something in the world. The question is: if we are made with perfect faculties by a good and omnipotent God, then how is error (any error) possible? What Descartes is going to argue is that the two faculties which are severally necessary conditions for error are themselves perfect; that one of them is such that it cannot ever be mistaken, and the other even as perfect in us as in God: and that this very perfection in us (our finitude being a necessary condition for our existing at all) is what makes error possible. 'For by the understanding alone I [neither assert nor deny anything, but] apprehend the ideas of things as to which I can form a judgment' (i, 174). Error cannot spring from the understanding, for it does not follow from my understanding something that I assert it, or deny it. As long as I do neither of these I cannot be in error. Understanding, in other words, is like entertaining a proposition. Nor can it be regarded as a fault in the understanding that I cannot understand everything, or even that I cannot understand more than I do. Ignorance is absence of understanding, not a fault in it. And omniscience belongs only to an infinite being, not a finite one.

It is, however, with Descartes' conception of will that we shall be chiefly concerned, since for him it is the will that plays the key role in the production of error; yet it is the same will that is the most Godlike power we have. 'I likewise cannot complain that God has not given me a free choice or a will which is sufficient, ample and perfect, since as a matter of fact I am conscious of a will so extended as to be subject to no limits' (i, 174). The understanding is certainly not so extended as to be subject to no limits. That does not make it imperfect in a finite being. The will therefore, Descartes seems to imply, could have been equally limited yet not imperfect. It has therefore more to it than is necessary simply for its not being imperfect. 'It is free-will alone or liberty of choice which I find to be so great in me that I can conceive no other idea to be more great; it is indeed the case that it is for the most part this will that causes me to know that in some manner I bear the image and similitude of God' (i, 175). Something of what Descartes means is clear. Will, or free-choice (or judgment), is an *original* activity, i.e. it is self-determining— a power to do one thing rather than another, to judge one thing rather than another to be true. And this means a freedom from determination by factors external to oneself *qua* thinking substance. In this we are like God, the absolutely active, original, and self-determining Being.

For although the power of will is incomparably greater in God than in me, both by reason of the knowledge and the power which, conjoined with it, render it stronger and more efficacious, and by reason of its object, inasmuch as in God it extends to a great many things; it nevertheless does not seem to me greater if I consider it formally and precisely in itself: for the faculty of will consists alone in our having the power of choosing to do a thing or choosing not to do it (that is, to affirm or deny, to pursue or to shun it), or rather it consists alone in the fact that in order to affirm or deny, pursue or shun those things placed before us by the understanding, we act so that we are unconscious that any outside force constrains us in doing so. (i, 175)

Now there appear to be two theses here, which I shall refer to as being connected with a strong and a weak sense of free will, and accordingly I shall describe them as the strong thesis and the weak thesis, respectively. The strong thesis maintains that having a free will is a matter of what we do, whether asserting or denying, or pursuing or shunning, something known to us by the understanding. Free will is a matter of choice or decision. In choosing or deciding, we exercise our freedom of will. Be it noted that it is in the choosing, or deciding to act, and not in the action itself that we show ourselves to be free, according to Descartes. In this sense freedom lies in the mind and not in the world of body, for we are presumably as free when we act unskilfully, or unsuccessfully, as we are at other times. Certainly there must be a logical connection between choice and decision on the one side and action on the other. For, as remarked above, we cannot claim to decide unless we think we might accomplish what we decide; and if we did not mostly know what we can and cannot do it would be pointless either to choose or decide. Nevertheless, we learn only by experience the sorts of things we can do; and this of course means that not only our practical freedom, but even our freedom to choose, or decide, rests upon a basis of contingency. The only escape from this would be to regard the will as free insofar as it is able to prefer one thing to another, whether it could bring it about or not. But this would amount to no more than freedom to value, or to appreciate, and not freedom to act. All the same to recognise something as valuable is not altogether unlike recognising a proposition as true. To affirm or to deny that something is the case may be just as possible when one cannot act on it as when

113

one can. And one can value truth just as much when one lacks the evidence to be able to claim it, as when one doesn't. Being unable to affirm or deny, through lack of gounds for doing so, is not unlike being unable to do what you would prefer to do because power is lacking. However, to repeat, in the strong sense, for Descartes, to have a free will is to be able to assert or deny in accordance with the understanding, or to be able to decide or to choose in accordance with our understanding of the possibility of success. Admittedly this fills him in a bit, but I don't think he would be entitled to complain.

The second, or weaker thesis is not quite certainly distinct from the stronger. By 'faculty of will' we mean 'that in order to affirm or deny, pursue or shun those things placed before us by the understanding, we act so that we are unconscious that any outside force constrains us in doing so'. Does he mean simply that, when we act, provided we are not aware of being compelled from without to perform the act, we are exercising a free will? Suppose this is what he means. It would follow that as long as our behaviour is not unintentional, as long as we are not aware of being compelled, we must be free. This sort of approach is certainly something of an answer to those who maintain that only when we are deciding, or choosing between alternatives, or following some set purpose, or something of that sort, are we really free. For most of our behaviour, on such a view, would certainly not be the expression of a free will. And yet we do in fact suppose it to be. We do not take ourselves to be under constraint, unless we actually feel ourselves to be. And when acting without awareness of constraint, we perhaps feel no less free doing what we simply happen not to mind doing, than doing what we are fiercely determined to. This kind of case requires no deciding or choosing. Yet we do not think that therefore we are not then free. Since the criteria for regarding ourselves as free are fewer than in the previous case, I have described it as the weaker thesis. But it is not crystal clear that this is in fact what Descartes intended by the preceding quotation. And indeed it might even be interpreted as the stronger thesis, not the weaker, as I shall now try to demonstrate.

The quotation in question appears also to state that for a will to be free not only must we affirm or deny, pursue or shun, but we must, as a condition for this to be possible, also be uncon-

scious of being constrained by outside forces. This almost suggests
that in acting we must at the same time be aware of being under
no external compulsion, and this is a criterion additional to those
required on the strong interpretation. But what is it to act in
such a way as to be unaware of external compulsion? Must there
simply be no external compulsion to attract our notice? Or must
we in addition be aware that there isn't? Obviously the formulation
quoted (which follows the French version pretty closely) is far
from precise. Thus the interpretation by which the weaker thesis
turns out in fact to be the stronger lacks the clear authority of
Descartes himself as this is manifest in the French version.
Hence we shall turn in a moment to the Latin version, but first
we shall consider the issues under discussion so as to formulate
them as exactly as possible.

I shall begin by arguing that the weaker interpretation cannot
be the correct one. The view that as long as I do not feel constrained, then, since I take it that I can do other than I do if I want
to, whether I want to or not, I am acting under freedom of the
will, may be one that conforms to our ordinary experience, but
for Descartes is neither here nor there. Ordinary experience is
precisely what he tilts against. For him the question is not what
is psychologically acceptable, but rather what is logically unassailable. And even that he has assailed. Now he is concerned
with the will, and (though he is in too much of a hurry to pay as
much attention to detail as we nowadays expect) especially with
the will regarded as free. But in the first place this will is something, let us remember he says, that stamps us with the likeness of
God. It is no ordinary thing, but rather the most extra-ordinary
thing about us. In the second place it is exercised when we decide,
or when we judge. Unless we do these things, the things in which
we act in a certain way as God himself does, we are not exercising
our will. In ordinary life we do all kinds of things in which we
manifest neither judgment nor agency. Much of this takes place
on a level hardly distinguishable from the animal. And there you
are. For right or wrong, Descartes most assuredly did not hold
that animals were made in the image and similitude of God.
Whatever will may turn out to be it is something special. To assert
that something is true, or to decide to do something (which
involves a power to contemplate, and to prefer something absent)

is no small thing. And so it is certain that, for Descartes, whatever is an exercise of will must be something special. Thus the first (and strong) interpretation of what Descartes means by will is at least part of what he must mean by it.

Consider again the phrase 'act so that we are unconscious that any outside force constrains us in doing so'. Descartes does not here say that we should be *aware* of not being conscious of such a force. Therefore the weaker interpretation of his theory as to what constitutes an exercise of free will is ruled out. How, then, can it be the case that we act so that we are unconscious of external compulsion? Suppose that I decide to get up and open my window now. Suppose also that I now feel my body making exactly the moves required to do this, but not that *I* am responsible for this. For instance I might try to sit down again, and find that I cannot do the opposite of what I am doing, even having decided to. I therefore discontinue, as I must, that decision and submit to what is happening. Clearly, then, I am not doing what I am *because* I originally decided to. Nor therefore can that original decision have any part in what I am now doing. Therefore my present action is not an expression of my free will. Suppose, however, that I do not discontinue my decision but decide that since this is what I want to do anyway I will just play along with what is happening. Now this is a case where I have decided to do a certain thing, and where I am not unaware of myself as being externally compelled to do the thing I should have done 'from myself' were I not under constraint to a like effect by something external to me. And in what sense could we here be regarded as exercising a free will? We may (or may not, according to taste) regard ourselves as lucky; but surely not as free. And this seems to me exactly what Descartes has in mind.

What is important for him is this. We should be doing what we have decided to do, or chosen to do, because—and only because—we have decided, or chosen, to do it. In other words, the proper explanation for what we are doing is either our reason for doing it, or the fact that we were not averse to deciding or choosing to do it even without being able to give a reason for it. In any such case we have, on Descartes' theory, acted freely. There does not also have to be a will pushing us to do what we have decided. Our decision is enough. If I *have* decided to do something now I do it now. If I don't, though I can, then either I have not in fact decided or I have decided to change my mind. The deciding or choosing, in this case *is* the willing. And this explains Descartes' indirect mode of statement. To be exercising freedom, we don't have to feel ourselves also willing what we have decided to do; it is enough if we don't feel something else compelling us to do it. Inner compulsions, acts of will, are as otiose for Descartes as they are for those who attack him for believing in them. The difference is that he knows what he thinks, and they don't.

One can put the matter another way by saying that for Descartes a man is free when he means to do what he does (very different from saying that he wills to do it), and when he means to assert or deny what he does. The position is even clearer in the latter case. For we can imagine a man who is told to believe a certain thing. He tries to and finds he can't. Can it be said that because he says the words to himself he is also asserting them to be true? No, for he may say them to himself out of fear, or out of habit, or out of a mistaken sense of obligation to say them. And if he tries to say them as if he believed them (initially, at any rate), this will not make him. His will is not freely expressed in his utterance of the sentence whether to himself or to another. If he *finds him-self* simply tending to say the words, whether he chooses to or not, his assertion is no more an act of free will than if he *finds himself* doing something whether he has decided to or not. Once he sees the words to be true, he does not need an extra act of will in order to affirm that they are. Such an extra act of will is not 'will' in Descartes' sense of this word, but merely the sort of compulsive act that we share with the beasts. Let us now consider the Latin version of the passage we have found it necessary to examine in this detail. Speaking of the faculty of will, he says that it consists:

in eo tantum, quòd ad id quod nobis ab intellectu proponitur affirmandum vel negandum, sive prosequendum vel fugiendum, ita feramur, ut a nullâ vi externâ nos ad id determinari sentiamus.[1]

A literal translation of this runs as follows: 'or rather it consists only in this, that we are moved to affirm, or deny, pursue or shun,

[1] *Meditationes de Prima Philosophia*, Librairie Philosophique (Paris, 1966), p. 57.

what the intellect presents to us, in such a way as not to feel ourselves determined to it by any external force.' And what way is that? Simply that we do it because what we do *is* what we have decided, and what we assert to be true *is* what we have seen by our intellect to be so. Whatever else the will may be for Descartes, it is not some kind of introspectible psychological force.

Yet free will does consist in doing something, whether theoretical or practical, and since what we do freely is what we'd rather do, so that we incline one way rather than another, it would seem that to be free is also to be inclined. But if we are *inclined* to do a certain thing how can it also be maintained that we are free in doing it? What, however, would be the alternative to this for a free will? It could only be that one is not inclined to do one thing more than another, to assert one thing as true rather than another, and so on. But if we are not inclined to do one thing rather than another, if we are equally indifferent to whatever possibilities present themselves to us, in what sense could we then be described properly as free? What reason could we have for doing anything, or believing anything? Indifference would appear to be incompatible with freedom. And yet Descartes seems, at first, to be unwilling to commit himself further than to say that indifference is not a necessary condition for the possibility of being free. Yet he soon sees that this is not enough. From saying that being free is not conditional upon indifference he goes on to say that freedom is in proportion to the degree to which one is inclined one way rather than another. Now whether one speaks of how much one leans one way rather than another, or is inclined one way rather than another, the degree in question is not a degree of intensity of willing, but a degree of commitment resulting from one's apprehension of the value of what one decides to do, or the grounds of what one asserts to be true. One cannot apprehend the true without judging it to be so, or the right without being inclined to the doing of it. Nor does Descartes suppose that there can be no such affirmation or inclination unless there are grounds for it. Some people seem to think Descartes is either stupid or dishonest when he claims that it is possible that a man whom God inclines to believe, or to act, may still be free in so believing, or so acting.

We cannot have reasons for all that we assert to be true, any more than for all that we decide to do. This amounts to a point

Aristotle made long ago. The trouble here is really to do with whether God inclines us in matters where there isn't really anything else that could be the ground of such an inclination; or whether there is, and God's inclining of us ignores or rejects it. In the latter case I do not think Descartes himself would be very happy. As for the former, where we find ourselves believing something, or deciding that something would be right to do, if we already believe in God why might we not maintain that not only are we indeed free, but that we have been vouchsafed by divine grace a freedom of will akin to the divine? At least this is not the obvious conceptual misdemeanour it might appear. The poet does not disclaim authorship for claiming also that the muse sang for him. Why, then, should we not regard the inspiration of the prophet, for instance, as the form his freedom takes?

From this point of view it is clear that indifference cannot be consistent with freedom because it is consistent with, and indeed is entailed by ignorance, which in turn is no condition at all for freedom. Whatever the proposition might be, refusal to assert its truth, or to assert its falsity, must be based upon ignorance of the knowledge that would sweep that refusal aside. Similarly whatever a contemplated action, or decision might be, refusal to act, or to decide, must be based upon ignorance of what the situation is and requires. One could not have this knowledge and remain indifferent. That it seems clear to me is Descartes' position. Thus it follows that the greater one's knowledge the more one is inclined (or disposed) to what amounts to an exercise of one's freedom. As for divine influence, it must not be forgotten that for Descartes God is still (i.e. even in the Fourth Meditation) seen as that which gives its very existence, not to speak of its capacity for freedom, to the self. And granted such a Being how could we logically deny to him the power to speak with greater directness to some than to others, and of more things to some than to others? To say that we are not free since God inclines us is like saying that since in a sense all knowledge is God's all of us are ignorant. Thus Descartes writes:

For in order that I should be free it is not necessary that I should be indifferent as to the choice of one or the other of two contraries; but contrariwise the more I lean to the one—whether I recognise clearly that the reasons of the good and true are to be found in it, or whether God so disposes my inward thought—the more freely do I choose and embrace it. And undoubtedly both divine grace and natural knowledge, far from diminishing my liberty, rather increase it and strengthen it. (i, 175)

One is free because one can act upon a proposition. One might by oneself reach that proposition, or be given it, let us say by an act of grace, but whichever way we come by it, to be able to accept it sufficiently to decide to act upon it because one is also able to see its truth is not only not incompatible with being free, but actually being it. Descartes does, of course, speak of God disposing our inward thought, and not simply determining it. It is not enough simply for God to dispose my inward thought, I must also lean towards the acceptance of that to which he inclines it. This seems clearly to hold both for thought and for action. By God's grace I may see the good, but by my own, in the end, I incline to the bringing about of it. It is willed by me because I lean towards it. God may dispose 'l'intérieur de ma pensée' without it being the case that he thereby makes *me* lean towards that to which he disposes it. If by disposing my inward thought he were also to make me decide to do something, or accept something as true, then certainly whatever I did in that case would be by his will and not my own; in which case I should not be free. But in that case it would not be I who decides or asserts for myself, but God. Therefore I could not in fact have asserted or decided at all. This is clear from Descartes' whole discussion of will. There is no room for compromise here. The whole point about the will is its autonomy. However I come by it it is my will if it is will at all. If my exercise of it is prevented, it has been withdrawn from me—a possibility which has not been ruled out by the fact that God endowed me with it. For whatever would not be self-contradictory for God to revoke, he presumably can revoke. But until he does I am in absolute possession of it. Therefore he can only dispose my inward thought in a given direction on condition that this does not necessitate my will. Thus there is a gap, and, it follows, a logical gap between my willing and his disposing of my thought. I can only close the gap by refusing to be free any longer. But that is another matter. Descartes does not say that the free will is uninfluenced by intellectual or other sorts of considerations: on the contrary, as we shall see. Ordinarily we have the power to dispose our own inward thought, though even here we do not always follow the result. We can 'refuse' by (or rather as) an act of will even our own inward dispositions, so why not God's? Provided we retain our will exactly the same considerations apply in either case.

Indeed, then, it is not on account of not being influenced that the will is free. We surely seek to be influenced by what is true and what is good. Does it follow from this that we are not free in so seeking, either? Since such values as truth and goodness are what we seek how could we regard them as external constraints when we meet with them? Not only are they, therefore, not constraints, but they are our very means to freedom. From the viewpoint of those who seek God, therefore, he is understandably the most reliable of those means. With him, a believer can consider himself as always free. And this is exactly parallel to the way in which the truth seeker seeks truth as the means to freedom. No wonder that Descartes scorns indifference as providing a picture of what it really is to be free. With God, or with knowledge, we cannot be, or remain, indifferent.

Descartes began by saying that to be free it is not necessary to be indifferent, and now he categorises indifference as 'the lowest grade of liberty'. On another level Descartes is saying something else. Indifference is not free will, but lack of knowledge. For with the appropriate knowledge, whatever the occasion, we couldn't be indifferent; we cannot know what to do, and remain indifferent to doing it. It is no more possible to know what to do without being moved to do it, than it is possible to see two and two as being equal to four, without judging that equivalence to be a true one:

Hence this indifference which I feel, when I am not swayed to one side rather than to the other by lack of reason, is the lowest grade of liberty, and rather evinces a lack or negation in knowledge than a perfection of will: for if I always recognised clearly what was true and good, I should never have trouble in deliberating as to what judgment or choice I should make, and then I should be entirely free without ever being indifferent. (i, 175)

This is surely a point that Socrates would have appreciated. In some things indifference would be the rational attitude, in others not. In the latter cases the rational attitude is not one of indifference, because some one thing or action would be better than the other; and we require the help of reason to know which. If, in these cases, we remain indifferent, it can only be through 'lack of reason', and not to know what ought to be done is not to be free at all.

Now in trying to free the concept of free will from the concept of indifference while at the same time preserving it from being assimilated to that of a causal system, Descartes falls with a kind of a dialectic inevitability into another trap. Inevitable, I think, partly because his link between knowledge and action, theory and practice *is* so close. He has said that it is not possible to know what one ought to do (in effect) and not be moved, in so far as one is a free being, to do it. Now this may be true. Perhaps God cannot do wrong, yet is free in exactly this sense.

It is difficult to understand how, for instance, an omniscient being would need to deliberate. For to deliberate is to try and discover by thinking what you would not know otherwise. There is no question of recognising without any 'trouble' whatever it is one ought to do. Descartes has proved too much, for in order to prove we are only minimally free when we are indifferent, he has proved that we are free in some stronger sense only when we cannot be indifferent because we are determined by knowledge to act in accordance with that knowledge, i.e. because we are determined.

On the other hand what Descartes has in mind may be that people act mainly not from knowledge, but opinion. Now Descartes has told us that to have an opinion that just happens to be right is not to have knowledge, but only the truth by accident. Similarly, to act rightly by accident is not to act from knowledge, nor therefore to be free; one's action may resemble an action which in those circumstances, i.e. if one had in fact acted from knowledge, would have been free, but is not itself so. To free the will, then, the first thing to do is to replace opinion by knowledge. But this itself requires an act of will to prevent opinion from speaking.

This is where doubt finds its first employment, namely, in banishing uncritical judgment. This is the first real link between will and judgment. But the next step requires not will, so much as knowledge. And this is where the Cartesian method of breaking down complex opinions into simple ones shows its advantage.

For if the simple elements of a complex opinion can be made simple enough we cannot help seeing whether they are true or not.

We cannot, however, be allowed to define freedom so that only an omniscient being could be free, that is, a being who could not but know the limits of practical possibility. We should consider Descartes' words about deliberation and recognition in relation to his method of analysis. We don't really need to deliberate; the method makes it unnecessary. Descartes has told us in the *Discourse*, that it isn't intelligence we lack but a method to free us from false or only accidentally true opinion. This will ensure knowledge, and thereby the possibility of freedom in our practice. All we need in order to be able to be free, i.e. to judge and to act in accordance with knowledge, is knowledge itself, and all we need, given acceptance of the Method, is a power to discipline ourselves. This looks as if we are asked to act as only a free person can act, in order to become a free person. And I think the answer is that this objection would be fatal were we not free to begin with. We cannot regard ourselves as not free, for we are thinking substances, and we do have at least the formal capacity for truth. Moreover, not everyone is equally custom bound. Descartes wasn't. To know about truth is already to be free, and therefore free to seek it.

Descartes sums up:

From all this I recognise that the power of will which I have received from God is not of itself the source of my errors—for it is very ample and very perfect of its kind—any more than is the power of understanding; for since I understand nothing but by the power which God has given me for understanding, there is no doubt that all that I understand, I understand as I ought, and it is not possible that I err in this. (i, 175)

Whatever be the reason for error, then, it cannot be imputed to God. From the empirical point of view, as from the metaphysical, God has been found to be no deceiver. Therefore knowledge ought to be possible not only of God as he manifests himself in us, but also of the world—even of its corporeal objects. Until, however, we know how it comes about that we do err, this possibility cannot be actualised.

Descartes' answer to this problem must be given in his own words:

Whence then come my errors? They come from the sole fact that since the will is much wider in its range and compass than the understanding, I do not restrain it within the same bounds, but extend it also to things which I do not understand: and as the will is of itself indifferent to these, it easily falls into error and sin, and chooses the evil for the good, or the false for the true. (i, 175-6)

To begin with he repeats that the will is (formally) as infinite as that of God, for that in fact is what he means, as we have seen. Secondly, since the understanding is not so wide in scope, we find ourselves tending to extend the scope of our will beyond the scope of our understanding. Thus we judge to be true what we do not understand to be so, for judgment is *assertion*, whether of truth or falsity. Thirdly, my power to extend judgment beyond my understanding arises from the fact that judgment itself is indifferent in relation to what is not clearly understood. In relation to what is clearly understood the will is not indifferent. This is the rational will. But removed from clarity of understanding the will so to say loses its head. Error, therefore, results when the will acts independently of understanding.

One cause of confusion here is Descartes' failure to observe that he is working not with one, but with two concepts of will. For in speaking of his own relation to his will he speaks of it as he also speaks of the relationship between his will and his knowledge, e.g. when he speaks of himself as restraining his will. Consequently he can speak of the will sometimes as being indifferent, sometimes as needing to be restrained (presumably by a further will) where no clear understanding is present to it. Certainly it is not always clear whether the subject of his assertion is himself, or his will; whether it is Descartes who sins and is in error, or his erring will. What one wants to know is whether the autonomy of the will constitutes or is other than the autonomy of Descartes. If the former he is working with one will (though not consistently), if the latter then with two; in which case we are faced all over again with an old problem which would appear in this connection as the problem of how to set up something that could serve as liaison between Descartes and his will, without itself being another will. In which case, what can Descartes have explained? For how is his will restrained or extended? But Descartes hasn't finished yet.

The one thing he wants to avoid saying is that when the will is not indifferent to an object it is determined by it. If we hold ourselves so that we understand clearly that something is true, or good, even so, as we have just seen, Descartes doesn't say that we must therefore be determined to belief or action by it. It is one thing to recognise something as good and true, but another to affirm or act upon it; and one thing, even, for God to dispose our inward thought in a certain way and another for us to make that direction our own. This we have seen to be Descartes' doctrine. But if asked to state the difference we are held up. Descartes is clear that to be compelled by an external cause is not the same as having a 'great inclination of the will'. And his method of proof is to present us with an example which is also important for its own sake. But in considering his example, in which he draws our attention to a certain contrast, we have, each one of us, the personal responsibility for deciding whether there is or is not such a difference, for us, as Descartes claims, and whether this difference is not something not merely due to the occasion, but something we find grounded in the very nature of the experiences under examination. Because he needs to find as perfect a case as he can, so that this distinction really shows, he takes a real case—the distinction will then be no less real. Thus he writes:

For example, when I lately examined whether anything existed in the world, and found that from the very fact that I considered this question it followed very clearly that I myself existed, I could not prevent myself from believing that a thing I so clearly conceived was true: not that I found myself compelled to do so by some external cause, but simply because from great clearness in my mind there followed a great inclination of my will; and I believed this with so much the greater freedom or spontaneity as I possessed the less indifference towards it. (i, 176)

To believe something, is to judge it true. But judging it is a kind of willing. Now to prevent, or restrain, oneself is a kind of judgment concerning what one restrains oneself from doing—and judgment, as remarked, is a kind of willing. Therefore, Descartes is saying that there was something he was unable to will himself not to will. Presumably, then, it is conceivable to him that he might have been able to will not to will, if not in the particular case he mentions, then in some other. The point I wish to distinguish is that he does in fact operate with at least a higher and a lower order of willing. For suppose that we are dealing with one will, and not two; then if we regard 'preventing oneself from believing' or 'refusing' as acts of will that are contrary to 'accepting', or 'believing', it follows that if we do believe what we clearly conceive to be true, we cannot at the same time prevent ourselves from believing it. The will cannot both do something, and prevent itself from doing that same thing.

In what sense of the word 'follows' does a great inclination of the will follow from a clearness of the mind? In neither the Latin nor the French version do we find anything entitling us to be more specific here. This is not, for Descartes, it is clear, a logical point, any more than the *cogito* itself is. And notice that Descartes insists upon speaking of a great inclining of his will, rather than of a determining of it. He speaks here in dynamic terms of finding his will inclining. And this still seems to me to leave open the possibility that it will not do more than incline. Perhaps it is not always easy to continue seeing clearly something which when seen clearly does so incline the will. Perhaps continuing to see something clearly itself depends upon an effort of will, even if only in keeping other things out of one's understanding. In finding ourselves inclining to believe (which is perhaps a clearer way of putting it than speaking about the *will*'s being inclined to believe, or inclining to) what we do recognise is that this is something *sui generis* and altogether different from the experience of being asked to believe, or told to believe, or commanded to. At least we can say that in this case something becomes related to the self as a work of the self. Believing is something I do. Thus, when you ask me why I believe, I give as my most obvious reason that it is because it is true, and not that it is because something, or somebody makes me.

Might it not be said, however, that to see something clearly and distinctly ('with a great clearness of the mind') is already to believe, and that therefore, the reason belief follows on clarity in a way that cannot be prevented is because it is in fact part of the actual understanding itself? From this of course it would follow that will and understanding are not such independent functions as might have been supposed. I consider it absolutely necessary for a proper understanding of Descartes' position to get clear on this point. Can we drive a wedge between understanding and believing such that however clear understanding may be it does not yet amount to believing, for believing involves also willing, which understanding does not?

The first thing to note is that most of the usual examples of things seen clearly are things we have already seen and asserted to be true, explicitly or otherwise, These are just the things we find it impossible really to doubt, that is, really to withold our assent from. On the other hand is this so obviously impossible? Nobody having read Descartes carefully can be so sure. Descartes has put everything at risk at some time or other. Now I want to show that there are in fact many cases in which we do come to accept as true what we recognise that we must in some sense have held true all the time. There are many expressions that point to this, though some of these expressions have more meanings than one. Many presuppositions in our everyday life are cases in point. We call them presuppositions precisely because we have not asserted them to be true, though if we had not in fact seen them clearly and even distinctly we could not have done or said other things. Many of our social, economic, political, and (especially) moral principles are never brought explicitly before us for decision as to their truth or falsity. Yet the moment we do stand them up for attention we recognise them for what they are. Kant, for instance, did not think he was recommending a new moral law. People had always recognised that certain things are right and others wrong. And this could only make sense if in some way they did have some understanding of the moral structure of things. Yet the truth of this moral structure could not be asserted until they did take a special kind of look at what they must in some sense have been looking at all their lives.

Descartes himself asks us again and again, in the *Rules*, as well as in the *Meditations* and the *Discourse*, to attend thoughtfully to the many ordinary truths there are. Then we shall see them to be true, for then we shall know that they cannot be doubted. But he doesn't suppose for a moment that the understanding had not previously recognised them clearly for what they were. The whole point, now we can see, about doubting, is that by doubting we activate the will in the most potent way possible. By seeking to join a non-truth-believing attitude to an idea that is clearly and distinctly conceived by the understanding to be true, we stimulate the will into a belief attitude that nullifies our previous effort to disbelieve. And it would be wrong to suppose that whatever we have not hitherto doubted we must have affirmed. Descartes seems here to have made a mistake of expression which gets in his own way later. Consider the beginning of his very first sentence in his *Meditations*. 'It is now some years since I detected how many were the false beliefs that I had from my earliest youth admitted as true . . .'. In what sense had he in fact 'admitted' them? Certainly not in the sense of affirmed, for otherwise the early Descartes cannot be taken by the later Descartes as the paradigm case of the unreflective intellect. To pick up information, as one does one's mother tongue, is hardly what Descartes would think of as an act of will. The pre-reflective mind at an early stage, at any rate, need have no truck with considerations relating to the truth or falsity of what is present to it. It need not at all follow that what one does not disbelieve, or what one now begins to doubt, one must previously have asserted (and therefore held) to be true. The whole point, for Descartes, of the autonomy and importance of the will is that an act of will is not like picking up information when one has no reason (nor looks for any) to reject it as false; nor is it like acting out of habit, or blind impulse, or mindless imitativeness; it is an act in which one identifies one's own self in a certain way with a meaningful set of words, or a change in the world.

This need not mean that understanding does not operate until will does. We cannot will what we do not already understand, or understand needs to be done by us. And there is a great deal of difference between the case where one tries to understand (as Descartes himself does) in order to be able to assert what is right to believe or right to do, and the case where one has understanding in the sense that without it one would hardly be conscious at all. We know what it is simply to gaze around, or stare in bovine fashion. We know too what it is to allow stray thoughts to wander round in our minds without its even occurring to us to ask ourselves whether they are true or false, or consistent. We also, to go a step further, know what it is to 'hold' certain things to be true, and others as false. But not so much because we know why they are, as because we so to say picked up their conventional truth values as if they were part of the very beliefs themselves. And that is not the same thing as seeing them clearly and distinctly in the sense in which there would then result a great *inclination in our will* to believe. For this sense would be more applicable where we are concerned with an enquiry—as indeed Descartes himself was. This is clear from an examination of the foregoing quotation. In an enquiry it is part of the rules to affirm as true only what the will greatly inclines one to, which it does only when one clearly and distinctly conceives something as true. Perhaps the chief point is that in a certain frame of mind such considerations as these could not even arise; and in another they not only do, but are decisive, since in that frame of mind (the investigator's) we intend them to be. Thus, if in fact we allow ourselves to do what the will greatly inclines us to, this is not because we are determined by some external cause, but because we are in that rational, human, frame of mind in which we are willing to be, or intend to be, moved only by truth. And here the investigation itself would not be possible unless we were sufficiently learned and disciplined to match our wills with our understanding. That is why he cannot be indifferent to a proposition seen clearly and distinctly to be true. How can this lack of indifference be regarded as a sign that he is not free? On the contrary, how otherwise could he be?

Now let us examine the case where he can be indifferent:

Now, on the contrary, I not only know that I exist, inasmuch as I am a thinking thing, but a certain representation of corporeal nature is also presented to my mind; and it comes to pass that I doubt whether this thinking nature which is in me, or rather by which I am what I am, differs from this corporeal nature, or whether both are not simply the same thing; and I here suppose that I do not yet know any reason to persuade me to adopt the one belief rather than the other. From this it follows that I am entirely indifferent as to which of the two I affirm or deny, or even whether I abstain from forming any judgment in the matter. (i, 176)

Descartes, here, is mainly concerned to show that where he has no reason to believe, or, where he lacks understanding, he is indifferent as to whether he affirms, denies, or abstains from 'forming any judgment' at all. His will, here, might even be described as being in abeyance. And indeed he talks in this place not of his will but of himself. 'I am entirely indifferent', 'I affirm or deny', 'I abstain from forming' and so on.

But what about the restraint? Does he have to restrain the will, or to restrain himself from restraining the will, or perhaps even encourage himself to restrain the will? What does he mean here? For on this account there ought to be none of the difficulty he speaks about in disciplining himself in his search for truth. And yet there is such a difficulty. Indeed that difficulty is partly what Meditation One is about, and it is not fully explained by Descartes till he gets to Meditation Six. 'Whence then come my errors? They come from the sole fact that since the will is much wider in its range and compass than the understanding, I do not restrain it within the same bounds, but extend it also to things which I do not understand; and as the will is of itself indifferent to these, it easily falls into error and sin.' The picture of 'the will' here is of an 'indifferent' will. Then it is Descartes who is responsible, not the will. But how can *Descartes* restrain, or extend, or perform any of these controlling operations, un*will*ingly? The will *is* Descartes, and another will is *in* Descartes. Which of these wills is such that Descartes cannot conceive God's will itself, as being (formally) greater? Sometimes it is the will that is indifferent, sometimes it is Descartes that is indifferent; sometimes it is the will that cannot be prevented, and sometimes it is Descartes who cannot be prevented; and all this matters because we are meant to be discussing error; and error, we have seen, is connected with a relationship between the will and the self, or between the understanding and one, or both, of two wills. In other words, involved in this whole discussion are relationships that Descartes doesn't even begin to discuss, but which he nonetheless uses. Having started by stressing the infinite nature of the will and its nature as something that is not checked from operating simply because of ignorance, he now stresses, instead, its indifference to operating except when the self clearly understands. There is much more to examine here than I have space for. But we shall return to this discussion.

Meanwhile, there is another matter ignored, despite its relevance, by Descartes, but not by one of the contributors to The Second Set of Objections. The question concerns whether it is wrong to do what you cannot see clearly and distinctly you ought to, and whether nothing done is right unless seen clearly and distinctly as what ought to be done. This is a point closely connected with the issues I myself have raised near the end of the second chapter of this book. There I argued that on Descartes' assessment of the nature of mind, human action of any sort upon the world, and therefore even moral action, cannot be regarded as part of man's essential nature. Basically the reason is that within the world where action takes place we can never have the certainty perhaps possible in the world where we only think. In Part 3 of Descartes' *Discourse on Method* he writes: 'My second maxim was that of being as firm and resolute in my actions as I could be, and not to follow less faithfully opinions the most dubious, when my mind was once made up regarding them, than if these had been beyond doubt' (i, 96). Thus, whereas in his theoretical enquiries the slightest dubiety is sufficient to cause him to reject them, in his practical life he will accept opinions 'the most dubious' as if they were 'beyond doubt', once his mind is made up. To me, at least, the basis upon which he does make his mind up is not clear. If all he means is that it is sometimes safer to do something—anything—rather than nothing, well of course. But mostly that is not so. Yet with the other sorts of case, the vast majority, he does not deal; the cases where there is time to consider, even if one cannot be sure one's consideration will yield indubitable truth—assuming one can indeed even talk about indubitable truth in the sphere of human action. In marked contrast with what he exclaims about in Meditation Four, Descartes seems not to question that we can, as thinking beings, be 'firm and resolute' in our actions, where we know these to be based upon 'opinions the most dubious'. To seek to influence one's will in this manner seems hardly the way to train it for the task Descartes advances. In our practice we instruct the will to follow a line, however improbable the information upon which it is based, then expect the same will to be under control when we instruct it to grant no assent to any theoretical propositions, however probable, if still not *more* than that.

Descartes has no difficulty in slipping almost unnoticed into a discussion of the case not where something is the most dubious, but where probabilities are equally divided. Here, of course, it is reasonable in many cases to do something rather than nothing; and when it is so reasonable it would be most unreasonable not to do it with as much firmness and resolution as one can command. The trouble is how to be certain that the probabilities *are* equally divided. Indeed, if one takes Descartes' theory about man's essence seriously, it is impossible to see how on that basis action is possible at all, as he dimly sees himself, though he does not feel capable, it seems to me, of facing the consequences. Again, in Part 3 of the *Discourse* he writes:

In the same way, making what is called a virtue out of a necessity, we should no more desire to be well if ill, or free, if in prison, than we now do to have our bodies formed of a substance as little corruptible as diamonds, or to have wings to fly with like birds. I allow, however, that to accustom oneself to regard all things from this point of view requires long exercise and meditation often repeated; and I believe that it is principally in this that is to be found the secret of those philosophers who, in ancient times, were able to free themselves from the empire of fortune, or, despite suffering or poverty, to rival their gods in their happiness. For, ceaselessly occupying themselves in considering the limits which were prescribed to them by nature, they persuaded themselves so completely that nothing was within their own power but their thoughts, that this conviction alone was sufficient to prevent their having any longing for other things. (*Discourse on Method*, i, 97)

In other words you don't do anything. Or at least what you do doesn't really matter. For if it did you *could* not do things simply because others do, and/or because you have to live with others. Yet is not this just what Descartes advocates—since is not his method what he wants others to pursue? 'For since I began to count my own opinions as nought, because I desired to place all under examination, I was convinced that I could not do better than follow those held by people on whose judgment reliance could be placed' (*Discourse*, i, 95). And this, apparently, Descartes finds, must be consistent with his first maxim of conduct, namely

to obey the laws and customs of my country, adhering constantly to the religion in which by God's grace I had been instructed since my childhood, and in all other things directing my conduct by opinions the most moderate in nature, and the farthest removed from excess in all those which are commonly received and acted on by the most judicious of those with whom I might come in contact. (*Discourse*, i, 95)

How Descartes could in fact find it possible to do all this, if he really believes the nature of the will to be such as he argues, I so far fail to comprehend. The will, let us recall, is the most

God-like thing about us, the similitude of God, as Descartes in the language of awe describes it. If this is so, what greater sacrilege than to subordinate it to the conveniences of practical life, even temporarily, so that Descartes could live 'my life as happily as I could'—of all things. There is something far from frank in this, surely, coming as it does from a man who proclaims constantly that the essence of mind is to be a thinking thing.

It follows from this position of Descartes' that it is not always wrong to do what you cannot clearly and distinctly see you ought to do, and I have just attacked him because, I argue, he had no philosophical justification for taking up his position. The contributor to the Second Set of Objections attacks him because he too doesn't see how Descartes can fail to be *opposed* to precisely that position. Descartes' wrigglings under this attack may prove instructive. His opponent begins by stating in brief the position he understands Descartes committed to in Meditation Four. He then draws from it certain consequences that trouble him, and which he obviously supposes ought to trouble Descartes no less.

Fifthly, if the will never goes astray or errs, so long as it follows the clear and distinct knowledge of the mind that governs it, but exposes itself to danger if guided by a mental conception which is not clear and distinct, note that the following consequences ensue:—a Turk or any other infidel does not only not err because he does not embrace the Christian [and Catholic] Religion, but in addition to this he does err if he does embrace it, since he does not apprehend its truth either clearly or distinctly. Nay, if this canon of yours is true, there will be practically nothing which the will may permissibly embrace, since there is hardly anything known to us with that clearness and distinctness that you want for a certitude that no doubt can shake. Beware then lest, in your desire to befriend the truth you do not prove too much, and, instead of establishing it, overthrow it. (ii, 28)

It is of note that the objector does not deny what he takes Descartes to be committed to maintaining, namely, that the will never goes astray when guided by clear and distinct knowledge of the mind. But if, as he takes to be the case, Descartes is also saying that the will always errs *unless* guided by such knowledge, then he wants to point out a consequence for practice, which is, in brief, that action would be paralysed. His position really is not that he does not value clear and distinct knowledge, but that he values the possibilities of human action even more. In other words one might say that for the objector it is action rather than thinking which he conceives to be the essence of man.

The specific position held by Descartes, as the objector sees it, is simply that we are in no danger of error when we act from clear and distinct knowledge, but we are in danger when we don't. His answer is that since usually we don't, if Descartes is right we are for the most part in danger, and therefore shouldn't act. Nowhere does the objector say that it would not be better to act from such knowledge; his claim is that we so seldom have it, that it cannot always be wrong to act without it. What he denies, then, is that we are never right to act unless we have this knowledge, not that we are safer when we do act from it. For even if we are, it does not follow that when we lack it, inaction is always safer than action. Yet in his reply Descartes writes:

Fifthly, I marvel that you deny that *the will runs into danger if guided by a mental conception that lacks clearness and distinctness.* For what can give it certainty, if what guides it has not been clearly perceived? (ii, 43)

Here he (deliberately?) misses the point of the objector, which is not directed against the view that we cannot have certainty without clarity, but against the view that we ought not to act unless we have that certainty. And if this is what Descartes asserts then he must refuse to admit action as part of the essence of man. For it is man's essence to think, and just as thinking does not entail being a body, so it cannot entail acting with body upon body. No wonder that when faced with the consideration that his philosophy makes the religious life impossible, he double hedges. But perhaps the most astonishing thing here is the statement which ends his reply to this objection.

But where only the contemplation of truth is involved, who has ever denied that assent must be refused when the matter is obscure and cannot be perceived with sufficient distinctness? But that this latter question alone is the subject of discussion in my Meditations is proved both by the very passages in debate, and by the fact that at the end of the first Meditation I made a statement in express terms to the following effect '*that I could not at this point yield too much to distrust, since my object was not action, but knowledge.*' (ii, 44)

His object may not have been action, but by informing his will of this fact did Descartes suppose that it would refrain from mis-behaving and would desist from refusing to act when he could not supply it with indubitable grounds for doing so? The will—made, as he tells us, in the similitude of God?

Let us return to the point in the Fourth Meditation where Descartes is examining the indifference of the will to things that are vague, or unknown, to anything at all that is not apprehended with perfect clarity 'at the moment when the will is deliberating upon them'. On this picture of the will, it is clear that it is not the will, but the 'self' that 'owns' the will that is now left with respon-sibility for error. Significantly, when he talks about the indifference of the will, he also talks about himself as the willing agent with whom the task now rests of matching the will to the understand-ing. And how is he able to do this? Easily, for he now treats himself as if he were the (extra) will, and then, in this dress, permits understanding to act upon him:

for, however probable are the conjectures which render me disposed to form a judgment respecting anything, the simple knowledge that I have that those are conjectures alone and not certain and indubitable reasons, suffices to occasion me to judge the contrary. (i, 176)

The knowledge that something is not knowledge, 'suffices to occasion me to judge the contrary', and this against 'the conjec-tures which render me disposed to form a judgment'. This would, however, explain how one breaks out of the sphere of opinion. If the one idea had not been clearer than the other then he couldn't have broken free ever: 'Of this I have had great experience of late when I set aside as false all that I had formerly held to be absolutely true, for the sole reason that I remarked that it might in some measure be doubted.'

How then are we to understand the working partnership between understanding and will? Descartes' heaviest guns now appear: 'the light of nature teaches us that the knowledge of the under-standing should always precede the determination of the will' (i, 176). It needs no argument, and indeed logically it can need no argument, that one should not judge as true what one does not see to be so. If one sees it, then, we cannot help judging it to be so. That takes care of itself. It is when we don't see, or don't see fully, that we have to restrain ourselves from judging. Now if the will is indifferent we should hardly have to restrain it. But if we are accustomed to believe something, or inclined for whatever reason to believe it, then we might have to restrain *ourselves*. Otherwise 'it is evident that I deceive myself', i.e. I fail to make proper use of my will. It will, so to say, *accept* being asserted of a proposition provided always that it cannot see the proposition to be false. But if it sees it to be true then it doesn't wait to accept the usage to which someone submits it, but indeed cannot be prevented from rushing in to put its own stamp of truth on what it sees to be true. One cannot *make* one's will free, but can only avoid acting in such a way as to prevent its being so. What does such action consist in? Either in committing it wrongly, in the first place, or in not striving for the *knowledge* that would commit it.

And it is in the misuse of the free will that the privation which constitutes the characteristic nature of error is met with. Privation, I say, is found in the act, in so far as it proceeds from me, but it is not found in the faculty which I have received from God, nor even in the act in so far as it depends on Him. (i, 177.)

But it should be noted that the whole argument now hinges about the meaning of the word 'misuse'. To misuse something is to use it, but not in the way expected by the person who describes your kind of use as a *mis*use. The will, for instance, was not made to resist misuse, i.e. its use for a purpose other than that for which it is supposed to have been designed. But shouldn't it have been? Or could God not do something with that degree of complication? Could a believer in God believe that? At least it seems undeniable that God permits me to misuse my will. In other words God does nothing to stop Descartes from judging something to be the case before he knows it to be so. Well, suppose God did intervene. Obviously Descartes would then not be able to believe anything that he did not know to be true. Therefore two states are open to him. In the one he cannot help but judge something to be true, and in the other he cannot help not judging it at all. In neither case can he help what he does, and therefore he is not free.

Here it is important for Descartes' theory that he should be identified with his will when he misuses it as well as when he does not. Otherwise it is no longer his will, but something God has made that happens to be part of him. Here I follow the translation of Norman Kemp Smith, which catches the particular subtlety I have in mind. What Descartes has to show is that man puts his will to such use as to constitute a *mis*use, since it leads him to falsity.

Nor, finally, ought I to complain that God concurs with me in framing those [wrongful] acts of the will, that is to say, the judgments in which I suffer deception. Insofar as they depend on God they are entirely true and good and my ability to form them is, in its own way, a greater perfection in me than if I were unable to do so. The privation in which alone the formal [i.e. actual] reason of error or sin consists has no need of concurrence from God since it is not a thing; and if referred to God as to its cause, it ought (in conformity with the usage of the Schools) to be entitled negation, not privation. For it is not in truth an imperfection in God that He has given me the freedom of assenting or not assenting to things of which He has not placed a clear and distinct knowledge in my understanding.[1]

I, a finite thinking substance, another individual in this universe, yet made by the infinite individual God, actually am able to do something Godlike, without lessening him. I am *made* so as to judge true whatever I see to be so. This power I owe to God. And even my indifference to what I do not see to be clearly true, I owe to God.

But where I judge falsely, that is not in my will (which of itself is only moved by knowledge) but me. The individual takes on the error. Insofar as I am will, made so by God, God would be responsible for any error; from the will alone error cannot arise. But insofar as I am *another* individual, God cannot be responsible; for if he is responsible for all that *I* will, then in what sense could I be another individual? Thus, either I am not an individual, or God is not responsible for my errors; but I am an individual, therefore God is not responsible for my errors. Thus my errors are not grounded in God. From this point of view error is not real, since what is not grounded in God can have no substantial being. Error consists only in failure to abstain from judging without knowledge. But the absence of what should have been, is not itself a thing, or even an act. Judging is an act and was not

---

[1] *Descartes' Philosophical Writings* (London, 1952), p. 238.

in itself error. The individual erred, not by judging as such, but by judging the proposition he did to be true, not knowing it to be so. Judging in the absence of the knowledge Descartes regards as a privation, but in the finite individual, not in God.

Though error, for Descartes, is the 'misuse' of the will, on the other hand, without the real *possibility* of such misuse there could have been no real possibility of finite individuality. The existence of error is entailed by the existence of finite individuality. For the only way in which the possibility of error might not be actualised is if God makes me so that

while still remaining free and while still with only limited knowledge, I should not yet err, viz. by endowing my understanding with a clear and distinct knowledge of all the things upon which I shall ever have to deliberate, or simply by so deeply engraving on my memory the resolution never to pass judgment on anything of which I have no clear and distinct understanding, that I shall never lose hold on that resolution.[1]

Descartes tells us that if he had been so made he would have been more perfect than he now is. But, would this 'perfection' not have been obtained at the cost of finite individuality? And is it not in fact just because of the value of finite individuality that Descartes himself also believes it better to be as he in fact is, than to have been created after the manner described? He himself writes that 'in the universe as a whole it is a greater perfection that certain of its parts should not be exempt from defect than that they should all be exactly alike.'[2] How extraordinary, if he really did believe not simply that variety is better than monotony, but that a universe in which a part is imperfect is a better one than one in which none is. And how extraordinary that Descartes could not (*if* he could not) see that God could not, metaphysical doubt aside, have created another individual as perfect as himself. In other words a world which cannot be good unless it has God in it, but thereupon is perfect, is better than a world not able to contain bad, or gain even from that. The perfect shows its incorruptibility in action—*against* the bad.

Therefore though my errors are imperfections since they lead me from truth, my fallibility is not an imperfection in a being such as myself, but rather a different kind of perfection. For it is only

[1] Ibid., p. 239.   [2] Ibid., p. 239.

138

by a special kind of effort that a fallible being gains truth. And perhaps our freedom consists not in being able to do or to judge rightly, but in our being able to do these things, when it is equally in our nature to fail, as to succeed, in doing what we are able to do, yet might not.

Here at last man is left to discover truth for himself. But whereas before there were authorities, now there is a method. At its heart we find: 'for so long as I so restrain my will within the limits of my knowledge that it frames no judgment save on things which are clearly and distinctly apprehended by the understanding, I can never be deceived.'[1] Descartes still insists it is better to restrict one's claims to knowledge to the very minimum, and proceed no further than the requirements of certainty permit. That way, revelation may take longer, but will be of truth. Authority can *give* the results, but mankind must work for them. There is something small and lonely in the voice of Descartes that speaks here. 'Since all clear and distinct awareness is undoubtedly something, it cannot owe its origin to nothing, and must of necessity have God as its author—God, I say, who being supremely perfect, cannot be the cause of any error.'[2] We, by our own efforts, share, insofar as a finite thinking substance may, his thoughts.

[1] Ibid., p. 240.

[2] Ibid., p. 240.

CHAPTER FIVE

THE SUB-TITLE of Descartes' Fifth Meditation is 'Of the essence of material things, and, again, of God, that He exists'. As this suggests, Descartes begins with the intention of re-opening the question of what material things are in essence. Perhaps he also intended, from the start, to pass on after he had considered these matters to consider a proof for the existence of God. On the other hand, perhaps Descartes had originally intended to deal with the essence of material objects only for the purpose of examining the operations of the imagination; but in considering his example of the triangle, he suddenly saw a connection between this and the various proofs and insights he had been having during the previous days concerning the existence of God.

That he should start by wanting to direct his new found confidence in the power of knowledge to an examination of the essence of material things is not surprising, for these are the things he has yet to rehabilitate. He has learned what to do in order not to err, and also how to discover what is true. Now firstly, what do we have in mind when we speak of material objects? Secondly, does anything corresponding to such ideas actually exist 'outside' consciousness? The second of these questions he deals with (as he may have intended before he began the Fifth Meditation) in Meditation Six. The first he probably intended to examine in the present Meditation—perhaps for all of it.

It is in the light of his affirmation, in the previous Meditation, that he would devote his attention only to those things which he perfectly understands, and 'separate from these that which I only understand confusedly and with obscurity' that we should examine his next step: 'But before examining whether any such objects as I conceive exist outside of me, I must consider the ideas of them in so far as they are in my thought, and see which of them are distinct and which confused' (i, 179). He has ideas of a corporeal world, but not proof of its existence. He now believes himself

140

able to distinguish between ideas he has a right to regard as true, and others he has a duty not to. What can he learn from his own ideas?

The class of ideas he notes to begin with are those he can imagine. Imagination deals with ideas connected with our experience of the corporeal world, but does not itself necessarily involve the actual sensing of corporeal things. And since Descartes for the moment is not concerned with the corporeal world, i.e. with sensory perception, the imagining he examines concerns rather the ideas of certain properties of corporeal things, namely those of which he can form clear and distinct ideas. He writes:

In the first place, I am able distinctly to imagine that quantity which philosophers commonly call continuous, or the extension in length, breadth, or depth, that is in this quantity, or rather in the object to which it is attributed. Further, I can number in it many different parts, and attribute to each of its parts many sorts of size, figure, situation and local movement, and, finally, I can assign to each of these movements all degrees of duration. (i, 179)

The first group of things imagined are modes of extended substance. Whatever the sensory qualities of any corporeal object, it must also have these properties—in fact all of them.

The idea of quantity, he has already argued, we clearly cannot regard as the idea of a property of a spiritual substance whether finite or infinite. Nor is it an idea which depends upon the special content of the senses. Which is partly (at least) the reason why it is clearly and distinctly apprehended. I can also imagine what might be regarded as an operation upon (and of the kind appropriate to) it. It can be cut up and numbered, the units resulting may be shaped or combined in different sizes. These I can move about either together, or relative to each other. I can introduce degree of duration in relation to the movements made. In fact these are the categories, so to speak, of extended substance. I can apprehend all of them distinctly; none of them depends in any way, for their being imagined, upon any of my senses for their content; all of them can be expressed in mathematical terms. These ideas are known by me distinctly and directly, through my imagination; they are not inferred, or deduced. I am aware of them by a direct familiarity with them, so that when I think about them, calculate with or upon them, I can in a real sense *see* what

I am doing, and that what, therefore, I validly infer from them to be true, must be.

But these ideas are so simple and direct that they can be known for what they are, and nothing is more certain than that what I so distinctly know to be so cannot be nothing, and cannot be known in any other way, even by God. Their truth is objective, though they appear to my imagination, and though I can call up or dismiss them, I cannot have fabricated them. For not only is there a vast number of them (surely too many for anyone to have constructed by himself) but I also grasp them, for, and as, what they were even before I grasped them. They relate to former experience much as the thought I am suddenly able to formulate relates to the thought I was trying to. Since these truths were somehow present before I thought about them, and when I couldn't have had a distinct idea of them, they could not have been constructed by me. But, Descartes is maintaining, since what is perceived clearly and distinctly must be true, if this truth has not been fashioned by me, its ground must lie in God, who is, then, the 'cause' of what is true in the idea, even though I myself am the cause of my having it when I do.

And what I here find to be most important is that I discover in myself an infinitude of ideas of certain things which cannot be esteemed as pure negations, although they may possibly have no existence outside of my thought, and which are not framed by me, although it is within my power either to think or not to think them, but which possess natures which are true and immutable. (i, 179–80)

What Descartes is talking about, the *structure* of extended substance, is not itself a possible perceptual experience, or, rather, a possible *sensible* object, for what has no sensory content cannot be experienced. Although it exists as part of the world of extended substance, that is a world which we know by thought, not by the senses. Though having no existence in the sensible world, something may yet exist. Moreover, what, though not framed by me, is clearly and distinctly perceived by me, must be framed by God. Descartes writes:

For example, when I imagine a triangle, although there may nowhere in the world be such a figure outside my thought, or ever have been, there is nevertheless in this figure a certain determinate nature, form, or essence, which is immutable and eternal, which I have not invented, and which in no wise depends on my mind, as appears from the fact that diverse properties of that triangle can be demonstrated, viz. that its three angles are equal to two right angles, that the greatest side is subtended by the greatest angle, and the like, which now, whether I wish it or do not wish it, I recognise very clearly as pertaining to it, although I never thought of the matter at all when I imagined a triangle for the first time, and which therefore cannot be said to have been invented by me. (i, 180)

The objectivity, the immutability, of the relations he discovers in these ideas, confers upon them authority. Though he here considers the idea of a triangle, the latter can also be a property of a physical object. But his imagination need not limit itself to picturing only the triangular physical objects he has seen. Yet neither has he any conceivable reason to suppose there is only a finite number of possible sorts of triangles. Therefore he could not possibly consider them all. In some respects, however, the one he does consider differs from none of them. Each imagined triangle may have a peculiar characteristic of its own, but to be a triangle each must have some properties which will apply equally to all.

And Descartes' triangle differs from all possible corporeal and all possible picturable triangles in that it is constituted by and only by those properties without which no triangle could be deemed one. The idea of a single set of properties necessary for anything whatsoever's being a triangle does not entail the existence either of a physical or of a mentally *pictured* triangle.

Relations between these properties entail each other, not just on the basis of some independent universal law, but simply because they can be 'seen' to do so. Descartes has already argued that we start from intuition and, in effect, expand it. We 'understand' because of what we see, or even, one might say, our understanding and our seeing are one and the same. Thus what Descartes describes as demonstrating the properties of a triangle could also be regarded as the coming to 'see' these properties. Did he really have to prove that the three internal angles of a triangle are equal to two right angles? Did he not see it until he had proved it? Did he, to put the matter another way, have to take it on trust from the logical validity of his proof that the proposition in question holds good? Put this way the question answers itself. But did Descartes mean this? So far, on the basis of almost everything he has said about method the answer is that he did.

And not only do I know these things with distinctness when I consider them in general, but, likewise [however little I apply my attention to the matter], I discover an infinitude of particulars respecting numbers, figures, movements, and other such things, whose truth is so manifest, and so well accords with my nature, that when I begin to discover them, it seems to me that I learn nothing new, or recollect what I formerly knew—that is to say, that I for the first time perceive things which were already present to my mind, although I had not as yet applied my mind to them. (i, 179)

One might almost say, bearing in mind the Fourth Meditation, that he knows much he has never affirmed. What he finds so well accords with his own nature, are the truths which though applying to corporeal substance are themselves modes of thinking substance operating on principles derived from *its* own nature. Thus, he has always known them, however confusedly, or obscurely, for otherwise his sensory input could never have furnished him with a knowledge of corporeal *objects*.

We are not, however, simply concerned with triangles. The example Descartes takes is admittedly drawn from the class provided by the activity of imagination, drawing upon sensory experience, perhaps, but nevertheless not subordinate to it. There is no end to the variety of figures he might have chosen or formed in his 'mind's eye'. He has made this point. The world of ideas is full of possible intuitions of the kind we have just been considering. The world of the mind, and therefore of the imagination, is full of insights that have only to be seen to be necessarily believed. It almost seems to be *constituted* by them; so that any one of them could, by some possible route, be related to any other.

The full force of Descartes' next move cannot be fully grasped if we think merely of this or that figure. We must think of all figure, and that *universal* necessitation which makes the corporeal nature of what we may apprehend possible. This, Descartes maintains, is in principle open to our intuition. The foundation of the empirical world is a necessary one, even if, so far, we cannot also claim that, being necessary as to its own character, it also necessitates the corporeal existence, in space and time, of the sensible world. Nevertheless, might there not be something, even if not corporeal, the existence or being of which *is* necessitated? Before attempting to answer this question, let us consult Descartes' own exposition, since we shall from now on be concerned in the precisest possible way with its argument.

One sentence in this meditation is surely the key one.

But now, if just because I can draw the idea of something from my thought, it follows that all which I know clearly and distinctly as pertaining to this object does really belong to it, may I not derive from this an argument demonstrating the existence of God? (i, 180)

Descartes has already given us good reason to suppose that all that he can intuit as clearly and distinctly belonging to something, really does—and indeed must—belong to it, i.e. be true of it. In relation to this thought let us again consider the triangle. The triangle I think of, *qua* triangle, and not some particular triangle, exists when I think of it—at least in the sense that it is true that I am thinking of a triangle; and what makes it so is that it is a *triangle* I am thinking of. Now it exists, for I see clearly and distinctly that what I am thinking of is, at least, more properly described as a triangle than in any other way. But what I can see to follow necessarily from something that exists must also exist, i.e. be true of the world. Thus it is as true of the world that in a triangle the three inner angles add up to two right angles as it is that in the world someone is thinking of a triangle, i.e. that in the world there is the thought of a triangle. And if it is true the triangle has such and such a property, then it is equally true that the triangle is something which has such and such a property, i.e. that this property characterises the triangle.

Now, throughout the Meditations, at intervals, Descartes has insisted that he is more certain that God exists than he is of any other single truth. The existence of God is presupposed by the very ground of the *cogito*, namely the doubt. But later, in the Third Meditation, we get a determined attempt to prove that the idea I believe myself to have of God, really is just that—an idea of God. There is nothing else it can be. Moreover, since it is *that* idea there is nobody but God who could have caused it. This is a reinforcing proof. For if God caused it then he must exist. Descartes, then, affirms not simply that the idea of God is present

to him, but that it is so no less than the imaginative pictures he
has so far in this Meditation been contemplating:

Certainly, the idea of God, that is of a being sovereignly perfect, is no
less present to me than is that of any shape or number; and I know
that an actual and external existence pertains to His nature no less
clearly and distinctly than I know that whatever is demonstrable of a
shape or number belongs to the nature of the shape or number.[1]

But this knowledge in neither case depends upon a deductive
proof, though such a 'proof' may lead one to a position from which
one can see the truth. The ordinary man has his idea of God, just
as he has his idea of a triangle, though he may have meditated upon
neither. Now there is a real difference, it seems to me, between
thinking of knowledge as apprehending ideas of something that
the ideas are in some mysterious way related to, and thinking
of it as the apprehending of what *it* is that is *thereby known*.
Descartes favours the second alternative. When he speaks of ideas
that 'so well accord with my nature', and that are so manifestly
so that it is senseless to question their validity, what he is saying
makes sense enough if we suppose him to be talking of insight
into the very thing he finds present, or presents, to himself. And
this is not the idea of X, but X itself. This gets away from the
representational theory of knowledge. Descartes didn't suppose
that his idea of himself only represented himself to his own mind.
That is a blundering thought. How would he know what the idea
was an idea of if he doesn't know that which the idea is an idea of?
But if he can know the former, then though he can indeed also
frame an idea of it, *it* isn't an idea, nor does he need an idea in
order to know *it*.

But Descartes insists that his knowledge of God is at least
not less certain than his knowledge of himself. It is not in his
awareness of his idea of his own limitation, or in his idea of a
something in relation to which he cannot but view his own short-
comings, but in his awareness of that very thing itself as it is
possible for such a thing to appear to a finite thinking substance,
that he stands as knower to thing known. He talks about ideas,
certainly, but his use of this term in the present connection is
compatible with his meaning by an idea simply a point of view,

[1] Kemp Smith, p. 243.

a perspective, a glimpse, or something of that kind. It doesn't follow that because in a given case you cannot be aware of all of something, what you apprehend cannot be the thing itself, but only an idea of it. Descartes in fact uses the word 'idea' in the sense of 'part of', and not 'picture' of, in the case we are now discussing. This might seem mistaken, on the grounds that we cannot know God himself at all, much less know him in his infinite majesty, and that therefore the most we can hope to know is an idea of him. But to know even only a part of something is sometimes enough to enable one to claim to know the thing as a whole, in a wider sense of 'know'. Thus, to use an example given by Descartes, we do not have to see all the sea to be entitled to claim we have seen the sea. And of course we could not claim to know God at all if this were to be understood as a claim to know all that can be known of him. But I have elsewhere in this book argued that we do claim to have some knowledge of God directly. We worship God, not the concept of God. And indeed, when we speak of God's being a person, one of the things we intend to convey is precisely that we in some way stand in some sort of personal, or personal-like, relation to him, i.e. that we are to some extent, however infinitesimal, acquainted with him—not with the concept of him. Nowhere in Descartes is it suggested that an argument for the existence of God which at no point made reference to an actual or possible personal experience could prove his existence. In a moment I shall discuss the way in which knowledge of the self and knowledge of God are related in the one act of thought. But before we come to that it might be worth taking a more careful notice of Descartes' views upon the way knowledge starts in us, for I have pointed out[1] already that Descartes is in some way as empiricist as Hume, in that for him knowledge must begin with particular experience.

But when we become aware that we are thinking beings, this is a primitive act of knowledge derived from no syllogistic reasoning. He who says, '*I think, hence I am, or exist,*' does not deduce existence from thought by a syllogism, but, by a simple act of mental vision, recognises it as if it were a thing that is known *per se*. This is evident from the fact that if it were syllogistically deduced, the major premise, *that everything that thinks is, or exists*, would have to be known previously;

[1] See p. 10 above.

but yet that has rather been learned from the experience of the individual—that unless he exists he cannot think. For our mind is so constituted by nature that general propositions are formed out of the knowledge of particulars. (ii, 38)

Not, be it noted, particulars out of general propositions. If then,
in this sense, knowledge of a particular is not formed directly
out of the experience by which we come to know the particular,
by what else can it be?

Any argument against the possibility of a direct knowledge of
God, based upon the special and infinite nature of a supreme
Being, can also be used to demonstrate that our ideas too cannot
properly represent him even as God. In fact innate ideas cannot
represent in the way adventitious ideas do: especially as they do
not stand for something that can be known through the senses.
Why, then, should we not suppose we can know something
directly? And why need we suppose that there is anything at all
less problematic about knowing ideas, than about knowing what
the ideas represent—the object that ideas claim to express? In
support of this view we may refer again to a quotation from
Descartes' Third Meditation (cf. pp. 98-9). Note that the dea of
God is known by the 'same faculty' as that by which I know
myself, and I know him as that very Being towards whom I
aspire. And there is not only 'the idea' of God within me, but
there is something else 'within' which that idea of God is 'contained' and that something else is not simply, therefore, that idea
of God, nor of course can it be God, as God may be thought of as
present to himself; but it is, as Descartes says, the actual 'image
and similitude' of God that he has placed upon me. And it is of
this that I take Descartes to be thinking when he speaks of what he
perceives when he perceives God by the same faculty as that with
which he perceives himself.

The suggestion that we must have God present to us only in
objective reality, i.e. in thought, because we cannot have God
himself present in our minds, is simply the suggestion that we
cannot encompass the mind of God in our own; and this says
nothing at all about whether we can or cannot know God directly.
Indeed, Descartes tells us in Meditation Three

For although the idea of substance is within me owing to the fact
that I am substance, nevertheless I should not have the idea of an

infinite substance—since I am finite—if it had not proceeded from some substance which was veritably infinite. (i, 166)

But it doesn't have to 'proceed' in the sense of come from where it was to where it wasn't before it came. Descartes has told us often enough that it is in the way we know ourselves (as, for instance, in doubting) that we know God. We know what zero means, without being nothing, and what 'infinite' means without being infinite. So why should we not know what 'God' means without being God? But how could we know what 'God' means unless somewhere we did have direct knowledge of him, however limited that knowledge must be, in the nature of the case—I say 'limited' and not 'inadequate', since for a human, perhaps the knowledge we can have of him is as adequate as we can bear. Unless we suppose that we can understand something of what God is, then no talk about him makes sense. In our knowledge of him we, as thinking substances, can easily be conceived as being directly characterised by what characterises him, though to a degree conforming to our finite nature. Otherwise there is no reason why our own finite substance should not assume from him those characteristics from which its own finite nature excludes it. Thus, our reflective idea of ourself emerges only from our awareness of these *perfections* we term God—not merely of our *idea* of those Perfections.

If the foregoing interpretation of Descartes' position is correct, then it is certain that he does not need to prove that God exists, since he has already shown him to. For what Descartes apprehends when he apprehends God, *is* God, and is not merely the idea of him. Therefore God is actually apprehended as existing. He could not be apprehended at all, otherwise. And in this respect, as we saw, Descartes' knowledge of himself as real, i.e. actually existing as himself, is in no different case. Moreover, from Descartes' point of view, it would be absurd to think that he, Descartes, existed, but that God, who conserves Descartes' existence, does not exist. And this, so far, can be considered independently of the question whether the existence in question, whether of Descartes or of God, is a necessary one.

Though Descartes is representationalist in respect of our knowledge of corporeal objects, he seems to me, looking directly at what he says, to be even insistent that in the case of innate truths there is no representation, but actual and immediate knowledge, though this knowledge, in the case of the idea of God, is of necessity partial; as he says, our power of understanding is not limited to representations, but only by its finite nature.

I have already spent more time than perhaps I should on this point, but it was necessary to prepare the way for the idea that God is no less immediately known to us than the triangle. But our knowledge of God is not merely on a par with that of the triangle. It has a reality greater than that of all other things whatsoever. Not to see that this is what Descartes means is to misunderstand him completely. I shall consider a few of his own statements from the point of view I here adopt:

It is certain that I no less find the idea of God, that is to say, the idea of a supremely perfect Being, in me, than that of any figure or number whatever it is; and I do not know any less clearly and distinctly that an [actual and] eternal existence pertains to this nature than I know that all that which I am able to demonstrate of some figure or number truly pertains to the nature of this figure or number, and therefore, although all that I concluded in the preceding Meditations were found to be false, the existence of God would pass with me as at least as certain as I have ever held the truths of mathematics (which concern only numbers and figures) to be. (i, 180–1)

Now the reason for this statement (which can be found repeated in other forms by Descartes) seems to me to lie at the very heart of Descartes' entire system of metaphysics. Descartes has argued repeatedly that God is not simply Creator, but also the great Conserver. Things were not only created, but stayed so. Nothing is closer to Descartes' central thinking than his conception of God as conserving *him*. In the first paragraph of Meditation Four he writes, we may remember, as follows:

And when I consider that I doubt, that is to say, that I am an incomplete and dependent being, the idea of a being that is complete and independent, that is of God, presents itself to my mind with so much distinctness and clearness—and from the fact alone that this idea is found in me, or that I who possess this idea exist, I conclude so certainly that God exists, and that my existence depends entirely on Him in every moment of my life—that I do not think that the human mind is capable of knowing anything with more evidence and certitude. (i, 171–2)

Descartes is here speaking of his knowledge of himself as depending for his very continuation 'every moment of my life' on God.

Descartes only knows that he exists when he thinks; but he is the *same* Descartes, whenever he thinks, because he knows himself to be so, and because he knows that he is not mistaken in this; and he knows he is not mistaken, because if he were this would amount to deception by God. And he knows God, a perfect Being, because he finds him actually present as, so to say, the upholder of his own self *qua* finite thinking substance. That is how he knows God. And though it may be dismissed as simply a logical requirement, it is a metaphysical requirement as well, that there can be none to conserve the conserver himself. In this sense the conserver's existence is the only real existence, for only God exists because it is his nature to do so. We exist only because and insofar as he confers some degree of that special perfection upon us.

Thus far we have considered the idea of God as Conserver of corporeal substance, and of finite thinking substance. But there is another kind of conservation it seems to me Descartes has in mind, which may be said to make knowledge itself possible. For the whole conception of God as not a deceiver appears to me to have its roots in a positive conception of God's nature as the Being who makes knowledge available to finite thinking substances, not simply by conserving them, but also *by conserving their very knowledge itself*—without which, of course, there could be no system of knowledge at all. I can rely upon my idea of a triangle to be always the same. I can rely upon all the truths I find within myself to be always the same. And I can rely upon my memory, when used 'properly'. The unity of knowledge is given by God, and on no other ground can it be explained. But our knowledge of God is, whether we are clearly and distinctly aware of this or not, the ground of that unity. This is what Descartes continues to explicate; and as we shall see, he means the ontological argument to take off from this position. That, in my view, is the actual purpose of Meditation Five, once under way, whether or not it was so originally.

From the foregoing discussion I conclude that Descartes believed himself to have an actual knowledge of God, however limited, without needing any further argument to demonstrate this; that is to say, he believed himself to know God as existing, or to know that on account of which the proposition 'God exists' is true.

But whatever can be known directly can also be represented, even if the converse does not hold. Thus, one can just as truly have an idea of what one knows when one meditates upon God, as one can have an idea of what one had for breakfast. In neither case does one have to engage again in the original experience. On the other hand, the concept of what one experiences immediately must conform to the formal reality which it expresses, for it to be the concept it intends to be. For when I intend to talk to someone who claims not to believe in God, about God, I can only succeed if my concept is in fact a concept of God, and not of something else or perhaps not even a concept at all. Therefore, what is essential in the formal reality of the thing must find a place in the concept. And since whatever is known immediately is thereby known as existing, and therefore, from a conceptual point of view, known to exist, the concept of God must find a place for the fact that I know God immediately in my very knowledge of my own immediacy.

The ontological argument, therefore, is a proof only in the sense that it is intended to be a formal proof (*une preuve démonstrative*) or, perhaps better, a formal presentation, of what we know already. Otherwise much of Kant's criticism would hold. But you cannot just drop the knowledge of God. Indeed, you cannot escape it. The question of whether God exists or not is not a question you can decide, on Descartes' view, as you happen to see fit; it is decided for you by the very nature of your knowledge of God. This is a point for which Descartes has contended again and again throughout the Meditations.

Even if he is wrong about this he cannot be nearly as wrong as Kant, who fails entirely to take this into account. One might almost say that for Kant, Descartes' six Meditations begin with the fifth, except that he can hardly have read that through either. But since he is by far the most famous and certainly the most influential opponent of Descartes in this matter, let us consider some of Kant's arguments as they appear in his section in the *Critique of Pure Reason* on 'The Impossibility of an Ontological Proof of the Existence of God'. I begin by quoting Kant's opening statement: 'It is evident, from what has been said, that the concept of an absolutely necessary being is a concept of pure reason, that is, a mere idea the objective reality of which is very far from being

proved by the fact that reason requires it.'[1] Now nothing that
Descartes has to say on this question depends upon its being true
that the existence of a perfect Being is proved only by the requirements of pure reason in Kant's sense, nor indeed entirely by reason
in any sense. Kant's sense of 'reason' is very different from
Descartes'. For the latter, as I have tried to demonstrate, what
we know isn't simply a formal concept of an absolutely necessary
being, but, in the measure possible for a finite intelligence, that
being himself. Whereas Kant's tendentious expression for this is
'a mere idea', to let us know that by means of the understanding
one cannot gain knowledge of whatever cannot be comprehended,
as to its content, by the senses. The idea stands sentinel at the
limits of human knowledge; it certainly does not afford us a
spectacle of what lies beyond. Moreover, it cannot even declare
that there is anything beyond; such, for instance, as God—a
perfect Being.

But Descartes never claims it possible to have a knowledge of
God through the external senses, nor an adequate (totally comprehensive) knowledge of him by any means whatsoever. He
makes this plain in his Reply to the First Set of Objections. And
when replying to the Sixth Set of Objections he insists that even
God's will is very different from ours, though it is this very will
that he declares so like ours that in respect of it we are made in
the similitude of God. Indeed Descartes had compelling enough
reasons for not even daring to claim the sort of knowledge of
God which could appear to the Church to imply less than an
infinite distance between man and God. But in any case, even for
Descartes (just as for Kant) there could not be such knowledge
through the external senses. Who more than Descartes had
maintained that insofar as we do depend upon the external senses
we cannot have any knowledge at all, less still knowledge of
God?

Still speaking of the 'mere idea' Kant writes: 'There is, of
course, no difficulty in giving a verbal definition of the concept,
namely, that it is something the non-existence of which is impossible.'[2] But this is just what Descartes himself pointed out
when distinguishing his account of the ontological argument from

---

[1] *Critique of Pure Reason*, trans. N. K. Smith (London, 1933), p. 500.
[2] Ibid., p. 501.

the one (Anselm's) put forward for attack by St Thomas. In his Reply to Caterus in the First Set of Objections, Descartes writes:

Now the argument to which he puts himself in opposition can be thus propounded. *When we understand what it is the word God signifies, we understand that it is that, than which nothing greater can be conceived; but to exist in reality as well as in the mind is greater than to exist in the mind alone; hence, when the meaning of the word God is understood, it is understood that God exists in fact as well as in the understanding.*

Descartes continues in reply to this:

Here there is a manifest error in the form of the argument; for the only conclusion to be drawn is—*hence, when we understand what the word God means, we understand that it means that God exists in fact as well as in the mind*: but because a word implies something, that is no reason for this being true. My argument, however, was of the following kind—That which we clearly and distinctly understand to belong to the true and immutable nature of anything, its essence, or form, can be truly affirmed of that thing; but, after we have with sufficient accuracy investigated the nature of God, we clearly and distinctly understand that to exist belongs to His true and immutable nature; therefore we can with truth affirm of God that He exists. (ii, 19)

This speaks for itself, and says a great deal. Descartes evidently does not think one cannot investigate the nature of God until one has discovered that he exists necessarily. How could one begin? One can have a pre-reflective knowledge of God as of much else. Only this does not have to be directly, or even indirectly translatable into terms of sense experience. And here lies what seems to me one of the fundamental weaknesses in Kant's position. He appears to hold that where the categories of the understanding have no application, there knowledge is not possible. But either this is just another stipulative definition of knowledge—or it is false. Kant's successors, such, for instance, as Fichte and Hegel, disagreed amongst themselves about many things but not in regarding Kant's system of categories as mistaken in being both incomplete and unsystematic. If they are right, reason, in Kant's account, lacks the universal and systematic applicability Kant himself claimed for it.

However it is less with concepts than with existence that Kant is here concerned. So he moves over from argument about the knowledge of God, to argument about his existence. His basic thought here is this: by including existence as part of the subject concept of something, we do, of course, make it necessarily true that that thing exists. However, this necessity of existence depends not upon anything in the thing, but upon the logical necessity of having to assert that the thing exists, once one has included existence (the concept of existence) in the subject concept, that is to say, among the essential predicates of that concept—the concept-constituting predicates. As we have just seen in Descartes's reply to Caterus, however, this argument cannot be directed against Descartes; and as we shall see to be true from further considerations, existence is not simply added to another bundle of predicates. Descartes discovers, he believes (and Kant seems not to have taken this into account) not simply that God exists, but that it is impossible to think as non-existent the Being he knows even from his pre-reflective days as God. And the impossibility consists in this, that to think it would entail, for Descartes, his being able to *think his own non-existence*. Descartes has argued that there is nothing he knows with as much certainty as he knows God. He has argued that in knowing himself he knows himself as sustained by something other than himself, and thereby given the self-identity that converts atomic pulses of awareness into a continuing and identical self. He has argued what amounts to this, that the very impulse to know, as well as the insight by the self that the self is limited in all sorts of ways, all presuppose our prior acquaintance with something that upon reflection by us can be seen to be that which we come to call by the name of God. There is not here any suggestion that we can have knowledge of this being *as* infinite. Descartes knows we can't, and has said it in answer to the protest that he is claiming superhuman knowledge in claiming knowledge of God. Even Kant has to suppose that he knows what he is talking about when he uses such expressions as 'unattainable completeness'. The difference between Kant and Descartes here is that whereas the former believes that what cannot be cashed in perceptual terms cannot be regarded as knowledge, the latter holds that what *can* be cashed in perceptual terms cannot. Thus Descartes doesn't claim either that he has perceptual or rational knowledge of God as an infinite object, but he nevertheless claims to have a knowledge of God without which no other form of knowledge could be knowledge, as we have seen, at all. For Descartes, as we have also seen him argue, the position might even be summed up by saying that for the human form of awareness to be even possible, God must exist. Whether or not he is right, it is clear that on Descartes' argument, we cannot regard 'God' simply as a name, or as an adventitious idea which could have been differently complex, or as a purely stipulated (or, rather, arbitrarily synthesised) concept. We cannot decide what we should or should not say about its nature, any more than in the case of the triangle. And though it is conceivable that nobody should ever have thought of a triangle it is inconceivable that anybody should not have thought, in however primitive a fashion, of God.

If Kant had bothered to take those considerations into account in the section we are examining he might have been less inclined to make his celebrated move of arguing that he could withstand the pressure to conclude God exists, by 'rejecting' the entire 'concept of an absolutely necessary being'. In a famous passage Kant writes:

If, in an identical proposition, I reject the predicate while retaining the subject, contradiction results; and I therefore say that the former belongs necessarily to the latter. But if we reject subject and predicate alike, there is no contradiction; for nothing is then left that can be contradicted. To posit a triangle, and yet to reject its three angles, is self-contradictory; but there is no contradiction in rejecting the triangle together with its three angles. The same holds true of the concept of an absolutely necessary being. If its existence is rejected, we reject the thing itself with all its predicates; and no question of contradiction can then arise. There is nothing outside it that would then be contradicted, since the necessity of the thing is not supposed to be derived from anything external; nor is there anything internal that would be contradicted, since in rejecting the thing itself we have at the same time rejected all its internal properties. 'God is omnipotent' is a necessary judgment. The omnipotence cannot be rejected if we posit a Deity, that is, an infinite being; for the two concepts are identical. But if we say, 'There is no God', neither the omnipotence nor any other of its predicates is given; they are one and all rejected together with the subject, and there is therefore not the least contradiction in such a judgment.[1]

[1] Ibid., p. 502.

Now Kant is concerned here with an argument in which, as he takes it, from the thought, and only from the thought, of something, the existence of that something thought about is concluded. What he wants to argue is first that we cannot conclude from thought to existence, second that the thought of God is no exception to this, and third that this holds equally when the thought contains as part of its complex the thought of existence as part of the subject concept.

It should be pointed out that for Descartes the proposition that God exists doesn't simply *happen* to be an identical (analytic) proposition, such that it makes sense to suppose that the subject concept is only constituted arbitrarily. Of course, even in this case, it would still be a contradiction to detach one of its predicates (constituent elements) and deny it of the subject concept. For the subject concept either would not, without the predicate, be the same, or (which is the case we are concerned with) it would still be intended as the same concept at the same time as the denial of the truth of something which once granted would eliminate one of the conditions necessary for the subject concept to remain the same concept. The contradiction that would ensue in such a case would be a purely formal one. Nobody would be concerned to take another look at the subject concept to see if what was left of it made sense even with a predicate withdrawn. Yet it might. So that the withdrawal of the predicate in question would not in itself render the remaining subject concept meaningless, but would change it in some regard. Now Descartes' conception of God is not a complex of parts only arbitrarily related. In Meditation Three he writes as follows:

Nor can we suppose that several causes may have concurred in my production, and that from one I have received the idea of one of the perfections which I attribute to God, and from another the idea of some other, so that all these perfections indeed exist somewhere in the universe, but not as complete in one unity which is God. On the contrary, the unity, the simplicity or the inseparability of all things which are in God is one of the principal perfections which I conceive to be in Him. (i, 169)

Thus Descartes' idea of God is not one that can be modified by the simple addition, or withdrawal of this or that predicate. It is conceivable that in some cases the withdrawal of a predicate from a subject concept might be found to leave us with something else, but still a concept, still something conceivable as a unit of some kind. In the case of the idea of a perfect Being, Descartes holds, it is different. The peculiar nature of this idea, as we shall later see he insists, is that if anything is taken from it, then it cannot any longer be the idea of a perfect Being, since such a Being could not lack what has been conceptually withdrawn and still remain a perfect Being, i.e. a Being to whom no perfection, whether existence or anything else be regarded as one can be lacking. One cannot even say that such a deprived concept can stand for something divine but less than a perfect Being; for whatever is less than a perfect Being is as far from divine, on Descartes' metaphysical account, as you or I are. Whatever it might be, it is not what Descartes is concerned about, or what he has even mentioned, or something the rejection of which makes a scrap of difference to his case. This is not that necessary Being of whose existence Descartes is more certain than of that of anything else whatsoever. It certainly is not any longer that which he cannot contemplate without recognising that it doesn't only exist, but exists by its own essence.

Is it anything? It may or may not be conceivable that something is omnipotent, or omniscient, or possesses some other perfection, or combination of them; but even if the possession of a single perfection makes sense, does possession of a selection of them, a combination which is limited insofar as it contains less than all possible perfections, hang together conceptually so as to make sense? Surely Kant must first show that it does; and it is not at all certain that this is possible. Instead, he conceives it meaningful to reject this or that predicate in an analytic proposition. Then he says that this would result in a contradiction. But in the case he would require to construct in order to meet Descartes, there could not be such a contradiction, for by withdrawing (assuming one could) a given predicate, one would be destroying the whole subject concept. There would thus not even be a contradiction, since there would not be a meaning-remnant of the original subject concept which the 'rejected' predicate could (if it still meant anything) contradict. I conclude, so far, that from the fact that Kant may sometimes meaningfully reject the predicate of an analytic proposition, it does not at all follow that it would make sense for him to claim that he could reject the predicate in a proposition of the kind that Descartes is concerned with when he claims that a Perfect being necessarily exists. And what kind of proposition this is we shall examine more closely later.

However, there is a further point. Not only is it not so obviously open to Kant as he may think, to deny the predicate in the case he ought really to be concerned with; he also certainly has no right to assume that he can, with any greater success, reject the subject concept, that is, the concept of a perfect Being. For Descartes has argued that above all things this is the one thought, namely, that of a perfect Being, that it makes no sense even to try to. And part of the reason, of course, is that in the first instance we do not meet it as one might some abstract concept far from intrinsic to the nature of the self, but, on the contrary, as something which is not simply the thought of a thing, but is in some degree the veritable experience of it. Possibly here the line between thought and being may be thinner than comfortable for Kant, but Descartes was not afraid.

We need not, perhaps, regard all innate ideas in this way, but *if* the idea is innate, necessarily, then how can it be rejected? If the idea of God can be rejected how can it also be innate? But if it is not, how can it be the same idea as the one which Descartes is really concerned with, and with which Kant too must be concerned if his argument is to be an argument against Descartes? Certainly it may appear that Kant was not entirely unaware of at least one of the difficulties here raised. He writes: 'The only way of evading this conclusion is to argue that there are subjects which cannot be removed, and must always remain.'[1] But when we see his way of answering this it becomes clear that despite appearances he has no insight whatsoever into the roots of the position he takes himself to be attacking. For he thinks it adequate to reply to this argument as follows: 'That, however, would only be another way of saying that there are absolutely necessary subjects; and that is the very assumption I have called in question, and the possibility of which the above argument professes to establish.'[2] But that this is an assumption for Descartes (whom Kant has in mind) is surely the most gratuitous assumption Kant could have made about him, of all people. In a dozen places Descartes had

---

[1] Ibid., p. 503. [2] Ibid.

produced one argument after another for his position, and
certainly I shall consider the central strand in Descartes' position
on this question shortly.

The ontological argument is not the only argument Descartes
uses to demonstrate the necessary existence of God. Even before
the Fifth Meditation Descartes has sought to show both that God
exists, and that he does so necessarily. The ontological argument
itself may even be regarded almost as a formal proof of this; and
because Kant does not understand the position of this argument in
Descartes' system, he treats it as if, from a purely formal point of
view, it could do what he supposed had been claimed for it. Kant
was right in a way to think it couldn't, but not to think that by
rejecting it as a formal argument he could reject the wider argument of which it is a part, nor the so-called concept of an absolutely
necessary Being. For the concept with which Descartes is concerned was not posited, but ineluctably given. We do not merely
posit God. The moment we begin to think about it we cannot
doubt it, for we cannot doubt what we cannot but think. Kant is
right, indeed, when he says that the only way of evading his
conclusion is to argue that there are 'subjects which cannot be
removed, and must always remain'. It *is* the only way, but he
himself can only maintain his own conclusion by arguing against
the position that there are such subjects. I myself have argued
that he has not succeeded in doing that. From this I conclude
that Kant can only 'reject' the concept of God on condition that
he doesn't *think* what he is doing.

And when Kant raises the question as to whether the proposition that this or that thing exists is a tautology, he seems to me
to repeat both his misunderstandings of Descartes, and also his
own insights. He writes:

We must ask: Is the proposition that *this or that thing* (which, whatever
it may be, is allowed as possible) *exists*, an analytic or a synthetic
proposition? If it is analytic, the assertion of the existence of the thing
adds nothing to the thought of the thing; but in that case either the
thought, which is in us, is the thing itself, or we have presupposed
an existence as belonging to the realm of the possible, and have then,
on that pretext, inferred its existence from its internal possibility—
which is nothing but a miserable tautology.[1]

[1] Ibid., p. 504.

What Descartes has claimed is precisely that the thought in us *is* the thing itself, since this is the only way in which *that* kind of thing, God, can be in the mind of a finite being. But the proposition that a perfect Being exists for Descartes, by the time he has reached the Fifth Meditation, is not simply analytic, but at least as necessarily true as the proposition, for him, that he himself exists. Kant is never more correct than when he writes:

By whatever and by however many predicates we may think a thing— even if we completely determine it—we do not make the least addition to the thing when we further declare that this thing *is*. Otherwise, it would not be exactly the same thing that exists, but something more than we had thought in the concept; and we could not, therefore, say that the exact object of my concept exists.[1]

For granted that we do think of God, we don't also need to add that he exists. In his Reply to the First Set of Objections, Descartes writes:

By similar reasoning I admit along with all theologians that God cannot be comprehended by the human mind, and also that he cannot be distinctly known by those who try mentally to grasp Him at once in His entirety, and view Him, as it were, from a distance. This was the sense in which, in the words of St Thomas in the passage quoted, the knowledge of God was said to be found in us only in a certain confused way. But those who try to attend to His perfections singly, and intend not so much to comprehend them as to admire them and to employ all the power of their mind in contemplating them, will assuredly find in Him a much ampler and readier supply of the material for clear and distinct cognition than in any created things. (ii, 18)

Having even in a non-cognitive manner attended no more than partly to God's perfection we already understand Him to exist. And, of course, to add after that 'and he exists' is then to compound precisely what Kant calls it—a miserable tautology. I don't say Descartes is right; I say Kant has not proved him wrong.

The opponents of the so-called ontological argument are right in one respect; one cannot deduce the existence of what is not of its nature existent. But then they conclude that Descartes was wrong. What they should have observed, however, is the other possibility, namely, that God's existence does not have to be

[1] Ibid., p. 505.

deduced. It is present in the knowledge I have of him. *That* is Descartes' position.

So far, then, there is no question of existence characterising God. A non-existing God cannot be characterised by existence; and an existing God does not need to be. To speak of existence as a property of God, is also misleading, for as we have seen it is not a property independent of his other properties. And just as some properties of things are less immediately clearly and distinctly perceived than others in the case of geometrical or arithmetical truths, so with truths about God. It is easy to know him as existent; but some thought is required before we can know him as necessarily existent, i.e. as eternally existent; and no doubt more thought might reveal more of his characteristics.

For being accustomed in all other things to make a distinction between existence and essence, I easily persuade myself that the existence can be separated from the essence of God, and that we can thus conceive God as not actually existing. *But, nevertheless, when I think of it with more attention, I clearly see* that existence can no more be separated from the essence of God than can its having its three angles equal to two right angles be separated from the essence of a [rectilinear] triangle, or the idea of a mountain from the idea of a valley; *and so there is not any less repugnance to our conceiving a God (that is, a Being supremely perfect) to whom existence is lacking (that is to say, to whom a certain perfection is lacking), than to conceive of a mountain which has no valley.*[1] (i, 181)

What Descartes thinks of, but with more attention, is the same idea of God that he had before. This time, however, he is concerned not so much with what might be said about God, but with what must be involved in the very concept of God, namely, that we could not even think the concept of a supreme Being unless not only did he have to be thought of as necessarily existing, but also unless he did necessarily and actually exist.

In the background is the view that existence itself is a perfection. Certainly one might challenge this, but it is not difficult to see that if God is a perfect Being, then so are all his works. We have seen how determined Descartes has been to establish this. Since whatever exists is either God, or God's work, whatever God, being perfect, could have made, it is better for him to have made than not to. Potentiality is not as perfect as actuality; parallel to

[1] My italics.

the way in which existence is more perfect than non-existence. Clearly, in this scheme of things the most perfect being will also be that which has a fuller measure of existence than anything else. And God, as the source (which we formerly argued) of all that exists, himself exists in a special sense; for since there is none other from whom he can receive his existence, or, by whom he can have been produced, he can only be an existentially autonomous Being; which is to say that he cannot be conceived as not existing. For only that which cannot exist except with help can be conceived as not getting that help, and therefore ceasing to be.

On this account it follows that if God did not exist nothing else could. And if God were not to exist, then, since as much power would be necessary to produce him as he would need in order to be what he is when not produced by anything other, only another God could produce him. It is easy to show that God, a perfect Being, (therefore the most really existing of whatever exists) cannot ever not have been, if anything at all is; and cannot ever cease to be, without it being true that he could not, after all, have been the source of his own existence. That is to say that in the case of God, essence and existence are not separable.

We may recall Descartes' insistence that the attributes of the perfect Being form a simple unity. And any interference with that unity would destroy it. But since no being could be perfect and destructible, the unity of the attributes is itself indestructible. But this implies that to know one attribute properly as an attribute of a perfect Being is to know all of them that the human mind is fitted to know. In this respect whatever is an attribute of a Being insofar as that Being is perfect is on a par with every other attribute of such a Being. In that case let us look again at the assertion that necessary existence is one of the attributes of a perfect Being. It might be said that this is not an attribute like any other, since whereas with less of the others, yet with this, the Being might be less perfect yet could still exist; without this none of the others, and therefore not even an otherwise perfect Being, could exist at all. But on Descartes' view you cannot have any of the other attributes of a perfect Being otherwise than in a Being who is entirely perfect. Therefore, no perfection of the perfect Being that makes him perfect could be possessed in isolation from the others. Thus, from Descartes' point of view, whether or not existence is or is not a predicate, necessary existence is certainly an attribute of a perfect Being and, as is the case with all the other attributes of the perfect Being, it is *no more the condition for their existence than are they for one another's.*

Hence, *if* I have an idea of a perfect Being then I have the idea of an existing perfect Being, not the idea of a perfect Being, plus also the idea of that Being's existing. We cannot properly be said to add to something what it already has. We have seen Kant argue that it does not follow from my having the idea of a perfect Being that such a Being must exist, for the idea of something's existing cannot of itself necessitate the existence of that thing. One answer to this is that if there is an idea of something the existence of which is not necessitated, that idea cannot be of a perfect Being. For suppose a being that is perfect in all things other than necessary existence. Then his existence with all his attributes is contingent. And, however perfect he might be, he surely could not be regarded as being as perfect as another being who had all the attributes of the former and also that of necessary existence. Nor could he even be regarded as equally perfect in all but this one respect. For by Descartes' definition of a perfect Being, it is impossible for any such being to have all the attributes of perfection minus one; and therefore it is impossible for such a being to have all the attributes of a perfect Being *except* the attribute of necessary existence. Thus unless necessary existence *is* an attribute of a thing, that thing cannot be a perfect Being, no matter what other attributes it has.

Not only should we give adequate weight to Descartes' repeated claim that it is impossible to think of God except as existing; it is equally important to remember his continual reminder that we cannot help thinking of God. The idea of God is not, for Descartes, something only contingently related to the fact of our existence, but on the contrary something which cannot be considered without being seen to be not simply an idea, but an idea which is the very ground of our existence, and therefore more than an idea. This insight is recovered in the consideration that on Descartes' account we cannot conceive even one of the perfections of God, if we try to conceive it in abstraction from the knowledge of its existence—its existence, that is to say, in that Being, the knowledge of which provides the ground for our recognition of the idea of God for what it is.

To return to the text of the Fifth Meditation, the point of Descartes' next example is now clear.

And we must not here object that it is in truth necessary for me to assert that God exists after having presupposed that He possesses every sort of perfection, since existence is one of these, but that as a matter of fact my original supposition was not necessary, just as it is not necessary to consider that all quadrilateral figures can be inscribed in the circle; for supposing I thought this, I should be constrained to admit that the rhombus might be inscribed in the circle since it is a quadrilateral figure, which, however, is manifestly false.

In other words, if he were to think a certain thing to be true, another thing would certainly follow from it, inescapably. Only he doesn't need to think that thing true, and indeed in the example he takes it isn't. As he says, continuing:

[We must not, I say, make any such allegations because] although it is not necessary that I should at any time entertain the notion of God, nevertheless whenever it happens that I think of a first and a sovereign Being, and, so to speak, derive the idea of Him from the storehouse of my mind, it is necessary that I should attribute to Him every sort of perfection, although I do not get so far as to enumerate them all, or to apply my mind to each one in particular. (i, 182)

At this point we get the following contrast with the geometrical example. First it wasn't necessary to think of the circle having such properties as to enable all quadrilateral figures to be inscribed in it. And secondly if we did it would be false. But in the case of God, while it is true that it isn't always necessary to think of the idea of a perfect Being, I cannot think of such a Being as non-existent. And there is also this difference: whereas there was no necessity for me ever to think of the figure in relation to the inscribing of quadilaterals inside it, or perhaps even of the figure alone, the circle, it is at least not so obvious that it is not necessary for me ever to think of God.

The awareness of someone who has thought about God may just as much include the awareness of God as necessarily existing, whenever he thinks of him, as the awareness of a mathematician may include the awareness of certain properties of a number, whenever he thinks of it. On Descartes' account, if it were not for our practical preoccupation with the senses, and if we were only to spend more time thinking about the properties of a perfect Being, and allow ourselves to consider these purely as attributes of a non-corporeal and perfect spiritual substance, we should acquire a familiarity with him akin to that which a mathematician has with a proof he has worked over many times. 'And as regards God, if my mind were not preoccupied with prejudices, and if my thought did not find itself on all hands diverted by the continual pressure of sensible things, there would be nothing which I could know more immediately and more easily than Him' (i, 183). Note the 'more immediately'.

We began this Meditation by discussing those things of which we could be as certain as we are, for instance, of geometrical properties; and we argued from this sort of example to the certainty of God's existence. Yet Descartes now seems even more certain about God's existence than about those very geometrical properties. Indeed, now he tells us that unless he has a prior knowledge of the existence of a perfect Being, no guarantee of the truth is available for *them*—his erstwhile models of objective necessity: 'For is there anything more manifest than that there is a God, that is to say, a Supreme Being, to whose essence alone existence pertains?' (i, 183). Nothing is more manifest. The truth which is the clearest and the most distinct, and even that which could be the easiest to know, which is not conditioned by any other truth, but is itself the condition of every other truth, is (what else could be?) that than which no conceivable truth *could* be more manifest.

For although I am of such a nature that as long as I understand anything very clearly and distinctly, I am naturally impelled to believe it to be true, yet because I am also of such a nature that I cannot have my mind constantly fixed on the same object in order to perceive it clearly, and as I often recollect having formed a past judgment without at the same time properly recollecting the reasons that led me to make it, it may happen meanwhile that other reasons present themselves to me, which would easily cause me to change my opinion, if I were ignorant of the facts of the existence of God, and thus I should have no true and certain knowledge, but only vague and vacillating opinions. (i, 183-4)

He seems to me to be wanting to say something very important here. If we stop at this point this will become apparent, whereas if we had continued it would have appeared from what follows as if he were only thinking about the fact that our memories may deceive us, or that our minds may be so constituted as to get things wrong for us. If God exists, then since his moral perfection is no less indubitable than his existence, he has not given us a brain to get things wrong by, or memories to take truth from us, serve us with lies, and play tricks that will confuse us into being unable to work out what is being done to us.

But when Descartes speaks of our having vague and vacillating opinions, now, as well as uncertainty as to what has gone before, one begins to understand something of the almost destructive uncertainty tormenting him. Is he not really asking for the same guarantee of the stability of the external world, as we know it through our thinking, as before he asked for our minds, or selves which likewise only a continuously creating God could sustain? Remember his argument against the proposal that we create our selves. The unity of selfhood that Descartes seems to be seeking is in a sense the unity of self-identity, but it is a unity that no self of a finite nature can, on Descartes' argument, be given by *itself*. Hence it has to rely on God for the ground of its very possibility. Here Descartes shows an almost painful sensitivity towards the nest of problems which later Fichte sought to solve by his conception of a self that acts in a sustained way according to a kind of dialectical pattern and in so doing makes consciousness possible.

However, it is conceivable that the self might be sustained by God and therefore be fit for knowledge, while the objective world doesn't itself possess that continuity of logical structure through time which permits knowledge. But on Descartes' argument this too is provided for by God, who not being a deceiver would not let us suppose that the corporeal world has properties that it hasn't. If and only if he can be sure of God, can he be sure at any time that triangles are in fact what we take ourselves to know them to be. The triangle was brought in simply to illustrate what is meant by the notion of objective necessity. But its being an illustration does not entail that our knowledge of the necessary properties of a triangle is immune to hyperbolic doubt. Only the idea of God transcends, by its own nature, our immediate apprehension. In this one case the idea by itself guarantees that the logical structure we perceive it to be holds beyond the momentary perception. It is God, not the triangle, that provides the paradigm case of objective necessitation. *Nothing* could be necessitated if God were not.

Descartes has had to suffer misunderstanding here, even by Arnauld. And since he has himself sought to correct these misunderstandings let us look briefly at the discussion between Descartes on the one side and Arnauld and the objectors in the Second Set of Objections on the other. In Meditation Five, towards the end, Descartes writes: 'For the rest, whatever proof or argument I avail myself of, we must always return to the point that it is only those things which we conceive clearly and distinctly that have the power of persuading me entirely' (i, 183). A little later:

And as regards God, if my mind were not pre-occupied with prejudices, and if my thought did not find itself on all hands diverted by the continual pressure of sensible things, there would be nothing which I could know more immediately and more easily than Him. For is there anything more manifest than that there is a God, that is to say, a Supreme Being, to whose essence alone existence pertains? (i, 183)

We see clearly and distinctly that God exists. Therefore it would be inconceivable to suppose it not true that he does. But when Descartes proceeds, it would seem that it is not, after all, the indisputable truth of clear and distinct ideas upon which his knowledge can depend, nor, therefore his knowledge of God's existence.

And although for a firm grasp of this truth I have need of a strenuous application of mind, at present I not only feel myself to be as assured of it as of all that I hold as most certain, but I also remark that the certainty of all other things depends on it so absolutely, that without this knowledge it is impossible ever to know anything perfectly. (i, 183)

Thus, if you didn't know of God's existence you couldn't trust even those clear and distinct ideas without which you cannot have any knowledge, nor, therefore a knowledge of God's existence. Now this certainly wears the formal appearance of a *petitio principii*, but an opening up of Descartes' position shows it to be anything but that, if my exposition and discussion can be taken as a guide. Arnauld states his case briefly.

The only remaining scruple I have is an uncertainty as to how a circular reasoning is to be avoided in saying: the only secure reason we have for believing that what we clearly and distinctly perceive is true, is the fact that God exists. *But we can be sure that God exists, only because we clearly and evidently perceive that; therefore prior to being certain that God exists, we should be certain that whatever we clearly and evidently perceive is true.* (ii, 92)

Since either thesis (God's existence, or the truth of clear and distinct ideas) depends upon, and only upon, the other, and neither can be known independently to be true, it emerges from Descartes' own position that each of his two most fundamental premises is, by itself, no basis for certain knowledge. Thus Arnauld.

One can reject as a premiss either that clear and distinct ideas constitute knowledge, or that God exists; and maintain in each case that the other proposition is independently true: thus, we may say that initially we cannot trust clear and distinct ideas, but we know God to exist in some other way and that his existence enables us to trust them. Or we may hold that we cannot initially trust our belief that God exists, but we can be sure that what we clearly and distinctly know to be true must be, since we find it impossible not to believe whatever we do so see—as for instance that we ourselves exist and that God does. But before we go on to consider Descartes' own reply to Arnauld we should note that though he refers Arnauld to his reply to a writer in the Second Set of Objections, that writer is not so much interested in showing that to start with either we cannot trust God to exist, or we cannot trust clear and distinct ideas to be true. He is interested in something even further back, namely, that Descartes cannot even begin his enquiry, since he cannot even know himself to be a thinking being, for this knowledge is only possible after he knows that God exists, with the consequence, for him, that his clear and distinct idea of himself as a thinking thing must be true. Thus Descartes can never get started—much less come to any such conclusion as that he has a knowledge of God, or that he has even one clear and distinct idea.

Now Descartes' reply to this suggests that the latter objector hasn't properly got the point; which is that without belief in God we cannot trust our memory—not therefore our memory that we have in fact seen clearly and distinctly what we think we have. Moreover, as we have elsewhere seen, Descartes insists that the knowledge of himself as a thinking being depends upon nothing but 'a simple act of vision' or 'a primitive act of knowledge' that rests upon nothing else, and being 'as it were a thing that is known *per se*' doesn't need to. Now this seems to me to evade an important question by what almost amounts to a diversion through making an otherwise interesting and valuable point. Is my knowledge of truths other than the existence of God also known by the same 'simple act of mental vision'? If so, then certainly God is not needed to secure them any more than he seems to be needed, on Descartes' reply, here, to secure my knowledge that I am a thinking thing. As for memory, I no less clearly and distinctly perceive that I have existed before this instant than that I am a thinking thing (and, if one thinks about it, I couldn't perceive the second without the first), or even that three is greater than two. How could I mean anything at all by such a statement if I were cognitively trapped from instant to instant? If God were needed to guarantee the possibility of memory, how could he not be necessary to guarantee the other possibilities too? Then Arnauld's argument, as well as that of the writer in the Second Set of Objections, would remain unanswered. Descartes entirely omits this problem when he replies to Arnauld:

For first, we are sure that God exists because we have attended to the proofs that established this fact; but afterwards it is enough for us to remember that we have perceived something clearly, in order to be sure that it is true; but this would not suffice, unless we knew that God existed and that he did not deceive us. (ii, 115)

One could, of course, reply to Descartes that perhaps one cannot trust one's memory of having established that God exists, or know that there is not an argument one has 'forgotten' which shows deception to be a possibility. Thus, in his selective remembering Descartes begs the question—even the easier version of the question to which he so oddly, and in my opinion unnecessarily restricts himself. For if he really meant 'For from the sole fact that God created me it is most probable that in some way he has placed his image and similitude upon me, and that I perceive this similitude (in which the idea of God is contained) by means of the same faculty by which I perceive myself etc.', why does he not use *this* as the basis for his reply? Indeed the very simplicity of the 'simple act of vision' or 'the primitive act of knowledge', although being too simple, or not complex enough, to contain error, could still not be so simple as to exclude God. For to be able to doubt that what is given is knowledge presupposes that what is given, already at the simplest, or most primitive level, makes reference, however obliquely, to the kind of knowledge, which, it has here been argued, only God could possess to put in our minds. After all, it should never be forgotten that it was in respect of our metaphysical, or our hyperbolic, doubt that Descartes felt it necessary to call in God—not just in defence of our individual memory claims. In the case of *any* single memory we can conceive what it would be to be mistaken, which of course is not to say it is equally conceivable that they all could be. But in the case of the truths that can only be doubted metaphysically we cannot conceive what it would be like to be mistaken (which is why they can only so be doubted). I raised very early in this book the question of how we can pass from ignorance to knowledge without already somehow possessing knowledge. In effect, Descartes denies that we can. God has been present all the time from the moment we began to think; and perhaps the entirety of Descartes' efforts can be said to be directed towards unearthing him. Knowledge is possible only because God is necessary. The fuller implications of this we are almost ready to examine.

There is no longer any fear of the instrument of knowledge having been diabolically warped. The hyperbolic or metaphysical doubts have been silenced. To doubt no longer makes sense, unless you can specify why one should. It is true people are mistaken, but that is only when they do not know how to distinguish true from false, when they have no method of approaching the truth, and when, perhaps above all, they have so far allowed themselves to depart from the standard of judgment that God has planted in them that their innate capacity for free choice, their free will, or, the rational exercise of their judgment has atrophied for lack of use. But this need not happen, and Descartes believes he has shown how to avoid it. As for dreams, to the objection that nothing that has been said yet helps us to distinguish between waking and dream, Descartes answers: 'But even though I slept the case would be the same, for all that is clearly present to my mind is absolutely true' (i, 184–5). If something present to the mind when asleep is clearly present to the mind in the same way as when awake, then if it is the clarity of a thing that makes it true, the truth is just as possible in a dream as when awake; and on occasion more so; for it is more likely that we get truth from a clear thing dreamt about than from a confused thought we have when awake.

We come now to a consideration as significant as anything Descartes has yet said. Expressions like 'clear and distinct ideas' abound so frequently, that they lose their freshness; and perhaps the hardest thing to do is to prevent this from happening. For there is a question at the back of all Descartes' thinking. Not: 'How can what I can clearly and distinctly see to be true be true?' but: 'How *are* clear and distinct ideas possible for a finite thinking substance?' The claim such ideas make is an *absolute* claim. Our understanding, Descartes has owned, can give us the very knowledge that God has, knowledge, that is to say, that however circumscribed in extent, is identical within the area circumscribed with that of God—from which truth it *draws* its certainty, and the impossibility of the will's doubting it. That is why Descartes recognises nothing as true that he does not also recognise as absolutely and unconditionally so.

But this sort of truth, precisely because it is absolute, presupposes the incorrigibility of its insights—which ordinary empirical experience never can give. Descartes may start by doubting the truth of information he has about the empirical world. But that is not what really worries him. For of course he knows as well as anybody that this kind of doubt presupposes knowledge in terms of which doubt is meaningful. What worries him is the reliability of the very knowledge itself out of which the vacillating, the vague, and the obscure, is built into shape. It is not merely the question whether there exists a world outside our consciousness that possesses a form of permanence; nor even simply whether we exist identically with ourselves when not thinking about ourselves, or indeed thinking at all. Nor is his worry merely whether our memories, empirically non-validatable, can be trusted. What seems to worry him, although in the Meditations this is not explicitly stated, is the question of how we can even identify our concepts, in their presentation to us, as self identical with what we take to be the previous presentation of the 'same' concepts. How, in other words, and to put it crudely, can we trust our recognition of what we know as being the same as when we knew it before? This problem applies to all knowledge. It applies to sense experience, to memories and to concepts, whether these are ideas in the subjective sense, or whether they are 'universals' in Plato's sense.

Thus, insofar as logic itself depends upon the continuity of the terms with which it deals, if we are mistaken, then though the form of logical argument be the schema of a possible truth-finding process, or truth-explicating process, it can never be known for certain to be more than that. As for the form of logical or mathematical argument itself, true we cannot but admit its validity when we clearly and distinctly apprehend it, but its claims go far beyond any possible experience, for we take it to be true not only when seen to be, but always and forever, whether seen or not. And we suppose in this not only that what we see is true within the four corners of our consciousness, but outside it. In this sense, indeed, we claim a knowledge that exceeds and stretches still further beyond the confines of any consciousness *we* could possibly envisage. In other words knowledge necessarily makes infinite claims, even when it is the knowledge of a finite thinking substance. And from within its own resources, by the very nature of its limited mode of existence, no validation on this level is even conceivable.

At this point it is clear what Descartes means when in Meditation Four he brackets natural knowledge with Divine grace. Here too he has been discussing the limitations of 'the faculty of comprehension', which is 'of very small extent and extremely limited'. What Descartes wants to say is that logical argument itself claims to be true independently of any actual argument (used or apprehended) exactly as a concept claims to be the same in a multiplicity of instances. Let us look again at Descartes' words:

Thus, for example, when I consider the nature of a [rectilinear] triangle, I who have some little knowledge of the principles of geometry recognise quite clearly that the three angles are equal to two right angles, and it is not possible for me not to believe this so long as I apply my mind to its demonstration; but so soon as I abstain from attending to the proof, although I still recollect having clearly comprehended it, it may easily occur that I come to doubt its truth, if I am ignorant of there being a God. For I can persude myself of having been so constituted by nature that I can easily deceive myself even in those matters which I believe myself to apprehend with the greatest evidence and certainty, especially when I recollect that I have frequently judged matters to be true and certain which other reasons have afterwards impelled me to judge to be altogether false. (i, 184)

The mere feeling of certainty is, as he has told us before, worthless. And I can persuade myself of having been so constituted by nature, because it is not logically impossible that I should have been. This is a point we have discussed in the chapter on Meditation Four. But the main point arising from this quotation is that Descartes is aware all the time of the claims of knowledge to apply beyond the sphere of any individual occasion of knowing. It is precisely this claim that gives unity to all our knowledge and precisely this claim is what he does not know how to answer except by an appeal to God.

Now if one is mistaken on this level, the level of hyperbolic doubt, one cannot be blamed. One deceives oneself by believing that what one sees clearly and distinctly to be true must be as true when one does not clearly and distinctly see it as when one does. This is a double deception on God's part, since we are deceived and at the same time suppose to ourselves that in this very respect we could not be. If God does not deceive us, we are not deceived. And if we are not deceived we are not self-deceived. And if we are not self-deceived then what appears to us to be the case when we see clearly and distinctly, *is* the case. And the question of whether we are dreaming or awake when we see something clearly and distinctly to be so is irrelevant to the question of truth. And this is the thinking behind the claim 'But even though I slept the case would be the same, for all that is clearly present to my mind is absolutely true.'

The justice of this view of what Descartes is here trying to do is perhaps borne out by the following:

But after I have recognised that there is a God—because at the same time I have also recognised that all things depend upon Him, and that He is not a deceiver, and from that have inferred that what I perceive clearly and distinctly cannot fail to be true—although I no longer pay attention to the reasons for which I have judged this to be true, provided that I recollect having clearly and distinctly perceived it no contrary reason can be brought forward which could ever cause me to doubt of its truth; and thus I have a true and certain knowledge of it. (i, 184)

There is, however, among all the things that I clearly and distinctly perceive to be true, one thing that stands in a special relation to all others. Once I have seen this to be true, I know it to be true independently of myself, in a way that is not quite similar to the others. For this is the knowledge of God. What I know of God can be seen by its nature to hold even when I do not think of it, or, to put it another way, God exists as what I apprehend him to be when I think of him, even when I am not thinking of him, or indeed of anything else at all. Thus he is clearly in a position, should he wish (and what perfect Being could wish otherwise?) to maintain that unity of my conceptual thinking, without which no world, or self, or human experience of any kind, would be possible.

Thus, those other truths which I apprehend, deductively or intuitively, are all of them dependent for their objectivity, or, one might also say, for their formal reality, upon God, who, necessarily existing, depends upon nothing other than himself. It is God who not only makes the world possible, but also makes intelligibility itself so. In this sense, though Descartes doesn't actually say so in the Meditations, *God* is the light of nature. *I could not possibly see anything at all as necessarily true if it were not for God sustaining, as well as everything else, that necessity.* If it were not for God, therefore, there could be no light of nature, no certainty of anything, no truth, and indeed nothing. And the difference between the light of nature and the teaching of nature, about which much will be said in the next chapter, may here, perhaps usefully, be summarised as follows. The connections we know through the teaching of nature are those which have been stamped in by practice because they have enabled us to survive; those we know through the light of nature are those which are revealed to us by a disposition of divine grace. We might not care to hear this kind of talk, but there is no reason to doubt that Descartes meant what he said:

And so I very clearly recognise that the certainty and truth of all knowledge depends alone on the knowledge of the true God, in so much that, before I knew Him, I could not have a perfect knowledge of any other thing. And now that I know Him I have the means of acquiring a perfect knowledge of an infinitude of things, not only of those which relate to God Himself and other intellectual matters, but also of those which pertain to corporeal nature in so far as it is the object of pure mathematics [which have no concern with whether it exists or not]. (i, 185)

This is the position Descartes has been struggling to establish for five Meditations. He has established the possibility of knowledge; it remains now for him to establish the existence of corporeal *objects*, and thereby the possibility of knowledge not merely of necessary truths, but also of those objects.

CHAPTER SIX

IN MEDITATION TWO Descartes had argued that mind is more easily known than body. The basis of the distinction between what is more and what is less easily known is not psychological, but epistemic. One is known indubitably; the other, however well known, is not known indubitably. Thus we begin with an epistemic and not simply an ontological dualism. Whatever material things may be, they can never be known to exist, or even be as purported, with the certainty minds are. Yet we cannot on that account dismiss them; something, at least, is problematic as to its nature in a way that minds are not, and is, therefore, that from which minds through meditation need to learn how to detach themselves. Descartes has shown, as he promised, that the soul is prior at least in the sense that what we most certainly and easily can know ourselves to be are souls, not bodies. He has now to show that despite this difference in epistemic status, bodies can also be shown to exist. He will then be in a better position to show that body is utterly unlike mind.

He could not claim knowledge of this in the Second Meditation, mainly because he could not be certain that in matters other than his own existence he was not being deceived. It required, as we have seen, three further Meditations to lay the foundations for his enquiry into 'whether material things exist'. Moreover, in Meditation Two, as he pointed out, he had not yet learned enough about the mind to be able to be certain of what could not be mind; which would not, of course, be the same as being certain of all that *is* in his mind. He never claims to know this, or that even if he could, he, a finite substance, could know that he did. But he does claim to have discovered what cannot be an essential part of his mind. And when he has examined the things he calls material things, he believes he can tell from their nature that they cannot be spiritual substances. As we shall see, not one of these claims went unchallenged, even in his own lifetime.

In certain respects what purport to be material things are capable of description in mathematical terms, that is, on Descartes' account, clearly and distinctly. In those respects, therefore, the existence of material things is at least possible. On the other hand, the truths mirrored in clear and distinct ideas are not possible truths, but necessary ones. That is certainly how Descartes saw 'pure mathematics'. For whatever he sees clearly and distinctly to be true, cannot be false. And now that he knows God exists, he knows that what we perceive clearly and distinctly to be true of anything must in fact hold of that thing's nature. Thus, we might prompt, if thought points to something beyond thought to a world of corporeal things, such a world must exist. But of course it doesn't follow from this that the same thought must also point to the precise *nature* of that world of corporeal things— or indeed that by the light of reason it ever can. Now, says Descartes,

the faculty of imagination which I possess, and of which, experience tells me, I make use when I apply myself to the consideration of material things, is capable of persuading me of their existence; for when I attentively consider what imagination is, I find that it is nothing but a certain application of the faculty of knowledge to the body which is immediately present to it, and which therefore exists. (i, 185)

It is a 'certain' application—a kind of knowing. The kind in which knowledge is turned outward from the mind to something else. This is the case in which we understand the object known, or understood, not to be simply part of an exercise of thought, and therefore not pointing beyond thought activity, but to be something of a quite different nature, and indeed that to which thought activity points. Something here acts like thought; it knows, but what it knows is so different from itself that only a contingent relation can hold between them.

Obviously Descartes must show the difference between the kind of knowledge which makes no such external reference, and the kind that does. For the latter in a way has the harder job to do, and yet seems to lack equivalent credentials. For the moment, Descartes is concerned less with the difference in the kind of object than with the difference between the kind of activity constituting knowledge. The kind of activity that makes sense without having to refer (even by similarity) to anything beyond the thinking mind itself, Descartes calls pure intellection, or conception: the kind that does not make sense without that kind of reference, he calls imagination. Sometimes we can both conceive and imagine the 'same' thing at the same time, as for instance a triangle, or pentagon. But at other times we cannot. We cannot, for instance imagine such figures as the chiliagon, though we can obviously think them. Thus some figures can be thought but not imagined (though the converse, of course, does not hold). Therefore, pure intellection is an activity independent of imagination. That imagination is (or involves) an activity other than intellection is brought out by pointing to one common factor which applies to triangle and pentagon, namely that they are viewed 'as present' with the 'eyes of the mind', or the 'power and inward vision of the mind'. In other words, by an activity which results in their being present analogously to the way they are in sensible experience. This explains Descartes' apparently glib step: 'And I easily conceive that if some body exists with which my mind is conjoined and united in such a way that it can apply itself to consider it when it pleases, it may be that by this means it can imagine corporeal objects.' The latter, if they exist, are causally related to the body with which my mind is conjoined, and through it alone (as Descartes, like Spinoza, maintains) can become known to the mind with which the body is conjoined. The power to imagine is analogous to the power to perceive through the senses, whereas the power of pure intellection bears no analogy whatsoever to sense perception, as is shown by its concern with matters which could never be understood, or clarified, by sense perception. Referring to the imagination, Descartes continues:

so that this mode of thinking differs from pure intellection only inasmuch as mind in its intellectual activity in some manner turns on itself, and considers some of the ideas which it possesses in itself; while in imagining it turns towards the body, and there beholds in it something conformable to the idea which it has either conceived of itself or perceived by the senses. I easily understand, I say, that the imagination could be thus constituted if it is true that body exists; and because I can discover no other convenient mode of explaining it, I conjecture with probability that body does exist; but this is only with probability, and although I examine all things with care, I nevertheless do not find that from this distinct idea of corporeal nature, which I have in my imagination, I can derive any argument from which there will necessarily be deduced the existence of body. (i, 186–7)

In other words, from the clear and distinct ideas of corporeal nature, which Descartes regards as the object of pure mathematics, and which he cannot doubt to be true, he cannot with equal indubitability deduce the existence of actual corporeal bodies. He can only see how, if they exist, the imagination is the faculty which is fitted to cope with them. Moreover, there is no doubt that the imagination, regarded as a faculty, is not part of the mind's essence. For Descartes can conceive himself as a purely conceiving, yet not imagining, being. He doesn't need to exercise the inward vision in order to think. His range and power of thought is vastly greater than it, as we saw. Therefore he can conceive himself not merely without it (which would be enough, he has argued, for him so to have been created) but as all the more comprehending for that.

But if the power of imagination is not part of the essence of thinking substance, what is it part of? It is not necessary to be able to answer this question here, but merely to observe that whereas pure intellection could not by itself relate him to something of another nature than his own (something with a different essence), imagination has at least the property of being related to something other than his mind as well as to it—since of course it is also true, as we saw, that we cannot imagine without also understanding what we imagine; and understanding as such is, for Descartes, a peculiarly pure activity of the mind. All that this shows, however, is not that there are material things, but another reason why, if there were, the imagination would be the natural bridge between them and mind.

Descartes next reminds us that he has, so far, been trying to get a proof of the material world only from an analysis of that corporeal nature which is the object of 'pure mathematics'. Even when he spoke of 'body which is immediately present' he had been thinking of body only within a mathematical frame of reference. Now he turns to the world as known through our senses.

But I am in the habit of imagining many other things besides this corporeal nature which is the object of pure mathematics, to wit, the colours, sounds, scents, pain, and other such things, although less distinctly. And inasmuch as I perceive these things much better through the senses, by the medium of which, and by the memory, they seem to have reached my imagination, I believe that, in order to examine them more conveniently, it is right that I should at the same time investigate the nature of sense perception, and that I should see if from the ideas which I apprehend by this mode of thought, which I call feeling, I cannot derive some certain proof of the existence of corporeal objects. (i, 187)

Now that he no longer fears deception he seems to adopt an almost naive realist position. He knows himself to perceive things 'much better' through the senses than by imagination, since after all through them they reach the imagination. Therefore why not go straight to the senses? From his idea of corporeal nature he cannot derive material objects; and he is not in a position to say that he knows material objects much better than he does those ideas; for without sense activity he could have no experience of material objects.

But if he is not being deceived now, neither could he have been before he had proved God to exist. Yet he did then find it possible to doubt. And though he could sometimes resolve those doubts on the non-philosophical level, on occasion he could not. But even when doubts could be thus resolved, they could never be completely resolved until he knew God to exist. What he now wants to do is to re-examine the situation from which doubts arise. For now, since he knows God to exist, he knows that when he has every reason to believe that a doubt is no longer possible, it isn't; for the power of thought, and its claim to know is validated in the validation of God's existence. From conception he finds (as Kant was to find later in his argument *against* Descartes' version of the Ontological Proof) he can derive no certain knowledge of material things. He returns then to the scene of his earliest doubts, for he is convinced that since God exists (and indeed even *though* God exists) if sense perception cannot assure him that material things exist, nothing can. But it is necessary to notice here that he will be concerned with the widest possible sense of 'sense perception', that in which he also calls it 'feeling'. This is important in his analysis because he is not going to argue only from external sense, but also from internal sense, and even from the kind of feelings which appear to lack location, as for instance emotions—at least the subtler ones.

First of all, then, I perceived that I had a head, hands, feet, and all other members of which this body—which I considered as a part, or possibly even as the whole, of myself—is composed. Further I was sensible that this body was placed amidst many others, from which it was capable of being affected in many different ways, beneficial and hurtful, and I remarked that a certain feeling of pleasure accompanied those that were beneficial, and pain those which were harmful. And in addition to this pleasure and pain, I also experienced hunger, thirst, and other similar appetites, as also certain corporeal inclinations towards joy, sadness, anger, and other similar passions. And outside myself, in addition to extension, figure, and motions of bodies, I remarked in them hardness, heat, and all other tactile qualities, and, further, light and colour, and scents and sounds, the variety of which gave me the means of distinguishing the sky, the earth, the sea, and generally all the other bodies, one from the other. And certainly, considering the ideas of all these qualities which presented themselves to my mind, and which alone I perceived properly or immediately, it was not without reason that I believed myself to perceive objects quite different from my thought, to wit, bodies from which those ideas proceeded; for I found by experience that these ideas presented themselves to me without my consent being requisite, so that I could not perceive any object, however desirous I might be, unless it were present to the organs of sense; and it was not in my power not to perceive it, when it was present. And because the ideas which I received through the senses were much more lively, more clear, and even, in their own way, more distinct than any of those which I could of myself frame in meditation, or than those I found impressed on my memory, it appeared as though they could not have proceeded from my mind, so that they must necessarily have been produced in me by some other things. And having no knowledge of those objects excepting the knowledge which the ideas themselves gave me, nothing was more likely to occur to my mind than that the objects were similar to the ideas which were caused. And because I likewise remembered that I had formerly made use of my senses rather than my reason, and recognised that the ideas which I formed of myself were not so distinct as those which I perceived through the senses, and that they were most frequently even composed of portions of these last, I persuaded myself easily that I had no idea in my mind which had not formerly come to me through the senses. Nor was it without some reason that I believed that this body (which by a certain special right I call my own) belonged to me more properly and more strictly than any other; for in fact I could never be separated from it as from other bodies; I experienced in it and on account of it all my appetites and affections, and finally I was touched by the feeling of pain and the titillation of pleasure in its parts, and not in the parts of other bodies which were separated from it. (i, 187–8)

He does offer certain explanations here for what he takes to be characterising features of material objects. They are regarded as independent of our minds because we experience them as independent of our wills, but dependent upon an objective causal order. This constitutes their objectivity. Their causal conditions (rather than causal relations) likewise contribute to the sense of their objective independence, inasmuch as they appear more lively, vivid, and distinct than the images and memories which I myself am capable of conjuring; hence, since I cannot have produced them, something else must. As for our judgment of what kinds of things material objects are, this depends entirely upon the fact that where we have no independent knowledge of a cause we attribute to it the characteristics of its known effects. All this amounts to so far is that this is how we come to believe that material objects exist: on this basis, certainly one could have no certainty that material objects exist.

And once more, as in Meditation Two, Descartes is obsessed by the incredible spectacle of the more dubious (and therefore the less real) corporeal world appearing to us more real than the indubitable (and therefore the more real) finite spiritual substance that knows it. Again the explanation is causal; we begin to use our senses before we do our reason; and by longer use, and greater frequency (not to speak of an initially greater usefulness and interest value) our feeling so monopolises our field of consciousness that we are unable, without practice, to exclude it from our attention when we seek to consider our own selves. My very idea of my self is shrouded by sense experiences, and is 'most frequently even composed of portions of these last'. The concept of the 'self' as housing in some entirely unintelligible manner what only makes sense when considered as a modification of extended substance is not a concept of the self at all. The self, in its essential nature, is to be grasped only by intellection. You can think of the self, but not imagine it, for whatever is imagined is meaningless as applied to mind: the application, for instance, of one form of imaginative activity, namely geometry, to spiritual activity of the sort that Descartes takes to constitute the self, is inconceivable; whereas its application to extended substance could not be more obvious. One characteristic of extended substance, if it exists, is that it should in principle be capable of being known, not that it should be capable of knowing. One characteristic of mind, on the other hand, is that it should be capable of knowing extended substance, not that it should be capable of being known by it. And however odd this kind of dispensation may seem, it is made even odder, where in order to fathom the mechanics of its possibility, assumptions are made which require that thought and extension each partake of attributes of the other, or enter into relations intended to explain the interaction between them, but which in fact are incomprehensible to thought, even if not to imagination. The one thing Descartes is sure of is that the mind-body problem cannot be solved on the level of the imagination, nor, therefore, by reference to the way ordinary language takes account of it. But in the stage at which Descartes is considering man's knowledge of the self, the spiritual nature of the latter is still obscured by the senses which can be driven off only by pure thought.

Even at this stage, however, we have learned to distinguish our own body from surrounding ones. This point has to be made because Descartes is going to argue that we can only know about other bodies through our own, just as we can only know about our own through one very highly specialised part of it. In certain respects we perceive our own body exactly as we perceive others, though obviously, for a variety of reasons that do not concern us here, we are limited in regard to how much of it is open to our direct inspection. But no doubt in principle we perhaps could see our entire body, just as we could any other. The first respect in which the difference shows is, as Descartes tells us, that our own body is the only one from which we cannot escape. But of course this is not enough. No doubt one could graft something on to a person at birth, so that he could not be separated from it without an operation. And it might even be so grafted that an operation for removal would kill him. That would surely still not be part of him, even if it possessed some function, provided he had no feeling in it, and no control over it. There is clearly a difference between something's being grafted on to one's body, and something's being an organic part of one's body. And it is not that we cannot be separated from it, but rather that we experience in association with it the sensations, pleasurable and painful, and the power of control which place us in a very special relation with our own bodies. Wherever something is so related to our body, I see no reason why it should not be regarded as an organic part of it, even though it has no genetic basis in us.

Yet the very sensations by means of which we identify ourselves with the body from which we cannot be separated lack what would be required for them to be part of a system of knowledge. Not only do they themselves lack clarity and distinctness, as we saw earlier, but their relations with each other and with bodies on the one side, and emotions on the other are all contingent. (We might distinguish emotions as mental feelings from sensations as bodily feelings.) So, therefore, are the relations between mental feelings and the perception of material objects that are known to cause pain, or, let us say, pleasure, as the case may be. And if this entire field is that of contingency, then upon what sure foundation can Descartes base the claim that material things exist? For between the self and material things every feeling that would appear to suggest to a mind that a world of material objects exists can be shown to command no rational authority for making that suggestion. All we know here we have learned from nature, as we shall see, and not from the light of nature. Thus it is not difficult to see that the picture of his world that Descartes had formed before ever starting to reflect was in no way built to withstand the assaults by doubt to which he began systematically, later, to subject it.

I find Descartes' opening attack, therefore, embarrassingly feeble:

But afterwards many experiences little by little destroyed all the faith which I had rested in my senses; for I from time to time observed that those towers which from afar appeared to me to be round, more closely observed seemed square . . . and so in an infinitude of other cases I found error in judgments founded on the external senses. (i, 189)

Obviously if he cannot trust his senses under optimum conditions (and one has no right to complain about the 'senses' having let one down if one uses them foolishly), then he cannot *know* himself to be in error. And although, in these conditions, he may still lack knowledge, his trouble isn't that he can't trust his senses, but that he doesn't *know* whether he can or not—quite another matter.

As to the internal senses, Descartes, speaking of error, says:

And not only in those founded on the external senses, but even in those founded on the internal as well; for is there anything more intimate or more internal than pain? And yet I have learned from some persons whose arms or legs have been cut off, that they sometimes seemed to feel pain in the part which had been amputated, which made me think that I could not be quite certain that it was a certain member which pained me, even although I felt pain in it. (i, 189)

I would point out, all the same, that there could be less illusion even here than Descartes thinks. The owners of phantom limbs do not suppose they don't feel pain. The pain is in them and not in the limb, for the limb is not there. But what does that prove? Certainly not that the pain is not in the limb when the limb *is* there. In one sense the pain is always in the person and never in the limb. For if the pain is in the limb and you cut the limb off you should get rid of the pain. Therefore in that sense the pain is always in the person. Which sense? In the sense that the pain is felt *by* the person *in* the limb, and not, for instance, *by* the limb itself. If it were, how could the *person* know it? The time to become alarmed is when one feels pain in some part of space one was never connected with. In the case above, at least one did have a limb there once. One is still connected with the space where that limb would have been, as any physiologist under-stands, and as Descartes himself understood well enough, as we shall see later in this Meditation. As he himself also pointed out, we don't feel pain in other people's bodies; or, for instance, in any part of space with which no limb of our own could have been causally connected at the time of the pain's being felt. Consider our reaction if we felt a pain a mile away from where our body is located, and then found that as we moved away from the point where the pain was felt, the point moved along with us. Phantom limbs are limbs that we know not to exist. But if we did have limbs where we now only have phantom limbs, then, where we now have real pain in our phantom limbs, we should instead have real pain in our real limbs. Only of course the pain itself might be due to now not having the limb; and that pain we logically could not have if we had a real limb. Finally, a man who looks at the space where his toes would have been if his leg had not been amputated and says that he has a pain in those toes that he knows himself now not to have, is not under any illusions whatsoever. He is simply not finding it easy to describe his condition—as we should expect. However little illusion Descartes has succeeded in finding in connection with external sense, I conclude that he has found considerably less in connection with internal sense.

Descartes now returns to the main attack. His chief concern is still with the existential import of 'material things', and he follows his usual pattern. On the one hand we show something we believed true to be false; on the other we examine why, since it must have been false all the time, we ever did believe it. Now in fact Descartes has performed both of these operations, but intends now to generalise the latter:

And as to the grounds on which I was formerly persuaded of the truth of sensible objects, I had not much trouble in replying to them. For since nature seemed to cause me to lean towards many things from which reason repelled me, I did not believe that I should trust much to the teachings of nature.

Of the reasons he had given for his believing in material things, he now mentions just the first, though he has shown himself capable of dealing as adequately as Hume with the second.

And although the ideas which I receive by the senses do not depend on my will, I did not think that one should for that reason conclude that they proceeded from things different from myself, since possibly some faculty might be discovered in me—though hitherto unknown to me—which produced them. (i, 189)

Since Descartes is not yet in a position to discount this possibility, he cannot know it is not the case. But he soon will. He will argue, in effect, that no faculty, the function of which is to produce ideas which are (as ideas of sensible objects are) of an intrinsically dubitable nature, can be part of the self, whose essence is to think, and whose existence and essence have been demonstrated to be as indubitable, for Descartes, as the knowledge of God.

At this point, then, he has, for the last time worked himself into the position of doubting again whatever cannot be demonstrated by the light of nature, including the existence of material things. The senses have easily been shown to fail to demonstrate the existence of an external world—more easily, even, than imagination was. The long haul back starts.

But now that I begin to know myself better, and to discover more clearly the author of my being, I do not in truth think that I should rashly admit all the matters which the senses seem to teach us, but, on the other hand, I do not think that I should doubt them all universally. (i, 189–90)

What he knows is that only clear and distinct perceptions are true, but that only a substance whose essence is solely to think can have such perceptions, i.e. knowledge.

Descartes set out, as he said, to 'recall to my memory those matters which I hitherto held to be true, as having perceived them through the senses, and the foundations on which my belief has rested . . . examine the reasons which have since obliged me to place them in doubt . . . consider which of them I must now believe' (i, 187). It is with the last that we now concern ourselves. Having proved that God (infinitely non-deceiving) exists, and that we need have no further concern with the possibility that things, selves, and thoughts, possess only a fugitive being, totally unrelated from glimpse to glimpse, except in our nature-inculcated habits of apprehending them, the metaphysical doubt that has haunted Descartes is formally dispelled. This, however, is not a signal for universal credulity. What has been shown is that not everything is false, not that everything is true. All we know now is that truth is attainable, not that we attain it whenever we think so; and this consideration places a new emphasis on the importance of finding the right way to make sure that what you think true is so, or that what you don't know to be true, you can by an unimpeachable method investigate. Verification, from now on, need only be empirical. It is no longer a case of disbelieving whatever it is not impossible should be false, but of asking oneself whether one has particular grounds for doubting. It must now make *sense* to doubt, for the *malin génie* lies dead. But from now on doubt is not acceptable unless the doubter does have such grounds. Doubting is now only a matter of suspending assent until you have investigated the question. Doubt, that is, has become a positive thing. It is now a reason for experimenting, or for searching, or for whatever else it is reasonable to suppose can settle the doubt. The suspect person now is the man who purports to be doubting though he can give no reason why he should, or no account of any meaningful alternative. For if he cannot, he merely suspects something is wrong but cannot explain why, or point to a single thing that he finds disturbing, or give a reason for thinking any alternative account better. Though possibly right, he is not entitled to expect that until he is proved right we must accept his judgment that something, since it *may* be false, should be treated *as* false.

Descartes now repeats his claim that whatever he can clearly and distinctly apprehend is true, together with his new argument that whatever he can clearly and distinctly conceive as separate, God can create so. If I can think of something in isolation, it is because it is separate as the particular thing it is, even within a complex. Its separate existence is not logically inconceivable, and therefore, since what is possible God can make actual, it is within the power of God to actualise this too. Descartes now states the classical case for dualism, drawing together the threads of various arguments that must by now be old friends.

and, therefore, just because I know certainly that I exist, and that meanwhile I do not remark that any other thing necessarily pertains to my nature or essence, excepting that I am a thinking thing, I rightly conclude that my essence consists solely in the fact that I am a thinking thing [or a substance whose whole essence or nature is to think]. And although possibly (or rather certainly, as I shall say in a moment) I possess a body with which I am very intimately conjoined, yet because, on the one side, I have a clear and distinct idea of myself inasmuch as I am only a thinking and unextended thing, and as, on the other, I possess a distinct idea of body, inasmuch as it is only an extended and unthinking thing, it is certain that this I [that is to say, my soul by which I am what I am], is entirely and absolutely distinct from my body, and can exist without it. (i, 190)

Let us recount. I exist, I am a thinking thing, nothing else is essential to me for my independence, this independence is clearly and distinctly known to me, and it is known to exclude body;

and since, also, body is known to exclude from itself what thinks (could you *see* a brain think?) I could exist independently of the entire universe of extended substance if God should will it. This mightn't exactly be somebody's dream of immortal bliss, but the implications are evident. Immortality is possible. At least, God could make it so. At any rate if we grant that the thinking substance is no less real than extended substance, i.e., not dependent upon the latter for anything of its own nature, then nothing that can happen to the body can in any way affect what is essential to the mind's remaining what it essentially is. Therefore nothing that happens to the body can destroy, or otherwise damage mind insofar as it is essentially mind; just as, one would suppose, nothing that goes on in a mind can as such make any difference to what goes on in a body.

The position we have just been considering is perhaps something of an 'ideal type' of dualist position. Descartes has made it easy for himself so far, because he has been considering thinking substance only insofar as it is purely so, i.e. an intellecting thing. But if it were to have an existence removed from material things, what could it intellect, except, presumably its own intellecting of itself, or whatever infinite series of intellectings are open to it? It is not easy to see, be it said, what such a mode of existence would be like. In this condition, what possible difference could there be between one finite spiritual substance and another? We would all be only too equal before God in our state of frozen loneliness.

In order to establish that body and mind are different, Descartes, as we have seen, considers mind or self at this point in the present meditation, as intellect only—thinking being to the self what attribute is to substance. The essence of thinking substance is to think, i.e. in the sense of intellection, and nothing else at all. Without intellection there is no self. There is not, in addition to thinking, a kind of cloudy extended substance in which the intellection inheres. In a self there is no non-thinking substance. To say that the self thinks is not to say that there is something, and that that something (an in itself non-thinking something) thinks. What thinks? I do. What am I? A thinker. But a thinker is only a thinker insofar as he thinks. Stop thinking and you stop being a self. The self stops. This self, however, is also a finite self. And this bothers me. For I do not see how a *pure* thinking being can be finite. How can pure intellection limit pure intellection? And if it can't, and if there is not, by definition, anything else to limit it, there cannot be a limit at all.

But there is also extended substance, and somehow thinking substance *knows* extended substance. It is as simple as that. But how? So we come back to imagination, and to sense perception. Though, in trying to keep his spiritual substance pure, Descartes disowns imagination and sense perception, when he has to explain how one substance knows another he claims them back. They are, both of them, now definitely identified as modes of thinking substance. The argument for this is surprisingly simple. That they are not essential attributes of the self is clear, we remember, from the fact that the self is possible without them. But they are not possible without it. Imagination and sense perception can only take place in a being that thinks. Therefore they are modes of thinking, but modes that relate to extended substance. They are, to thinking, what figure or number is to extension. One might even hold that just as number and figure may be regarded as modes of extension that point to thought, so imagination and sense perception may be regarded as modes of thought that point to extension. Certainly, without imagination and sense perception there could be thinking, but no knowledge of extended substances; without figure and number and the other formal properties of extended substance the latter could not be known by a self with even the most perfect imagination and sense perception.

At this point, Descartes' position is haunted by the ambiguity of his expressions 'think' and 'self'. Before Descartes has resolved his hyperbolic doubts, he knows only that he is a thinking thing. His essence, as we have seen, cannot be anything more than his power of intellection, for only in the exercise of that power does he remain within the realm of the indubitable. He does find it impossible to doubt that he *seems* to imagine, sense-perceive, and so on. But all these ideas lack the coherence of knowledge. He seems to have a body, but to know this is to know something only about himself, as for instance that he is a person who can only regard himself as seeming to know, in other words, as one who doubts, or, as he has already said, a thinking thing.

This, however, is not knowledge about anything other than himself. Yet when Descartes accepts that there is a world of material things, including his own body, he would appear to be laying claim to know that mind though he be, he is also closely conjoined with a special material body—his body. But he cannot know this merely by intellection. Therefore his nature is seen as comprehending the very real power of imagination, sense perception, and feeling. Thus thinking is no longer merely intellection, but also whatever other activities are required for him to know himself not merely as a purely thinking essence, but as a man. Descartes the man may also be regarded as essentially a thinking being. But 'thinking' is now co-extensive with all exercise of whatever faculties enable us to know ourselves as men.

The question, however, is: What is it that thinks? Descartes says he is a thinking thing, and that this is indubitable. It does not, however, follow that because it is indubitable that he is a thinking thing, it is equally indubitable that the thing that thinks is necessarily different from that which is extended. A materialist has no difficulty in conceiving that a brain thinks; indeed that, he would say, is precisely what its function is. Only the self does not know itself to be a brain, i.e. does not know its brain to think, in the way it knows itself to. This is not simply the point that the brain is a material thing and is therefore not properly known to exist, as, for instance, the self is. For even if we could know the brain to exist, indubitably, (and since we cannot conceive this to be so except by hypothesis let us adopt that hypothesis) we could not know ourselves as being the brain that thinks, as we do know ourselves as that which thinks. Firstly, we might be said to know that a brain can think—at least in the sense of its being a necessary condition, as far as we know, that there be a brain, before anyone is known to think, in the way we, as external observers, believe them to. But we cannot be said to have that knowledge of the brain thinking that we have of ourselves thinking. From the subject's point of view, not only can we not think of ourselves as being brains (a meaningless proposition), but neither can we think of brains as thinking (another meaningless proposition). On the other hand, it would be strange to suppose that I, a thinking thing, at least, (as I know myself to be) should know better what is not myself, than what is. But it would be stranger still for me not to know myself at all. Yet if I am a brain, or any kind of physical object, what would it be for me to know this? Especially what would it be for me to know this thing, not merely as something I know, but as my *self*? But above all, Descartes has argued that I cannot doubt my own existence; that is to say, that when I try to do this, by thinking, I fail. But since, on his view, we do have to depend upon the goodness of God to know that things other than the self exist; and as when we say we know ourselves to exist we do not even mean the brain (or body); and since, also, we can at some point doubt the existence of any corporeal thing, we cannot be a corporeal thing, since we cannot be that which we can doubt. For I know the difference between being aware of my body and being aware of myself. For one thing I cannot, on Descartes' account, be aware of my body without also being aware of my self; but I can be aware of myself, as when engaged in pure intellectional activity, without being also aware of my body. Hence, whatever else I may be, I cannot be a body.

Descartes' position, to sum up part of it, is this: he clearly and distinctly perceives that his essence is to think. He can clearly and distinctly think of himself with no other attribute. He cannot think of himself at all as extended substance. He no more knows what it would be for him to be extended, than what it would be like for an extended thing, whatever its form of organisation, to think. Why does he bother to call himself a substance at all, seeing that he knows nothing more about himself than that he thinks? Something thinks. How does he know? Because *he* is that something. But he is not aware of himself as a substance in any other sense than that in which it might be said that whatever can actually exist, is something essentially different from what can only be an object of thought. He can, certainly, form the concept 'self'—or perhaps we should say *a* concept. In this sense abstractions presuppose an abstracter, and thoughts a thinker. One might put it this way: if there is an experience of any kind, whether of a material thing, or of the abstractest possible concept, then something exists, namely that for which these are what they are, and which perhaps even produces them. And that is why Descartes cannot escape calling himself a substance. This has nothing to do, in my opinion, with identity or continuity through time. The question of how long a substance lasts is not something to be determined by it, but, on Descartes' view, by God.

Now what can it mean to insist, as Gassendi and others do,

that when Descartes thinks of himself as a thinking substance, he cannot know that this substance is not a material body? Not only has he no reason to think he is; he cannot even make sense of the words 'thinking material substance', as for instance he can of the words 'a material thing moves, or is divisible, or is so and so far from another material thing'. To choose examples less favourable to Descartes, can we give sense to 'a material thing is hot, is red, stinks (which makes a less ambiguous point than 'smells')'? Yes, because in each case we think of someone for whom it is or does these things. Now suppose I said that X, a material object, smells; not would smell if anyone smelled it, but smells. The immediate reaction is now to interpret 'X smells' as a description of an activity, namely, a smelling activity being engaged in by X. Now I maintain that there is only one way of making sense of this, and that is by regarding X forthwith as the outward expression of that which (perhaps by means of that very outward expression) has the smelling experience. I can make sense of a material object *reacting* to a smell, or recording it in some perceptible form, since for this there are possible explanations; but not if the reaction is one of smelling, where, by smelling, I mean that an experience is being had such as that which I have when I would describe myself as smelling X (as distinct, let us say, from sniffing at it). In other words, in order to make sense of the words 'X smells' under the conditions I have just described, we are *compelled* to introduce into the situation a subjective element—a self. For Descartes, the man who says it is his body that thinks can give no meaning to these words; and if the man goes so far as to add that he *is* his body, so that walking and thinking are equally done by him, he continues to be uninformative. According to Descartes, it is not, strictly speaking, the self that walks, any more than it is the body that thinks. And should it be urged, nevertheless, that it is at least possible, Descartes would surely reply with the words he uses in his letter to Clerselier:

Hence it is the most absurd and extravagant error that a philosopher can commit, to wish to make judgments which have no relation to his perception of things. Yet I fail to see how my critic can avoid the censure of having fallen into this error, in the greater part of his objections; for he does not wish each individual to stand firmly by his own perceptions, but claims that we should rather believe the opinions or fancies he pleases to set before us, though we wholly fail to grasp them as perceptions. (ii, 129)

Descartes is still the supreme empiricist, but with it he combines the fearless rationalism which had never forgotten not to believe what cannot be clearly and distinctly perceived to be true. And perhaps Descartes' argument against his opponents here is just that they cannot claim to *know* that they are bodies, or even how they could be.

It has, however, been urged against him, and especially by Gassendi, that he, Descartes, has as little right to claim to know what he is, as he has to claim to know that he is not an extended thing. For what does he know when he knows only that he is a thing that thinks? The answer, says Gassendi, is 'nothing'.

far from having a clear and distinct idea of yourself, you seem to be wholly without one. This is because, even though you recognise that you think, you do not know of what nature you, who think, are. Hence, since this operation alone is known to you, the chief matter is, nevertheless, hidden from you, namely, the substance which so operates. (ii, 197)

Gassendi here is pursuing Descartes with the proposition that to say what one is not (as for instance that one is not an extended substance) is not to say what one is. He not only denies Descartes' latter claim, but also his former. And to Descartes' claim that materialists lack knowledge of themselves as extended substances, Gassendi opposes his own claim, namely that Descartes must admit himself to lack knowledge of the thinking substance he takes himself to be. (He is at least in good company with Hume here.) Unfortunately Descartes is too irritated at this point of his reply to do more than re-iterate something of what he has already said, together with an answer to Gassendi's illustration of a blind man whom he likens to Descartes:

This brings up the comparison in which you may be likened to a blind man, who, on feeling heat, and being told that it proceeds from the sun, should think that he has a clear and distinct idea of the sun, inasmuch as, if anyone ask him what the sun is, he can reply: it is something which produces heat. (ii, 197)

Now this alone shows what I have earlier maintained more than once, namely that Gassendi has never had the slightest glimpse into the profounder levels of Descartes' thinking. Let us suppose that the blind man is not told anything. Then would he have any idea of the sun at all, as distinct, perhaps, from conjecturing that something (perhaps even something specific) causes him to have the feeling of heat? Moreover, supposing even he is told, could he be in doubt whether a later denial of this might not be true? Of course he could. And of course, if he were not told he would have no particular reason to think of a 'sun'. Whereas the whole point of what Descartes had to say in Meditation Two, which they both have in mind at this point, is that we cannot deny the self. For this denial must fail to take hold where what is denied is seen in the very light of the attempted denial itself to be false. Moreover, we don't have to be told about the self. The self is the very last thing we should be said to know only by hearsay. One cannot know anything, Descartes has repeatedly maintained, without knowing the self to know it, i.e. without knowing oneself as a knower. Perhaps Descartes is wrong, but Gassendi hardly demonstrates this. In his reply, Descartes writes:

Nor is your comparison of me to that blind man just: firstly, because the act of knowledge which apprehends a thing that thinks is much more extensive than our apprehension of a thing which warms, as it is much more than that of anything else, as was shown in its proper place. . . . You, however, not only know nothing more than I do of mind, but do not even have knowledge of the very thing I recognize in it; so that in this comparison it is rather you who play the part of blind man, while I, along with the whole human race, could at most be said to be one-eyed. (ii, 231)

By 'at most' he means, clearly, that the only charge possible here is that people may not see as much as there is; but they do see something. All minds have some knowledge of themselves.

However, Descartes here leans upon certain metaphysical positions, which he deals with more fully in his later work, *The Principles of Philosophy*, especially in Part One of that work. What is perhaps of primary importance here, is Descartes' insistence that neither in the case of body or mind can we have an actual experience of something which is neither, but is that in which each mysteriously inheres. Descartes was as certain as Locke about this. There is no knowledge of substance, of whatever kind, except by their attributes; and extension and thought may both be regarded as the most general attributes characterising their respective substances.

Now Descartes has defined imagination and sense perception so as to make them unintelligible save as referring to something other than thinking substance. But a substance other than thinking substance must have attributes such that it would be as meaningless to attribute them to thinking substance, as to speak of matter thinking, or a memory having weight.

The importance of this stage of his enquiry can hardly be overestimated, for the entire difference between substances, on Descartes' repeated assurance, consists in their attributes differing in such a way that we cannot clearly and distinctly perceive how a synthesis, or collection of one grouping of attributes, could include any attribute of another grouping. Descartes can not only think, imagine, and sense perceive, but also move his body in various ways. This body itself has length, breadth and thickness, figure, weight, as well as other properties it is the business of the physical sciences to understand. But they must be properties of something; yet not, as we saw, thinking substance. Hence there must be another kind of substance, such that it makes sense to speak of these properties belonging to it, as it does to speak of imaginings, and sense perceivings, and doubtings, as properties of a thinking substance. Except in a thinking being none of these properties can be conceived as existing; and without extension none of the others can, either.

Whatever it is that makes sense of my putting length and shape in the same basket with each other and not in the same basket with doubt, and whatever makes sense of my putting imaginings and sensing in the same basket with each other, and not with motion, is that which in each case, whatever other content may also be compatible with this, Descartes means by 'substance'. It might be argued that if I can conceive a substance separate from attributes, God can create it etc. But I cannot. Therefore for me to say he can is not in fact for me to state anything. The failure is mine, not God's.

Now my faculties of imagination and intellection have this in common—I can at any time set them into operation. In this respect imagination is nearer to intellection than to sense perception. The way to activate sense organs is by using them, i.e. by 'applying' them to something outside (or inside) the body. If there is nothing to apply them to, they cannot be used. The faculty of sense perception can produce a certain sort of experience when it is stimulated from outside itself in a certain sort of way, and under a fairly specific range of conditions. The outside thing must (or must it?) then be said to have the faculty of stimulating the other faculty. But what is meant is clear enough in what Descartes says. Whatever can operate, so to say, by self-stimulation is an active faculty, and what can only operate when stimulated from outside itself is a passive one. Like Kant, Descartes cannot quite suppose that in sensory experience we are active in just the same way as in some of our other mental activities. Only Descartes is thinking here of sense perception itself, whereas Kant, of course, is thinking mainly of the manifold of intuition. But like Kant, again, he finds himself unable to suppose that his sensed experiences are not the effects of something which is not itself part of himself, but which corresponds in some way with its effects.

But Descartes wants to justify his claim that the cause of his sense perception lies outside himself, and is not some 'hidden' faculty of the soul. The factor in sense experience which is a faculty of the self, is passive, as we remarked. Now, since it requires also an activating source (faculty) the question is this: does this source lie in the same self as the passive faculty, or does it lie elsewhere? At this point Descartes might be considered over-eager to ensure his conclusion. He intends to get rid of the active faculty that is the source of our sense perception. He intends to expel it from the self entirely. He is not an idealist. He does not think that the mind itself, whose essence is pure intellection, manufactures the raw material of sense perception. Why does the active faculty that sets off the passive faculty of sense perception not lie in the same self as it? Because the active faculty is something that cannot be conceived as a property of a thinking substance.

But this active faculty cannot exist in me [inasmuch as I am a thing that thinks] seeing that it does not presuppose thought . . . it is thus necessarily the case that the faculty resides in some substance different from me in which all the reality which is objectively in the ideas that are produced by this faculty is formally or eminently contained. (i, 191)

The active faculty cannot be in me, for what it produces in the passive faculty is not thought, but a perception of something; and that something, the objective reality of the idea, especially in the case of our knowledge of material things, lacks the properties to constitute it an attribute of thinking substance, since, among other reasons, its formal reality is inconceivable as characterising a purely unextended substance, and only conceivable as characterising an extended one. Moreover, as Descartes has pointed out, the activity (and therefore the corresponding faculty) is not under my control. I can, within limits, act so as to break the causal linkage between the passive and the active faculties (as for instance by closing my eyes, or thinking hard about something not physically present) but that is not the same as controlling what I shall receive by the passive faculty if I don't interfere in that way.

Perhaps unnecessarily at this late stage Descartes takes a last look at the possibility that the active faculty is in God:

But, since God is no deceiver, it is very manifest that He does not communicate to me these ideas immediately and by Himself, nor yet by the intervention of some creature in which their reality is not formally, but only eminently, contained. For since He has given me no faculty to recognise that this is the case, but, on the other hand, a very great inclination to believe [that they are sent to me or] that they are conveyed to me by corporeal objects, I do not see how He could be defended from the accusation of deceit if these ideas were produced by causes other than corporeal objects. (i, 191)

I do not find this convincing, even within Descartes' system. Descartes has shown repeatedly that the light of nature can dissipate what otherwise we have 'a very great inclination to believe'. If we still lean upon our inclination to believe that material objects are the causes of certain of our ideas, when the light of nature is unhelpful, can we accuse God of deceit if in fact they are not? Especially if by believing what we are inclined to we ensure our survival, where by disbelieving it we would ensure the opposite. A knowledge of the objective source of my ideas, whether as material objects, God, or angels, is without survival value. To complain at not having it, therefore, is to complain that God has given me insufficient natural light, as well as to accuse him of deceiving me.

If the active faculty, then, is not in me, nor in God, nor in some other spiritual substance, what can it reside in other than what we take it to, namely material things? This doesn't help as much as appears, for unless we have a clear and distinct idea of at least one material thing, the information is not firm enough to constitute knowledge. And Descartes has not advanced from the position that we only have clear and distinct ideas of material things insofar as in some respect they are comprehended, as he has put it, in the object of 'pure mathematics'. To this extent they are independent of us, and obey the formal requirements of pure mathematics. This constitutes their element of objectivity. They obey their own rules and not ours, and they require as their 'content', not spiritual, but extended, substance. This may be taken to provide something other than a self, in which it perhaps makes sense to say an active faculty resides, and from which the passive faculty of sense, which is somehow in the self, receives the modifications which constitute the individuated objective reality, or finite thoughts, with which our ideas become identified. There is no cosy naive realist theory for anyone here. If Descartes is right it is no wonder we find it so hard to understand what it is for something to be external to the mind.

Moreover, Descartes is still stuck with secondary qualities. All he knows so far is that he cannot accord them the same ontological status as primary qualities, i.e. the properties of things insofar as they are clearly and distinctly perceived. The primary attribute of material substance is extension; the primary qualities, as I have said, are the clearly and distinctly perceived properties of extension. Therefore, what, on account of their being extended, we think about material objects, as, for example, that they exist outside our minds, is (and indeed must be) true.

Hence we must allow that corporeal things exist. However, they are perhaps not exactly what we perceive by the senses, since this comprehension by the senses is in many instances very obscure and confused; but we must at least admit that all things which I conceive in them clearly and distinctly, that is to say, all things which, speaking generally, are comprehended in the object of pure mathematics, are truly to be recognised as external objects. (i, 191)

It is clear that secondary qualities are not to be accorded this recognition. There is at least one objection to be made to this theory, namely, that Descartes cannot complete it until he has also explained how it comes about that the secondary qualities that qualify material things possess all those properties he mentions, such as liveliness, a distinctive clarity, and so on, by which he distinguishes them from the memories, and images, that we produce from ourselves. He has explained away some of the other distinctions he made in his pre-reflective years, but he has not, so far, explained away this one. It may of course be maintained that if he had in fact set much store by this distinction he would not have been as unsuccessful as he claims in trying to distinguish dreams from waking experiences. But this consideration would lead us too far afield. What does here concern us is the consideration that for Descartes what confers its objective status as a material object, upon anything, is indeed, as he has already told us in Meditation Two, the class of properties by means of which we understand it to be a material object. And the paradox, of course, is that we don't understand by our senses.

No doubt with these considerations in mind Descartes turns next to examine those elements in his experience of corporeal things which are not clearly and distinctly perceived. Since the light of nature, so far from assuring him that these elements are as objective as are the clear and distinct elements, seems to me to rule this possibility out entirely, why then do we find it impossible to discard our belief in them? What Descartes' answer amounts to is that we cannot entirely discard, for reasons we shall shortly examine, the teaching—as opposed to the light—of nature. But this is partly because if there is a belief that we cannot discard, although it is something the light of nature does not illumine, we can trust God that it contains some truth. Nature cannot be a necessary source of deception any more than God can;

for by nature, considered in general, I now understand no other thing than either God Himself or else the order and disposition which God has established in created things; and by my nature in particular I understand no other thing than the complexus of all the things which God has given me. (i, 192)

In short, God (and his work) being good, whatever either leads me to believe to be true should be treated as no less true than if the light of nature itself had been capable of leading me to it. So Descartes:

As to other things, however, which are either particular only, as, for example, that the sun is of such and such a figure, etc., or which are less clearly and distinctly conceived, such as light, sound, pain and the like, it is certain that although they are very dubious and uncertain, yet on the sole ground that God is not a deceiver, and that consequently He has not permitted any falsity to exist in my opinion which He has not likewise given me the faculty of correcting, I may assuredly hope to conclude that I have within me the means of arriving at the truth even here. (i, 191–2)

If the teachings of nature, then, are to be trusted, and if it is nature that teaches us that there is a world of material objects, then we have the best possible reason that we can have for believing that material objects exist.

But at this point Descartes makes a sudden switch, and begins to consider the teachings of nature not with respect to what we may take ourselves to know about material things by means of our external senses, but with respect to what we feel in our bodies that makes us know them as our own bodies.

But there is nothing which this nature teaches me more expressly [nor more sensibly] than that I have a body which is adversely affected when I feel pain, which has need of food or drink when I experience the feelings of hunger and thirst, and so on; nor can I doubt there being some truth in all this. (i, 192)

Previously he has been concerned to prove that material things exist, now he seems equally concerned to prove that whatever else he may be, he *is* also, himself a material thing. It may be worth a closer look at what Descartes is doing here. When, in the first Meditation, he was considering the reliability of the senses as a source of knowledge of the external world, he asked how he could deny the evidence of his own senses when they related to such experiences as those of his own body. He was searching for the best possible evidence. Even this evidence turned out not to be good enough, related as it was to the external senses, and to powers of action, and not to such experiences of inner sense as 'the feelings of hunger and thirst and so on'. Now, however, when on the one hand he is compelled by his own arguments to accept the evidence of his senses, yet, on the other, is still unable to grant this evidence more than problematic status, he expresses his plight in an almost despairing attempt to find greater reliability in inner sense experience than in outer. He is surely more certain that he is in pain, or hungry, than even that he is perceiving his own body. There is nothing, he says, that nature teaches him more expressly (nor more sensibly, he significantly adds) than that his body (or, that it is his body) is affected when he has these inner feelings. There is no doubt that Descartes in his final writhings is still seeking something sufficiently cogent to guarantee the evidence for the external world more effectively than his external senses have seemed able to. What he is saying here is surely that he knows there are material things for he knows himself to be one.

But this knowledge he never confuses with intellection. The finite thinking substance which Descartes regards as his essential self is not required by its thinking nature to be able to 'have' feelings. It is still not by the light of nature that Descartes knows there to be a necessary connection between his body as known to him by his outer senses and as known by his inner ones. It is by the teachings of nature that he knows that his body (as perceived by the external senses) is affected in various ways in a steady relation to his experience of various feelings.

Now what is the status of these feelings? Why should they be more reliable than outer perception as evidence for the existence of an external world? If they are not then the gap between thought and extension, mind and matter, is not closed by them. But it is evident that Descartes by now has lost his sure tread. Let us in all humility ask one question. Why does Descartes think the evidence of inner sense might (even if only just might) give him more certainty than that of outer? It can surely only be because he finds himself more immediately affected by it. What are these immediate effects? It can't be simply because you can escape from outer but not from inner experience, since Descartes has made the standard point that we have no choice in the former case. There are illusions of course in both cases, but there is surely a difference between the illusion of a searing pain and the illusion of something's being a certain colour, or shape, or distance. But what is the difference between something's being in fact a searing pain and something's being only the illusion of one? We know what it could be to be under a perceptual illusion, but under what specifiable conditions would you admit to being under an illusion when you suppose yourself to be feeling a searing pain?

To be more immediately affected by pain or hunger is therefore to be tied down more than by the external senses for the simple reason that it is difficult to make sense of the kind of distinction we may illustrate by being in a searing pain and being under the illusion that you are. As we shall see, just as there is not much false about false hunger to the person suffering from it, phantom pains are by no means less painful by reason of the non-existence of the limbs in which they are felt. Now this immediacy of feeling is more immediate to the self; therefore deliverances of feeling, being more immediate, would look as if they relate the self more directly to what they are feelings of (in this case feelings of the state of a particular body) than external sense experience ever could. Hence in feeling experience the self knows 'itself' not merely as a thinking thing but also as an extended one.

It is true that Descartes does at times use the word 'think' so as to include in it feeling. It is not, however, in thinking as feeling but as pure intellection that we discover the human essence, as Descartes himself maintains. He can conceive himself as existing, though neither feeling, nor perceiving. Feeling is only contingent in relation to the essential self just as perceiving is, but also as thinking could never be. He cannot even be as certain that he feels as that he thinks; and much less so that what he feels is in fact a particular material thing which he identifies as 'owned' by himself—'my body'.

It remains that Descartes has not succeeded in closing the gap that still taunts him: in the end inner sensings provide us with no privileged insight into what it is actually to be a material thing, and indeed Descartes' entire position would be undermined if it could make sense to say that a thinking thing can know what it is like to be an extended thing. Whatever knowledge we can have even of our own body by inner sensing differs, in the end, from our knowledge of it by our outer sensing in a way that is not essentially different from the way the knowledge we get of a thing by one sensory modality differs from the knowledge we get of it by another.

Having first shown that his essence is thought, then that all the same he knows something, corporeal body, whose essence is the very contradictory of thought, namely extension, Descartes now seeks to show that he is not simply a thinking substance, but also an extended one. He is not asking general questions about how body can affect mind, or *vice versa*; nor is he concerned to discuss the metaphysical possibility of such a relation. He is concerned with the facts, from as close as he can get to them, and with the proper description of them. It is true that he has argued that there are two substances, one extension, and the other thought, which so far from having anything in common, may even be defined in terms that constitute each a negation of the other. But he rejects the view that this implies the impossibility of any sort of causal relation between 'them. In his famous letter to Clerselier about Gassendi's objections to Descartes' replies to the Fifth Set of Objections, he writes concerning 'how the soul moves the body if it is not material', and 'how it can receive the specific forms of corporeal objects', as follows:

Likewise these objections, among other things, presuppose an explanation of the nature of the union between soul and body, a matter of which I have not yet treated. But to you, for your own benefit, I declare that the whole of the perplexity involved in these questions arises entirely from a false supposition that can by no manner of means be proved, viz. that if the soul and the body are two substances of diverse nature, that prevents them from being capable of acting on one another. (ii, 132)

Descartes does not hold it unreasonable to argue that when the evidence is such that it is difficult to see how certain things can fail to stand in some sort of causal relation, the fact that one cannot specify precisely how they accomplish this in no way weakens the evidence, or even brings it about that it makes less sense to suppose they don't interact, than that they do. Descartes is certainly not disposed to regard all relations between thinking things and material things as entirely co-incidental. And there must surely be something wrong with any argument that maintains that wherever an enquiry cannot be pursued by pure intellection, no explanation can be regarded as more rational than any other. And what Descartes is about to do is precisely to investigate an area of experience, where intellection unaided could do no more than maintain a paralyzed silence.

Nature teaches Descartes, he says, that material things exist and that one of those is related in a unique way to him, namely as his. To repeat, what nature teaches him are the things he cannot know by the light of nature, and unless the existence and goodness of God guaranteed their truth, he could not here claim to know, certainly not in the sense that such knowledge could not even conceivably be mistaken. For nothing not clear and distinct throughout is knowledge, and though in respect of its mathematical properties a material object is known clearly and distinctly, in respect of its sensible properties, as we have seen, it is not. Thus, when Descartes claims truth for nature's teaching concerning the existence of material things, he is not advocating a form of naive realism. Secondary qualities have been epistemically separated from primary ones, and do not in fact possess the external form of existence that naive realism seems to maintain. Rather he seems to be arguing that although nature teaches us that material things exist, it does not follow that she also teaches us that this knowledge is equally evident by the light of nature. Now just as Descartes has been at pains to distinguish between the light of nature, and the teaching of nature, so he will now be at pains to distinguish, where that distinction becomes necessary to save his entire system, between the teaching of nature, and what he calls certain habits of forming inconsiderate judgments on things. For, let it be said at once that Descartes is still terrified of the possibility that even the trimmed claims for the teaching of nature may collapse under examination.

Nature teaches him that only in one of the material things that exist, and not in any of the others, are there feelings that he also knows to be his. To say they are his is to say that they do not belong to the body through which alone he experiences them in the way that its mathematical properties do, nor even in the way that its colour, or the sound it makes, does. For the colour of his body does not characterise him in the way the pain in his body does. The feeling in his body is not present in his consciousness in the way that its colour is. His body is coloured, but he is in pain. Admittedly his pain can be anaesthetised away, just as the colour of his body can be shut out by closing his eyes; but the absence of pain constitutes, for him, a change in himself, that is to say, in the condition of a being who thinks, and whose thinking includes, in its widest sense, as Descartes has argued, feeling (such as pain) as well. The absence of the colour of his body cannot meaningfully be said to constitute for him a change in himself. The thing that thinks, and is in pain, is not the thing that is red.

But though the thing that thinks is also the thing that has the pain, having pain is not like thinking. For in the first place, says Descartes, in effect, I can conceive myself as existing without any feeling whatsoever, but not as existing insofar as I engage in no thinking whatsoever. In the second, it is by the light of nature that I know that (and what) I think, but only by the teaching of nature that I know myself to be in pain. For what I think, is clearly and distinctly known to me, but though my pain may be said to be known clearly to me, it cannot be said to be known clearly and distinctly, if only because there is always the possibility of illusion present in our experience of pain. We may know by the teaching of nature that material things exist, just as we may also know by it that feelings do. But what the teaching of nature cannot provide us with is the kind of analysis of these experiences which alone would enable us to have indubitable knowledge of them through and through. Thus feeling is like sense perception in this respect, but like thought in being experienced as a condition of the thinker, and not a condition of a material thing. On the other hand, since thinking is possible without feeling, as Descartes has argued, there is no necessary connection between the two, so that nothing about feeling can be deduced from the fact that we think. Now since it is by feeling that I know myself to have a body, even my knowledge of my own body is not as certainly known to me as my knowledge of myself as a thinking thing. For I cannot deduce from the fact that I think, the fact that I have a body. All I can deduce it from is the fact that, for instance, if this, and not if any other, body is fed, my feeling of hunger will cease. Thus feeling is a kind of knowledge of a body, even though one's own body, and therefore as a state of consciousness (or mode of thought) it is necessarily confused.

The reason for this should be noted. There cannot be between mind and body the same kind of articulation as that between one idea and another in the same mind. For mind and body, as Descartes never ceases to argue, are each, in themselves, what the other is not. There is not anything they can be understood to possess in common by means of which there could take place the kind of articulation that might enable the mind to have as clear and distinct an idea of body as it has, or can have, of ideas. This might be regarded as the price mind has to pay for being in the corporeal world at all. It has to make do with second best. And this is only a further expression of what Descartes has already remarked; as is also the recollection that intelligence ceases to be limited by this fact if it simply takes note of it. This, after all, is the object of the method of doubt.

Perhaps what Descartes should have concentrated on bringing out at this point is the fact that knowledge by feeling is not simply knowledge of the body, but also something more than knowledge, namely a tendency, stronger or weaker, that leads one to act with reference to that feeling. It has in short a practical element. In contrast to one's thinking, one's feeling must point to the world of material things, since it is because of what is there the case, and is either acceptable or not, that our feeling has the practical reference it has. And this certainly has less to do with what is the case, than with what it does or does not suit us to be the case. For, of course, if we know what people feel we are better placed for making accurate predictions about them than otherwise. This point is perhaps worth making now, for if there is a distinction between the passive and active content of a feeling, in other words if what we call 'feeling' contains an element which is not feeling, but an actual or incipient drive of some sort, then when we speak of feelings being clear, or confused, or true, or mistaken, we ought to be clear to which element of the feeling we wish to apply these predicates, the affective, or the conative. From this it follows, then, that as well as teaching us what is the case, nature may be regarded also as teaching us what requires to be done. But we shall return to this point shortly.

If I am right, then some of what Descartes takes to be the difference between a man understanding his situation in respect of his body, and feeling it, is not simply the difference between two kinds of knowing, the clear and distinct on the one side, and the obscure and confused on the other, but rather between the clear and distinct apprehension of what is the case for any person in that situation; and the feeling of what is the case for the observer himself, together with an actual or incipient tendency to act in relation to that feeling. However comprehensive might be an individual's understanding of his own situation as being in the world with his body, unless he has something that can move him to relevant action, there could be no guarantee that he would ever do anything to his advantage. He may have the power to act, but unless there is also feeling for certain conditions and against others, then even with the knowledge of those conditions he would have no motive for action. He needs the lot.

There is no doubt that Descartes seeks to identify the mind with the body as far as any compatibility between the two is possible. The mind knows the body as its own because, as we saw, only in conjunction with this body does it, a thinking thing, feel; in other words feel as *if* it were in fact a body, or feel one with it—which, as has been argued in this book, on Descartes' account no mere body could. The kind of unity Descartes seeks to introduce here is, as we have seen, not of a deductive kind. It is closer to some organic model, such as the unity of the written word and its meaning, or the unity of diverse sense data that form one material thing, or the unity of a visual or auditory pattern with the feeling, or the value judgment that accompanies it. There is no shortage of models, though indeed this may also be a model of its own kind, and in its own right. Descartes is only too well aware of such considerations. To suppose anything intelligent, or even intelligibly relevant, has been said about him by describing him as a Dualist is to have read him (if one has read him) with closed eyes upon the page. Let him speak for himself:

Nature also teaches me by these sensations of pain, hunger, thirst, etc., that I am not only lodged in my body as a pilot in a vessel, but that I am very closely united to it, and so to speak so intermingled with it that I seem to compose with it one whole. For if that were not the case, when my body is hurt, I, who am merely a thinking thing, should not feel pain, for I should perceive this wound by the understanding only, just as the sailor perceives by sight when something is damaged in his vessel; and when my body has need of drink or food, I should clearly understand the fact without being warned of it by confused feelings of hunger and thirst. For all these sensations of hunger, thirst, pain, etc. are in truth none other than certain confused modes of thought which are produced by the union and apparent intermingling of mind and body. (i, 192)

All the difficulties here, in my view, are well understood by Descartes, and rest upon certain metaphysical positions. Descartes never pretended that these could be understood on the level of imagination, much less that of feeling, but only by an activity of thought in which understanding trusts itself without perceptual crutches—crutches whose modern form is 'ordinary language'— the language which even by definition is concerned with life, and not with an understanding of it.

What emerges from the present examination of Descartes' attempt to relate mind and body to the individual is that he makes room, in his analysis, for the fact of human agency, and thus for the existence of material things other than his own body, which are factors in the situation with which he as an agent may have to reckon. Some material things will be seen as the possible causes of what we desire, and others of what we seek to avoid. Now since our interest in these things is practical we are bound to form some picture of the external objects which we take to be the causes of our experiences. Might one then conclude that the need to become familiar with the field within which we may be required to act must drive us to suppose that these external objects are in themselves precisely as our ideas of them are? And might it not be that this is even what nature teaches us? This, of course, would be fatal to Descartes' position. He cannot allow that secondary qualities, or feelings, could possibly characterise (inhere in) extended substance. But if nature teaches us that they do, then we are being deceived, for we cannot correct this teaching by means of any other faculty. Descartes now has to find a way of allowing that there really are external things; but at the same time he must maintain the position that whatever these external things are, being extended substances they are metaphysically disqualified from housing the secondary qualities by which we know them:

And certainly from the fact that I am sensible of different sorts of colours, sounds, scents, tastes, heat, hardness, etc., I very easily conclude that there are in the bodies from which all these diverse sense-perceptions proceed certain variations which answer to them, although possibly these are not really at all similar to them. (i, 192)

His next move must be to show that they are not similar at all. For since reason cannot assure us of it, if it can be shown that the teaching of nature doesn't, then there is no necessity in the nature of our condition for us to assume it ourselves.

For the moment, then, Descartes is concerned not merely to show that nothing we perceive by the senses can, by its nature, characterise a material thing, but that if we look carefully we shall find that we are not in fact impelled to suppose this to be so, as indeed would be the case if nature had really taught this to us:

But there are many other things which nature seems to have taught me, but which at the same time I have never really received from her, but which have been brought about in my mind by a certain habit which I have of forming inconsiderate judgments on things; and thus it may easily happen that these judgments contain some error. (i, 192–3)

The examples he gives of these 'inconsiderate judgments' which are here pertinent are warmth, colour, taste and perspectival appearance. Now his point is that though (perhaps by association) we have formed the *habit* of supposing qualities such as these to reside in material things, there is, to put the case at its weakest, no compelling reason to suppose they do. This is to say, that insofar as our judgment is a theoretical one, concerning how the world is, we have no rational foundation for it; we do not see clearly and distinctly that things must be like appearances, we can therefore doubt that they are, and cannot therefore claim to know, in what is for Descartes the only proper sense of that word, that they are. His key remark is surely this: 'For it seems to me that it is mind alone, and not mind and body in conjunction, that is requisite to a knowledge of the truth in regard to such things' (i, 193). In other words, the nature of material things, insofar as it cannot be known by a mind engaged in its essential activity of thinking, cannot be known at all.

All the same he is no Idealist. Speaking of the feelings of heat and pain we get from a fire, he says:

there is at the same time no reason in this which could persuade me that there is in the fire something resembling this heat any more than there is in it something resembling the pain; all that I have any reason to believe from this is, that there is something in it, whatever it may be, which excites in me these sensations of heat or of pain. (i, 194)

And we should observe that he does not want to be mistaken on this score. For as well as arguing that we are not entitled to conclude that things are in themselves what they appear to be to us, he is also in this very place arguing that it does not follow from there being no appearances that there are no things. In view of the historical importance of Descartes in this very connection let us quote him:

So also, although there are spaces in which I find nothing which excites my senses, I must not from that conclude that these spaces contain no body; for I see in this, as in other similar things, that I have been in the habit of perverting the order of nature, because these perceptions of sense having been placed within me by nature merely for the purpose of signifying to my mind what things are beneficial or hurtful to the composite whole of which it forms a part, and being up to that point sufficiently clear and distinct, I yet avail myself of them as though they were absolute rules by which I might immediately determine the essence of the bodies which are outside me, as to which, in fact, they can teach me nothing but what is most obscure and confused. (i, 194)

What I perceive by the senses, taken in conjunction, of course, with what I feel as a body,

teaches me to flee from things which cause the sensation of pain, and seek after the things which communicate to me the sentiment of pleasure and so forth; but I do not see that beyond this it teaches me that from those diverse sense-perceptions we should ever form any conclusion regarding things outside of us, without having [carefully and maturely] mentally examined them beforehand. (i, 193)

Sense-perception teaches me how to regulate my body, in relation to material things, so as, presumably, to maximise 'the sentiment of pleasure' and minimize that of pain. Any other employment of sense-perception is a misemployment, and the consequent deception a self-deception.

Is it, however, true that if we confine our judgments involving sense perception to matters of practice only, there is no need for us to err? Is it possible that our senses, and our feelings can be wrong, if not in respect of what they appear to be, then in respect of what they tell us to do? Descartes hasn't a great deal of rope left. Suppose what nature 'teaches' us to do is not the best thing to do; suppose it is even the worst. Suppose that having marked off the proper sphere of sense perception and feeling, we still cannot trust them even there. In other words, what if even the correct employment of our faculties misleads us, will God not be a deceiver? And is such a being God at all? And if there is no God, are we not back where we started from, but this time with all hope of knowledge gone for ever?

He writes:

But I have already sufficiently considered how, notwithstanding the supreme goodness of God, falsity enters into the judgments I make. Only here a new difficulty is presented—one respecting those things the pursuit or avoidance of which is taught me by nature, and also respecting the internal sensations which I possess, and in which I seem to have sometimes detected error [and thus to be directly deceived by my own nature]. To take an example, the agreeable taste of some food in which poison has been intermingled may induce me to partake of the poison, and thus deceive me. It is true, at the same time, that in this case nature may be excused, for it only induces me to desire food in which I find a pleasant taste, and not to desire the poison which is unknown to it; and thus I can infer nothing from this fact, except that my nature is not omniscient, at which there is certainly no reason to be astonished, since man, being finite in nature, can only have knowledge the perfectness of which is limited. (i, 194)

The point of all this is that even with respect to action we cannot be sure that we may not even be doing the worst thing, unless we can know every detail relevant to the outcome of what we propose. And that action is not simply a matter of doing what we are directly impelled by nature to do, but often involves complicated means-ends relationships, assumptions, calculations, and empirical knowledge depending upon memory and even hearsay is, in the human condition, inescapable.

But when it comes to the sort of case where we are mistaken in doing an action to which, in total, we are directly impelled by nature, that is another story. That we are sometimes so impelled even when we know it to be bad for us, Descartes does not discuss here, though he has himself pointed this out in another connection. Yet what he does discuss is in a way more fundamental. Descartes has no room for even the slightest possible moral flaw in God. It is not enough for Descartes that God does not always deceive us; nothing less will do than that God never does. There is not only the consideration that if he ever deceives us, then he is at least capable of deceit, and that when he does deceive us we are none the less impelled to believe than when he does not. There is the further point that for him ever to do so would show first of all that his nature does not exclude the intention to deceive; and secondly, that since our natural impulsion may have no bearing upon the truth, it is again possible that for all we know his power of deceit is exercised upon every finite mind, and without respite.

Since the things we desire to do are correlated with our bodily condition, it is conceivable that our bodily condition should be such that by doing what we desire we bring about a condition destructive of the body. Since this is the opposite of what we intend, between our intention and our well-being on the one hand, and our natural impulsion on the other there is a relation such that by following our natural impulsion, that is, by doing what nature teaches us, we are deceived into doing what is contrary to our own interest and intention. That all this deceit is in full conformity with the laws of nature, is irrelevant to a possible charge of a breach of good faith. We do not act, here, in conformity with our understanding of how the laws of nature operate to affect us in a particular case. We are not simply pilots, as Descartes has said. We don't have to measure the saline content of our bodily fluids to know when to drink. We depend upon certain mechanisms to speak to us through our feelings about what in this or that case the welfare of our body requires us to do. If this mechanism breaks down—and as we know only too well it can—we are, or we can be, as helpless in our own defence as a new born baby, and without suspecting this to be our condition. Now because we have bodies we have to have these mechanisms. And because these mechanisms are material things, bound precisely by the laws of nature and interacting with a material environment under conditions where the operation of natural law and the interest of a body, insofar as somebody lives and feels by it, are not always in harmony, unless miracles become the order of the day, we are always at risk.

Nevertheless, it might be argued, it is difficult to believe that the omnipotent, and omniscient Being we call God, could not have found some system of natural law which related our minds and bodies in such a way that our deception would be a causal impossibility. Yet, Descartes maintains, whatever system he chose would still be limited by the fact that it operates upon extended substance. It is in the very nature of the latter that the trouble lies, the very fact, as we have pointed out already, that spiritual substance, and material, (or extended) substance, are so diverse that each constitutes what can actually be described in terms of the negation of the other. In other words, the disparities between the two kinds of substance are such that, as we noted above, no precise articulation between them is possible.

Whatever other disparity there may be, the one that here engages Descartes is the

great difference between mind and body, inasmuch as body is by nature always divisible, and the mind is entirely indivisible. For, as a matter of fact, when I consider the mind, that is to say, myself inasmuch as I am only a thinking thing, I cannot distinguish in myself any parts, but apprehend myself to be clearly one and entire; and although the whole mind seems to be united to the whole body, yet if a foot, or an arm, or some other part, is separated from my body, I am aware that nothing has been taken away from my mind. And the faculties of willing, feeling, conceiving, etc. cannot be properly speaking said to be its parts, for it is one and the same mind which employs itself in willing and in feeling and understanding. But it is quite otherwise with corporeal or extended objects, for there is not one of these imaginable by me which my mind cannot easily divide into parts, and which consequently I do not recognize as being divisible; this would be sufficient to teach me that the mind or soul of man is entirely different from the body, if I had not already learned it from other sources. (i, 196)

I think it is quite vital to understand the foregoing quotation. My mind is multiple in the form of its expression but unextended and therefore indivisible. It does not so to say lie alongside or parallel with the body. It is not something that we can think of as permeating the body. The mind is not open to the body's influence throughout the whole of the body, but only at one part. The mechanism of this influence is not something that need concern us here; the main thing to understand is that the area in question, a tiny part of the brain, is held by Descartes to be connected with the rest of the body in such a way that nothing that can happen in or to the body can register in our minds unless it registers itself within this part of the brain, and also, in particular, upon that specific element of this part of the brain fitted to receive a signal of that specific sort. This is the last link in the chain of extension. After that, or at the same time, its nature is registered 'objectively' in the mind. Indeed if we could stimulate mind as if it had been stimulated by the *sensus communis* we could do away with the *sensus communis* as well, and the need for extended substance altogether. The contrast between mind and body makes possible between them only one form of interaction, which itself is the root of a kind of formal deception. The passage quoted continues:

I further notice that the mind does not receive the impressions from all parts of the body immediately, but only from the brain, or perhaps even from one of its smallest parts, to wit, from that in which the *sensus communis* is said to reside, which, whenever it is disposed in the same particular way, conveys the same thing to the mind, *although meanwhile the other portions of the body may be differently disposed*, as is testified by innumerable experiments which it is unnecessary here to recount.[1] (i, 196)

It might, of course, be argued that if one corporeal structure can interact directly (even if only on the level of communication) with mind, then interaction between the whole body, at every point, and mind, is also not inconceivable. But the reply might be that the body, apart from the part so constructed as to house the *sensus communis*, has a multiplicity of functions which they could not perform if they were constructed like it. Hence if they were like it, there would not be anything *to* communicate to the mind.

Now, whatever happens anywhere in the body is connected with its appropriate centre in the special area (*sensus communis*) whose function it is to draw together into one common location all the feelings and perceptions of the body. Between any physical 'incident' in the body, which is capable of reaching consciousness, and the centre to which it is attached in the *sensus communis*, there will be some system, simple or complex, of neural connection. Suppose this to be a single nerve. Well, whatever happens at the distal end of the nerve will have to travel right along till it reaches the proximal end. But since each nerve can produce one and only one effect in the *sensus communis*, provided that the nerve

[1] My italics.

is stimulated anywhere at all along its length the effect in the *sensus communis* will be the same as if it were stimulated at the actual point of the incident. Thus, as we remarked just now, if I were only to stimulate the appropriate centres in the *sensus communis* I could produce in the mind exactly the same effect as if what it supposed so actually was.

Descartes knew all about phantom limbs, as we saw. Using the very body which in itself may be perfect for its work, one can in fact produce illusions which are as real to the mind as if they were not illusions at all. Deception is indeed possible. And in sickness, when our bodily apparatus becomes affected detrimentally, we do suffer illusions of various sorts—and all in strict accordance with the laws of nature. For the condition of the body being what it is, and the affected centres in the *sensus communis* being what they are, these effects are all just as predictable, on the basis of natural law, as any physical fact.

The nature of mind and the nature of body are such that the best and most useful way in which they could have been brought together advantageously to promote human experience is in accordance with the plan in fact followed. No other, if we think about it, is even possible. For if there was to be a mind and body composed into one, and capable of the automatic reactions necessary for remaining alive and avoiding pain, there had to be a bodily *sensus communis* in close contact with mind; and the former had to be linked with the rest of the body by a system of nerves that could not get direct access to mind, nor indeed any access at all, save through the appropriate centre in the brain. One is really left with the picture, of one's body as almost, but just not quite, severed from one's mind. Yet all this is the only possible condition under which that 'apparent intermingling' of which Descartes speaks can occur. Thus Descartes' conclusion at last overtakes him: 'From this it is quite clear that, notwithstanding the supreme goodness of God, the nature of man, inasmuch as it is composed of mind and body, cannot be otherwise than sometimes a source of deception' (i, 198). With this admission, wrung, I should think, from Descartes despite all his hopes to the contrary, his whole case surely yawns wide open again.

Nevertheless suppose we do grant that after all deception is still possible. But is there a deceiver? God at least had no hand in that. He made the world, but even he couldn't 'do' the impossible. And the two 'things', extended substance and thinking substance, are just so entirely other each to the other, that even to have brought them together as he has requires a sort of standing miracle, or at least something that itself cannot be explained by any laws. Descartes, I am afraid, is now granting that the possible deception of man by his very own body is *necessary* if mind and bodies be wedded as they are in us. To demand of God that he should have made conditions not requiring this is to demand the inconceivable, i.e. not to demand anything of him at all. Since the impossible is the impossible, even God cannot bring it about, but he could do the nearest meaningful thing, and he did—he made us.

But this is not enough to suit Descartes' case. For even if God is not any kind of deceiver, and even if he did all that he could conceivably do, the outstanding fact, and one with which Descartes can surely never come to terms, is the fact that clear and distinct perceptions are not always the criteria of truth. If before you can be sure that yours are, you have to get a check up on your body, then the case is truly subverted. Further, who will check the checking up? But most depressing of all, for Descartes, surely, is the plain fact that the very correlation between mind and body that gives us truth, or rather, that makes truth possible, makes deception also possible. Yet, if we have already recognised deception then let us find out what to correlate it with, and with what to correlate the cases where we have no honest reason to doubt. And this is actually the direction in which we do advance. Medical treatment operates by the *reason* of the specialist, rather than by the *feeling* of the sick. If science is the expression of intellection in the field of physical facts, then to rely on science is to keep as close to the light of nature as the subject matter permits. Just as in the sociology of knowledge we seek a concrete sort of objectivity by investigating certain historically conditioned categories of thought not obvious otherwise, so perhaps here, Descartes might say, to reach concrete truth, one has to investigate just how closely it can be affected by the workings of the body—and learn how to allow for it. But in that case the concept of absolute knowledge is gone for good, and with it the possibility of knowledge by pure intellection.

But did Descartes really consider that one could have absolute and unconditional knowledge of extended substance? Perhaps all that we can ever hope to do with extended substance is *use* it. The ideal of pure knowledge here has merely a regulative function; we cannot *know* what is 'outside' mind. But were we right to concede that God could really not have arranged mind and matter in a more profitable partnership? It might be argued, indeed, that God has made us on the cheap, or at least on the most economical basis, since he made us so that we should not be deceived as long as we were healthy, but no longer: when he could have built into us mechanisms we are hardly (perhaps) likely to need, but which would be needed badly if at all, and which would monitor the information input received whenever there had been some interference with the normal bodily mechanism. There could have been more control nerves, feed back and oscillatory mechanisms, electrical low (or high) frequency circuits of one sort and another that would be able to take account of everything that happened to the body concerned; so that the central element operated only when other circuits had monitored for all possible faults. We would have been more complicated than we are, and a bit more trouble to God, but if he really were opposed to our being deceived, then he could have done all this, and more, with no greater difficulty than he, the perfect Being has found already. But this argument may be dismissed by the simple consideration that the need for a monitoring system to check a monitoring system would here set up an infinite regress.

Certainly, before any one nerve sends its message, it could be made to feed it through other systems. But these could be damaged. But just as one can take care not to fall into error when one is well, so perhaps, as rational beings, we can also take care not to fall into error when we are not. And meanwhile we can take some comfort from the knowledge that statistically speaking we are not deceived.

In the end Descartes finds no single path to certainty. We just have to be desperate enough, as he was, to use every means we can.

For knowing that all my senses more frequently indicate to me truth than falsehood respecting the things which concern that which is beneficial to the body, and being able almost always to avail myself of many of them in order to examine one particular thing, and, besides that, being able to make use of my memory in order to connect the present with the past, and of my understanding which already has discovered all the causes of my errors, I ought no longer to fear that falsity may be found in matters every day presented to me by my senses. (i, 198)

The most that Descartes had even the vestige of a right to claim here was that falsity is not always found in matters every day presented to him by the senses. Similarly, though a cross check by more than one sense may lessen the chance of error, how could it obliterate it altogether? As for memory, it is precisely because knowledge by memory is not knowledge by clear and distinct perception that Descartes may be said to have had to call God in, as we may recall, in the first place. It is with a tired voice indeed that the great philosopher now speaks to us. Otherwise he might have argued that he had at least shown that even if some trace of error is ineradicable from the human condition this is not due to bad workmanship by God, or to God's indifference to deceiving us, but is the price the spirit pays, by its very nature, when it consorts with mortality. What Descartes has really shown is that in their respective natures thought and extension are such that one necessary condition for a thinking thing to know a material thing is that a disconnecting element can anywhere, and at any time, be present. It is only when a thinking thing does not have an extended thing as its object that knowledge in Descartes' sense is possible, if he really has also shown that his doubts as to the very possibility of knowledge by a purely thinking being are groundless in the face of God's goodness. He has certainly not so far established a firm and permanent structure in the natural sciences, but it is less obvious that he has done nothing towards laying the foundations.

But Descartes can hardly re-instate the waking world of the senses without returning to the subject of dreams. For it was because he could find no mark by which to distinguish a waking experience from a dream experience, that he felt able to apply the method of doubt to his sense experience, in the first place. Now Descartes had resolved, after satisfying himself that God existed, and that knowledge was possible, not to doubt unless he had some good reason to.

However, if he seeks, at this late stage, for the mark distinguishing the waking state from the dreaming, would not his entire investigation require to be started anew? But he doesn't. There is still no intrinsic sign, by which a dream can be distinguished from waking. But now that Descartes believes that memory, sense-perception, understanding, knowledge of causal connections, are to be trusted, these provide for him a context within which individual experiences, whether waking, or dreaming (or dare we say the memory of dreaming?) may be placed for examination. There is no waking experience he cannot imagine as possibly a dream, nor remembered dream as possibly a waking experience. So he ends the Meditations with something of a whimper.

And I ought in no wise to doubt the truth of such matters, if, after having called up all my senses, my memory, and my understanding, to examine them, nothing is brought to evidence by any one of them which is repugnant to what is set forth by the others. For because God is in no wise a deceiver, it follows that I am not deceived in this. But because the exigencies of action often oblige us to make up our minds before having leisure to examine matters carefully, we must confess that the life of man is very frequently subject to error in respect to individual objects, and we must in the end acknowledge the infirmity of our nature. (i, 199)

In plain language, then, it is still always the case that in following sense-perception, or feeling, or the teaching of nature, we can never 'in respect to individual objects', or on any given occasion, claim to know that we cannot then be mistaken, or, in other words, claim knowledge.

But he now *knows* this, whereas at the beginning of his Meditations, as I stated the matter, he could not know even this. Moreover, he now knows that what he doesn't in the complete sense know, is of far less value to him than what by the very same process he now knows he does know, namely, the existence of God and the soul. To some extent he can afford to regret the infirmity of his nature as a human creature—especially in public. Did he reckon this regret a high price to pay for the success of his undertaking? That he did not is evident from his own account written a little while after the Meditations had been completed, when he had had time to observe the reactions to it. At the end of the Synopsis he then wrote of his Meditations we find this:

All the errors which proceed from the senses are then surveyed, while the means of avoiding them are demonstrated, and finally all the reasons from which we may deduce the existence of material things are set forth. Not that I judge them to be very useful in establishing that which they prove, to wit, that there is in truth a world, that men possess bodies, and other such things which never have been doubted by anyone of sense; but because in considering these closely we come to see that they are neither so strong nor so evident as those arguments which lead us to the knowledge of our mind and of God; so that these last must be the most certain and most evident facts which can fall within the cognizance of the human mind. And this is the whole matter that I have tried to prove in these Meditations, for which reason I here omit to speak of many other questions with which I dealt incidentally in this discussion. (i, 142–3)

When Descartes is taken seriously as a philosopher, instead of being interpreted as a fawning coward, it is clear and distinct enough from his works, as I have tried in this book to show, that he means here exactly what he says. He would have been a fool not to pay the formal respect which he considered the price of his freedom to give the world what he believed to be the most valuable gift it could receive, but still not so foolish as those who cannot distinguish the essential from the formal in his very close and sustained argument. The only way for a philosopher to attack Descartes is to attack his argument; and this would be true even if the driving power behind Descartes' great work were nothing more than the desire to stand well with the Church.

I shall turn, in conclusion, to his somewhat neglected dedicatory note to the Meditations, for there we may find what the driving power really was, and with it another approach than seems customary to Descartes' Meditations. His remarks are addressed 'To the Most Wise and Illustrious the Dean and Doctors of the Sacred Faculty of Theology in Paris.' The key sentence reads:

And, in truth, I have noticed that you, along with all the theologians, did not only affirm that the existence of God may be proved by the natural reason, but also that it may be inferred from the Holy Scriptures, that knowledge about Him is much clearer than that which we have of many created things, and, as a matter of fact, is so easy to acquire, that those who have it not are culpable in their ignorance.

In other words, even if there is no particular merit in believing in God (and why should there be?) there is blame attached to not believing; for knowledge of God 'is so easy to acquire' that no real excuse is open to those who fail to acquire it. This makes sense, for otherwise how could they be blamed? And if they are blameworthy, then this can only be because they failed in what was possible.

This indeed appears from the Wisdom of Solomon, chapter xiii, where it is said '*Howbeit they are not to be excused; for if their understanding was so great that they could discern the world and the creatures, why did they not rather find out the Lord thereof?*' and in Romans, chapter i, it is said that they are '*without excuse*'; and again in the same place, by these words '*that which may be known of God is manifest in them,*' it seems as though we were shown that all that which can be known of God may be made manifest by means which are not derived from anywhere but from ourselves, and from the simple consideration of the nature of our minds. Hence I thought it not beside my purpose to enquire how this is so, and how God may be more easily and certainly known than the things of the world. (i, 133–4)

Descartes in fact is saying that men can be saved by their intellects as well as by their faith. The mistake is in failing to try for what is possible—for every creature with a mind. Indeed, blind faith is not enough, Descartes has argued. For if we have no conception of God whatsoever, then to 'say one believes that *God* exists' would 'be the same as saying that one believes that *nothing* exists' (ii, 130). A little earlier, in this same letter to Clerselier, he had written:

Even in the matter of the truths of the faith, we should perceive some reason persuading us that they have been revealed by God, before determining ourselves to believe them; and though those who are ignorant do well to follow the judgment of the more capable, touching those matters that are difficult of apprehension, it must nevertheless be their own perception that tells them that they are ignorant and that those whose judgments they wish to follow are less ignorant, otherwise they would do ill to follow them, and would act as automata or as mere animals rather than as men. (ii, 129)

Thus Descartes may have conceived of his work in two ways: firstly as bringing to a knowledge of God (and the soul) those who lacked it completely; and secondly as bringing to blind and incoherent faith such intellectual apprehension of the nature of

God as a finite being can have, which alone can give that faith any meaning and human reality. What Descartes has, at bottom, been arguing through the greater part of the Meditations is that intellect alone cannot help but have what amounts to a knowledge of God; and that in every case where this knowledge is absent the reason is always (and can only be) that sense-perception and feeling have been allowed to mist over the clarity of pure intellectual vision. Indeed, his second Meditation could be regarded as an exercise preparatory to dispelling that mist, and his remaining Meditations the report on what he was thus able to see no less clearly by reason than had formerly seemed possible even by faith.

INDEX

Action: relation to thinking, 48; logically related to choice and decision, 113; link between knowledge and, 121–3; motive for, 209

Actuality of God, 85

Adventitious ideas: nature of, 59; different from innate ideas, 148

Affection, a class of thought, 58

Agency, knowledge of our, 48–9

Alexander, Samuel, 68

Animal experience, compared with ordinary human experience, 40

Arch deceiver (see *Malin génie*), invincibility of, 44

Archetypes, relation to copies, 71

Aristotle, his concepts of formal and efficient cause, 93

Arnauld: on doubt of existence of body, 44–8; on the self-derivation of God, 92–3; his interpretation of 'self-derivation' criticised by Descartes, 95; on the circularity of Descartes' reasoning, 168–9

Attributes, their relation to modes, 61

Autonomy of rational thought, 17

Belief: relation to doubt, 4; a necessary condition for error, 18

Berkeley, compared with Descartes on waking experience, 53

Body: perceived by the mind, 37; relation to thinking, 48; nature of unity of mind and, 209

Brain, materialistic view of, 192

Caterus: on cause and effect, 67; and Descartes on relation between ideas and external objects, 70; on knowledge of God, 99

Causal relationship, three possible types of, 65

Causality, compared with logic, 63

Cause (see Efficient cause, Eminent cause, Final cause, Formal cause): Descartes' conception of, 67; power of a, 71; the only real, 71

Certainty: only grounds for claiming entire, 6; of one's own existence, 42

Clear and distinct ideas: God guarantees truth of, 81, 96–7; relation to doubt, 81; the absolute claim of, 172

Clear and distinct perceptions, 37; reliability of, 52–3; not always the criteria of truth, 218

Clearness and distinctness: criterion of, 55; relation to thought, 74; lacked by sensory ideas, 78

Cogito: relation to agency, 48–9; relation to God, 145

Confused perception, 37

Conservation: relation to creation, 89; makes knowledge possible, 151

Corporeal substance: how describable, 11; origin of idea of, 79–80

Creation, relation to conservation, 89